JEAN KORTERING

SAY AMONG THE HEATHEN
THE LORD REIGNS
Evidences in Southeast Asia

REFORMED
FREE PUBLISHING
ASSOCIATION
Jenison, Michigan

©2022 Reformed Free Publishing Association

All rights reserved

Printed in the United States of America

No part of this publication may be reproduced, stored in a retrieval system, or transmitted in any form or by any means—electronic, mechanical, photocopying, recording, or otherwise—without the prior written permission of the publisher. The only exception is brief quotations in printed reviews.

Unless otherwise indicated, Scripture cited is taken from the King James (Authorized) Version.

Scripture marked NKJV is taken from the New King James Version®. Copyright © 1982 by Thomas Nelson. Used by permission. All rights reserved.

Italics in scripture quotations reflect the author's emphasis.

Cover design by Amy Zevenbergen
Interior design by Katherine Lloyd, the DESK

Reformed Free Publishing Association
1894 Georgetown Center Drive
Jenison, Michigan 49428
616-457-5970
mail@rfpa.org
www.rfpa.org

ISBN 978-1-7368154-4-1
Ebook ISBN 978-1-7368154-5-8
LCCN 2022944435

This collection of stories is dedicated with love
to the grandchildren of Jason and Jean Kortering who,
at whatever age they were from July 1992 to September 2002,
gave up their grandparents for the Lord's work in Singapore.
May these writings help to bridge the gap of separation.

CONTENTS

Author's Foreword vii
Acknowledgments ix
Introduction. 1

Part One
Evangelical Reformed Churches in Singapore

1   The Early Years 9
2   Our First Singapore Experience 20

Part Two
Personal Conversion Accounts

3   It Was Only a Picture 31
4   Christ, the Lord of Romance 37
5   My Sister Was Given Away 43
6   They Tore Up My Bible 61
7   My Young Days Were Full of Danger 74
8   Baptism Was a Big Issue 85
9   I Was Delivered from Demons 97
10   This Time It Was a Story 114
11   Suffering for the Reformed Faith 119
12   The First ARTS Student 130

Part Three
Mission Trips

Myanmar—January 5-19, 1996   143
Myanmar—November, 1997   168

Myanmar, 1999	173
Myanmar, 2001	194
Myanmar—January 16-23, 2006	213
India—April 10-May 1, 1998	227
Home, Sweet Home	263
India, 2000	265
India, 2002	280
Hyderabad	298
India, 2006	302
Philippines—May 20-31, 1999	317
Penang, Malaysia—October 19-25, 2005	335
Epilogue	351

AUTHOR'S FOREWORD

Say Among the Heathen the Lord Reigns was written primarily for the children and grandchildren of Rev. and Mrs. Jason Kortering to give an account of their labors in Singapore, India, and Myanmar during the years 1992 to 2006. This new edition published by the Reformed Free Publishing Association includes only a few changes, made with the author's approval. The content and style of writing remains the same as the first edition.

Jean Kortering
July, 2022

ACKNOWLEDGMENTS

The writing of this book would have been impossible without the help and involvement of others. I greatly appreciate the willingness of those who took their time to share their conversion experience with me and also agreed that I could use their story so you, the readers, can learn more of God's goodness and power to save those whom he has chosen in Christ. Their desire and mine is that all praise be to God alone. I will not list their names here because in several cases a pseudonym was used, but my thanks to each one of you nonetheless.

My thanks to Amy Loh Lai Yin, who so graciously consented to work out the cover design of the first edition. It was very expertly done and greatly appreciated.

A big task fell on Hiew Peng, and she handled the challenge very competently and quickly. When I learned that the printer had to have the document set up in a computer book program, I became desperate; who would I turn to? Hiew Peng has the necessary know-how, and she very capably assisted. Thanks so much, Hiew Peng.

When I called to SRC Publications and Distributors in Singapore to inquire about publishing, imagine my surprise when I found out I was speaking with Lim Beng Young, a friend in the church. Beng Young assisted in every possible way he could in arranging the printing process and bringing this endeavor to its completion. I am very grateful to him for all his help.

And thanks to my dear husband, who was always there with encouraging words, for putting up with all my many questions and my spending so much time at the computer. Thanks to our entire family for all their enthusiasm and eagerness, and their willingness to share ideas when asked.

Active in Missions (AIM) agreed willingly to assume the responsibility of the distribution process in the USA. Without their help, this book may have been limited only to our immediate family. A special word of thanks to them.

And I also wish to thank Tan Poh Choo and Fiona Tye Siew Hua for their part in the distribution in Singapore. Above all else, thanks be to God for all his many blessings each step of the way. There were times when I almost felt like giving up on the whole idea, but with talking it over and prayer for the Lord's direction, we were led to the conviction that it should be done. It was amazing for us to see how God graciously provided and opened doors in order to finish the work. "Praise God from whom all blessings flow."

Jean Kortering
March 24, 2007

INTRODUCTION

First I must acquaint you with some background information of Grandpa's ministry in the Protestant Reformed Churches (PRC) and then explain the purpose for this collection of stories. Grandpa was ordained in 1960 and served in seven churches.

- 1960–1966   Hull PRC, Hull, Iowa
- 1966–1970   Hope PRC, Grand Rapids, Michigan
- 1970–1976   Hull PRC, Hull, Iowa
- 1976–1979   Hope PRC, Redlands, California
- 1979–1984   Loveland PRC, Loveland, Colorado
- 1984–1992   Grandville PRC, Grandville, Michigan
- 1992–2002   Hope PRC, Grand Rapids, Michigan
              Minister-on-loan to Evangelical Reformed Churches in Singapore (ERCS)
- 2002   Emeritus minister in Grandville PRC, Grandville, Michigan

In 1991 the PRC Contact Committee asked Grandpa to spend six months in Singapore to help Covenant Evangelical Reformed Church in working through some difficulties, and also to give lectures on various subjects for the church leaders. Grandville PRC, where Grandpa was serving as pastor, agreed to release him for six months, so in August of 1991, we went to Singapore for the first time, and we returned to the United States and Grandville PRC in late February 1992.

During our stay in Singapore, the ERCS asked the PRC to "loan" a senior pastor to them for an extended length of time, for the purpose of helping to develop their mission work and theological training. Upon our return to the USA, Grandpa received that call to be the minister-on-loan (M.O.L.) to Singapore, and at the same time he received the call to labor in Northern Ireland. As we considered those calls, we could only wait upon the Lord and reflect on how he had guided our lives.

Grandpa and I were married in 1957, and in the first ten years of our marriage, the Lord blessed us with five daughters. The Lord ended our family there; it was necessary for me to have surgery, due to a tumor, a year after Carol was born. We knew then that there would be no more children in our family, but our hearts were filled with gratitude that the Lord had already given us five children. Now as we considered the calls, we could see the Lord's leading even in that. Under God's guiding hand, the girls had all married good Christian husbands within a ten-year period from 1979 to 1989, so we no longer had family responsibilities. It was indeed a great blessing for us to know that our daughters were all established in God-fearing homes.

During the eight years in Grandville (1984–1992), Grandpa's parents and invalid brother and my mother were all taken to glory. You might have noticed how many years we served in the "western" churches, away from family. We were especially thankful that we were in the Grand Rapids area during the declining years of our loved ones, but now even the concern for elderly parents did not have to be considered.

We were still young (if you call fifty-six and fifty-eight young), and the Lord had given both of us good health, so from that point of view also, we were able to leave as there were no ongoing medical needs.

We also reflected on how we were brought up. The value of a godly upbringing is immeasurable, a tremendous blessing, and we pray that all you grandchildren will truly treasure your Christian upbringing as well. There is not a doubt in our minds that the instruction we received from our parents instilled in us the desire to submit ourselves to God's will and to have him be first in our lives.

Believe you me, we did a lot of talking, and the Lord showed us clearly that there was no other way but that we should go and serve him in Singapore. That doesn't mean that all the details fell easily into place. We were living in a parsonage, meaning that there was

INTRODUCTION

a house full of furniture that had to be disposed of. That wasn't the most difficult part—with five daughters, one of them could surely use this or that, and it was neat that most of our things could easily find a place in their homes. We also had a huge garage sale, and then many leftover things were brought to the mission. I can vividly recall how, while I was doing all this sorting of things (and remember that's exactly what it was—just things), little tugs of pain would creep in. The greatest hurt, though, was facing the fact that we would be leaving behind all our dear families, the girls and their husbands and those precious grandchildren. I know there were many, many times I sang in my heart the following hymn; it helped me to stay focused and press on.

> *All the way my Savior leads me*
> *What have I to ask beside?*
> *Can I doubt his tender mercy,*
> *Who through life has been my guide?*
> *Heav'nly peace, divinest comfort,*
> *Here by faith in him to dwell!*
> *For I know, whate'er befall me,*
> *Jesus doeth all things well.*[*]

So it was that in July of 1992, Grandpa and I said our tearful goodbyes to all our loved ones. Over the years there would be times of homesickness and loneliness, but we would always have to remind ourselves to stay focused. Attitude goes a long way, and having self-pity never helps. Some of my friends would say to me, "I could never do what you're doing," or "What a big sacrifice you're making, being away from your family." I'm no different than anyone else; there were struggles, but God supplied our every need. I always preferred to think of our years in Singapore as a privilege rather than a sacrifice—a sacrifice would make me feel it's something I'm doing, whereas a privilege to do this work is really a rich blessing given to

---

[*] Fanny J. Crosby (1875).

us by the Lord. There are comparatively few who have that privilege, and the Lord in his goodness had given that to us.

The PRC graciously provided that we were able to come home for a few weeks each year. One of the grounds for that decision was family. They realized that we were leaving family behind and that would be difficult for us. Each year we certainly treasured those times we could spend with family, seeing everyone again and enjoying fellowship with them. But there's no getting around it, we missed out on the growing-up years of our grandchildren, and that wasn't easy. (I'm dabbing my eyes as I write this, as the thought is still painful.) I'm sure it wasn't easy for all the parents and grandchildren either, as we all had to have a giving attitude in this situation, but the Lord understood this as well, and he supplied sufficient grace for that need.

Over all those years, we could not do what many other grandparents are able to do. My anticipation of being a grandparent was that we would always be there for the grandkids, they would be welcomed in our home anytime, we would spend lots of time together, talking and doing fun things, etc. However, that was not to be our portion, except for the time before we went to Singapore, which I certainly do remember and treasure. Even now in our retirement, we are not around as much as we would like to be, for again, the Lord has called us to work in Singapore under difficult circumstances (September 2005–March 2006). We are once again assisting CERC since their minister, Pastor Cheah Fook Meng, passed away, and help was needed in supplying their pulpit.

There is something, however, that we can do that other grandparents cannot do, and that is to share with our grandkids the many joys and experiences of having labored in Singapore and other countries. While we were living in Singapore, we considered the possibility of writing a book to tell of the Lord's work in that country. Since that idea did not materialize, we decided to use this time while we are in Singapore once again to share with you, in writing, the many blessings we received from the Lord's hand while here. There have been good times and difficult times, joyful times and sad times, but

INTRODUCTION

through it all the Lord has been faithful and good, and we praise and extol his love and grace.

Some of the stories in this collection are the true-life stories of dear friends we personally know. The stories will help you to understand the people with whom we worked. Compared to what we are accustomed to in America, you will find that many of the situations referred to are very unusual. We are not writing these down simply to be entertained by their uniqueness, but rather to see God's guiding hand in calling his children out of darkness into his marvelous light. All the people I have interviewed have agreed to share their story only for the purpose of acknowledging God's hand in their life and bringing honor and glory to his name. At certain times a pseudonym will be used to protect an individual's identity. Some stories are written as first-person accounts so that we can enter into their life and see the greatness of God's electing grace as they experienced it.

All the effort of this endeavor will certainly be worth it if by reading through these stories, you realize anew the urgency we have to daily pray for missionaries and missions and at the same time to appreciate more fully the great blessings you children have in family, church, and school.

With much love to all our precious grandchildren,
Grandpa and Grandma
(Grandma is the writer, Grandpa the encourager)
November 29, 2005

Part One

Evangelical Reformed Churches in Singapore

The day thou gavest

The day Thou gavest, Lord, is ended,
The darkness falls at thy behest;
To thee our morning hymns ascended,
Thy praise shall sanctify our rest.

We thank thee that thy church unsleeping,
While earth rolls onward into light,
Through all the world her watch is keeping,
And rests not now by day or night.

As o'er each continent and island
The dawn leads on another day,
The voice of prayer is never silent,
Nor dies the strain of praise away.

The sun that bids us rest is waking
Our brethren 'neath the western sky,
And hour by hour fresh lips are making
Thy wondrous doings heard on high.

So be it, Lord: thy throne shall never,
Like earth's proud empires, pass away;
Thy kingdom stands, and grows forever,
Till all thy creatures own thy sway.[*]

---

[*] John Ellerton (1870).

Chapter 1

THE EARLY YEARS

The Evangelical Reformed Churches in Singapore (ERCS) had their very beginning in the 1960s as a Bible study group in Monks' Hill Secondary School. In order to give you a little background, I had an interview with Johnson See, who was involved right from the beginning and who also was instrumental in making contact with the PRC. Another source of information was a paper written by Pastor Lau Chin Kwee entitled "Our Church History."

Singapore was a very different country in the 1960s from what it is today. The population has increased so much in Singapore that the majority of people now live in high-rise apartment buildings, whereas back then, about thirty or forty families lived close together in a kampong (village). The houses in the kampongs were constructed of woven bamboo sheets or bamboo logs with a zinc roof, and some of the houses were even built on stilts. The people were generally poor, and the homes were simple, but those who experienced that kind of living look back with fond memories. Kampong living was a more relaxed atmosphere, and the kids could run about freely and have fun together as there weren't all the demands of school studies like there are today.

Upon entering a kampong, there would be an idol or a picture of a god, which the village people prayed to. They believed this idol could protect them, give them good grades in school, help them to pass their examinations, keep them healthy, make them rich, and give them good luck and blessing. If all these good things didn't happen in their life, it was their own fault—perhaps they were not worshiping their ancestors or the gods enough or were not doing as many good deeds as they should.

About 98 percent of the original church members came from such non-Christian homes. They were brought up in the Chinese religions, Buddhism and Taoism, with the main characteristic being the worshiping of ancestors. Ancestor worship is done regularly, but there is also a special time of the year called Qingming when the Chinese people visit the graves of their close relatives, or the temples where the ashes are stored if they had been cremated. The people make these visits to show their respect but also to worship the ancestors and seek blessing for the family. There was only one Christian family in the village where Johnson lived, and this family had to endure much teasing and mocking from all the young village boys.

It was at Monks' Hill Secondary School that Johnson first learned about Christianity. (Secondary school 1–4 in Singapore is comparable to grades 7–10 in America.) At that time the Singapore government did not hold such a strict hand over what could and could not be done in the schools. At this school was a Christian teacher by the name of Mr. Goh Seng Fong who taught science. Mr. Goh organized a Bible class and used the science laboratory as the meeting place. Johnson said he was just walking along one time during recess and noticed a gathering of students, who were singing. Mr. Goh was very kind and said to him, "Come along and join us." This group of students met every day with Mr. Goh, singing and praying together, and also listening to a lesson from the Bible. Many young people came to know the Lord through these Bible classes, and that is also the early beginning of the ERCS.

Johnson said that when he became a Christian, his parents and siblings were not aware of what he was doing. Both his parents needed to work as the family was very poor; consequently, parental control over the children was somewhat lacking. When Johnson reflects back, he marvels at how he was used as an instrument in God's hand. Since kampong living was a friendly environment, the houses were not locked, and the children were welcomed in all the homes and were quite free to roam about and do as they pleased. Although he did not go to a Bible school, when Johnson became a

Christian, he started talking to the kampong people, and when there was an opportunity, he would bring them along to hear the gospel. Slowly his brother, sister, and some of the village people—nieces, nephews, Elder Siew Chee Seng, Geok Lay (wife of the late brother James Tay), and others—came to know the Lord.

When talking about his home situation, Johnson shared that when he was young, his parents frequently quarreled. He spoke with his mother about the Bible and asked her to go along to the Chinese service at Life Bible Presbyterian Church. His mother experienced that whenever she went to church, she had a certain sense of peace within her. One night when the parents quarreled, Johnson slammed the door in anger. The Lord struck his conscience that as a Christian, he should not behave that way to his parents, so he kneeled down and cried for forgiveness, praying for his parents and also praying that God would glorify himself that night.

As it is common for people to throw things when they are angry, his father, in a rage, took the idol and threw it down and broke it. If his mother was already a Christian by that time, Johnson didn't remember, but from that time onward, there was no idol in their home. "Actually, this action of my father made no sense to me. Why would my father destroy the idol? But from a spiritual point of view, I was praying for my parents and that the Lord would glorify himself, and here was an answer to my prayer. It was only much later when my mother consistently went to church that my father also went along with her. Eventually both of them attended Life BP Church, were baptized, and confessed their faith."

Johnson said, "At the time when I became a Christian, my younger brother Chuan Hoo wasn't a Christian. In fact, he was very anti-Christian. Once when Life BP Church conducted a gospel meeting, I invited the rest of the kampong boys to come along but I did not invite him. However, my brother did come to that meeting—I think he was spying on me. I remember the gospel meeting is 'Christ Is the Answer.' At that very meeting he was converted; that is how he came to know the Lord. Looking back, it is really how the Spirit works, it is really a miracle. Like in the kampong, how do you expect those people to know the Lord?"

Now to get back to the Bible study at Monks' Hill Secondary School. In the beginning it was associated with the Singapore Youth for Christ (YFC). Seeing the importance of church membership, Mr. Goh encouraged the students to join Life Bible Presbyterian Church. In the following years, many of ERCS's church members were baptized in Life BP Church while still being actively involved in the Monks' Hill YFC. Rev. Tow, pastor of Life BP Church, allowed a Baptist missionary to preach from his pulpit, and this missionary was also allowed to speak regularly at the YFC Saturday club meetings. The missionary went on to organize the Harvester Baptist Church, and some members left Life BP Church and were rebaptized by this pastor. Around this time Monks' Hill YFC terminated their association with Youth for Christ and became the Monks' Hill Bible Club, still under Mr. Goh's leadership.

Mr. Goh also became involved with the pastor of Jesus Saves Mission (JSM), a ministry in the kampongs of Singapore. Many combined meetings were held between JSM and Monks' Hill Bible Club. An attempt was made to integrate this combined group of young people into the mainstream life of Life BP Church by making it a department of Life BP Church Sunday school and changing its name to Gospel Literature and Tract Department (GLTD). This did not work out—the GLTD continued to function independently, and it was obvious that the GLTD members would not blend into Life BP Church. As Johnson recalled, "At that time we were going through a real struggle. On the one hand, Life Church looked at us as being traitors and not grateful for their help, and on the other hand, JSM looked at us as compromisers."

In 1972, Mr. Goh left his position as a science teacher to undertake theological training in the United States. At that time, the members of GLTD were mostly students and only a few older working people, but they willingly gave their savings to help Mr. Goh as he set off to study at a Baptist college. For a while the group of young believers was like sheep without a shepherd, quite lost and not knowing what to think or do.

It was at this time that Johnson began to lead the group. He was already attending Polytechnic but "Early in the morning, I would take my backpack and go to Whitley Secondary School to evangelize. You just wouldn't believe it. You know Kim Fong, Patricia, and Kim Neo, I would go to their school and teach them Bible study, and afterward go to the other school." Before Pastor Lau became a minister, he was a teacher at Dunearn Secondary Technical School, and he followed the example of Mr. Goh by conducting Bible classes at Dunearn. Pastor Lau became a regular speaker for the GLTD group at that time.

Then there was another interesting development. Quoting from Pastor Lau:

"In the midst of all this, another event took place that showed the Lord's good pleasure that this group should become an instituted church, but not of the Baptistic persuasion. Out of the blue, we were asked to organize three lectures for two Protestant Reformed ministers who were passing by Singapore. I wonder how these prominent men (a professor of theology and a senior minister) felt when they stood before a group of young people, speaking about the Reformed faith. Later, I learned from Professor Hoeksema that it was beyond his wildest dreams that those lectures could ever spark a Reformed movement here in Singapore. God's ways are higher than our ways and his thoughts transcend our thoughts. We devised our ways to have a church under the Baptist minister, but the Lord directed our steps toward becoming a creedal church confessing the three forms of unity.

"The lectures did not have as much effect as the literature that was left behind by the ministers. Among the literature was the three forms of unity, the first question and answer of which so thrilled my heart that I devoured the Heidelberg Catechism wholeheartedly and began to teach it the following year at the Saturday Club meetings. Other Reformed literature, like books by A. W. Pink, were also read to the spiritual benefit of our souls.

"After these Reformed lectures, another important man came into the life of the GLTD. He was Mr. Ong Keng Ho, who was instrumental in the organizing of the lectures. A recently returned Colombo Plan scholar, Ong Keng Ho came to know the Protestant Reformed Churches through an Orthodox Presbyterian Church in Christchurch, New Zealand, where he was a member while studying there. He was, among us, the most Reformed man at that time of our development. Later, he was one of the five elders who were ordained at the time of the institution of the Evangelical Reformed Church in Singapore."

After the visit of Professor Homer C. Hoeksema and Rev. Cornelius Hanko, Mr. Lau Chin Kwee studied more of the doctrines of the Reformed faith and taught these to the GLTD while Johnson taught more of practical Christianity and provided leadership to the group. The GLTD was at a crossroads in 1975, which was about a year before the return of Mr. Goh from the U.S. The leaders were talking about the future of GLTD: should it remain status quo as part of the Life BP Church, or should it work toward the establishment of a church with Mr. Goh as its first pastor? The latter was the inclination of the majority of the executive committee as well as the majority of the membership. In preparation for Mr. Goh's return, the group rented a place on River Valley Road for its Sunday worship services. The meeting place was a vacant kampong house, which they could rent from Johnson's father. The GLTD members were just young people at the time, so they had to save every cent in order to pay the rent. They still used Life BP Church for the Saturday meeting, but on Sunday they went to the kampong.

By the time Mr. Goh returned, many others had joined the group, not only from Monks' Hill Secondary School, but from other schools as well. Mr. Goh returned to Singapore as Rev. Goh Seng Fong, a missionary of a Baptist church in the United States. He was received joyfully and sincerely as he was expected to become the first pastor for the GLTD. Rev. Goh introduced the congregational form of church government, with himself as the moderator of all the congregational meetings where all the matters of the church were decided. Rev. Goh was also very zealous in pushing his view of baptism by immersion. He was the speaker for the annual December camp meetings, and whenever he came across the word "baptize" or "baptism" in the KJV, he would read it as "immersion" or "immersed."

Around this time Johnson was due to go to Scotland for studies, but before he left, there was a crisis; an ultimatum was given to Rev. Goh. A debate was organized between Rev. Goh and Mr. Lau Chin Kwee on the issue of baptism. Rev. Goh was a pastor, and Mr. Lau did not have his theological training as yet. The outcome after this debate was that Rev. Goh left GLTD. A few members left with Rev. Goh, but most of the members remained with GLTD. Even many who during that time had been baptized by immersion by Rev. Goh chose to remain. On the subject of baptism, Johnson agreed with Mr. Lau, but on the subject of limited atonement he agreed with Rev. Goh.

Quoting again from Pastor Lau's article:

"Coming to the pure Reformed faith from our type of background, the most difficult doctrine to accept was the doctrine of limited atonement (the doctrine that states that Christ died for the elect only). For years we had been preaching the gospel after the Arminian way of universal atonement. Without Christ being stated as dying for all men, head for head, how can there be a gospel to preach? That being our understanding, an acceptance of the doctrine of limited atonement could amount to the cessation of evangelism. While this need not be necessarily the case, many could not see the consistency of preaching limited atonement and yet calling all men to repentance and faith in Christ. A few leaders left GLTD and went back to Life BP Church."

Providentially, during Johnson's stay in Scotland, he was able to attend the Church of Scotland and the Free Church of Scotland. During this time he was led to a better understanding of the Reformed faith. It was through the reading of a book entitled *Life by His Death* (an abridged version of *The Death of Death in the Death of Christ* by

John Owen) that he came to understand more clearly the doctrine of limited atonement. His love was for the group in Singapore, and he continued to keep in touch with them while he was away.

Pastor Lau expresses his own call to the ministry this way:

"1978 saw my admission into the Far Eastern Bible College. My call to the ministry clearly had to do with the doctrine of grace that the Lord was pleased to reveal to me in 1976. The teaching of the Heidelberg Catechism in that year to the young people and the knowledge I had of the rampant Arminianism in all the churches I knew impressed deeply in my heart the necessity of upholding this glorious truth for the glory and honor of the God of our salvation. The burden that I should be the one to take up the cross and follow the Lord to spread the truth (since God was pleased to reveal the truth to me) grew heavier toward the end of that year as the return of Mr. Goh drew near. Knowing the spiritual state of most churches, I had no confidence that Mr. Goh would return a Calvinist. I left my teaching job at the end of 1976, after enjoying that profession for six years."

The seed of the Reformed faith was sown when Prof. Hoeksema and Rev. Hanko visited in 1974. By 1977, Johnson was consulting Prof. Hoeksema over the issues confronting the GLTD. This led to an official request for help by the GLTD to the PRC in 1978. The first emissaries to come to Singapore were Rev. James Slopsema and Mr. Dewey Engelsma. Their mandate was to investigate if there was a group viable to be organized as a Reformed church. For a time the PRC sent taped messages for the group to listen to. The next thing was for the group to be registered with the government so that they would be able to sponsor a missionary working among them. In January 1979, the GLTD was registered as the Gospel Literature and Tract Society (GLTS).

The next delegation sent to Singapore from the PRC was in 1979. Rev. Marvin Kamps and Mr. Dewey Engelsma came then, and the request was made through them to the PRC for a missionary to help in organizing the GLTD into a Reformed church.

Around this time Johnson was going to go from Scotland to the U.S. as a student, but he needed a sponsor. He was put in touch with Pastor denHartog (probably through Rev. Slopsema). "I asked Pastor denHartog to be my sponsor. He was so kind; he said why don't you come and stay by me?" Johnson tells what a culture shock it was for him. "Everything was so big—the Greyhound bus, the seat is so big you can sleep in it. At Pastor denHartog's house, everything was so big, the fridge was king-size. And the American people were big." He stayed with the denHartogs for the first few weeks, and then Pastor denHartog helped him arrange a trip to visit some other PRC churches and families. Johnson recalls visiting the Korterings in Redlands, California; he thought we were poor people, five daughters and no sons. In the Asian culture, daughters marry out of the family, but a family keeps their sons. He explained that our daughters would be taken into their husband's family, and we would be left alone.

While Johnson was staying with the denHartog family, Pastor denHartog had the call to go to New Zealand as missionary. Hope PRC had a trio for Singapore and Pastor denHartog's name was on that, but the call to New Zealand came first. Johnson thought Pastor denHartog was the right person for Singapore. He said if anyone goes to Singapore, they must be able to adjust their whole life. Johnson had visited other PRC churches and "was very stumbled" to see the PRC men smoking. From a Singapore perspective, smoking is sinful, and only non-Christians will smoke. Pastor denHartog was also against smoking; therefore, he must be the right man for Singapore. He said to Pastor denHartog, "Why don't you go by faith. Don't accept the call to New Zealand; see if you receive the call to Singapore."

In 1980 Pastor Arie denHartog and his family came to Singapore to labor as the first missionary pastor. It was also during that year that Pastor Lau left Singapore to begin his studies at the PRC seminary. After the saints in Singapore studied the three forms of unity with Pastor denHartog, and the constitution of the GLTS was amended to be a constitution of the would-be church, the Evangelical Reformed

Church in Singapore was instituted on January 24, 1982. At that time, five elders and three deacons signed the formula of subscription. There were more than ninety founder members for the new church.

In September 1982, Pastor Lau completed his studies in the PRC seminary and returned to Singapore to become the first pastor of the ERCS. In 1983, Mr. Jai Mahtani left Singapore to study at the theological school of the PRC. It was toward the end of his time in the U.S. that a new congregation was formed: Covenant Evangelical Reformed Church in Singapore. As Pastor denHartog was planning to leave by the end of 1986, the CERC Session called Candidate Mahtani to be their pastor. Pastor Mahtani was ordained in October 1986, and Covenant church was instituted in September 1987.

Pastor Lau closes his account with:

"Let us praise the Lord, the Almighty and God of our salvation, for he alone has done wondrously, carrying us along with him and often without our being aware of what was happening until a later time when we have opportunity to recall his goodness and to praise him. Amen."

It was in August 1991 that we first appeared on the scene for a period of six months. In July 1992, we moved to Singapore to take up the work of minister-on-loan.

Pastor Cheah Fook Meng completed his studies at the Theological School of the PRC in 1996 and became the new pastor of Covenant Evangelical Reformed Church. After laboring in CERC for nine years, the Lord took him in death to his eternal home in glory on August 29, 2005, at the young age of forty-one years.

Paul Goh also studied at the PRC seminary. He returned to Singapore and was ordained to serve the churches as minister-at-large, being available to preach in the two congregations and also involved in the mission activities of the denomination.

One of the highlights of our tenure in Singapore was the establishment of the Asian Reformed Theological School (ARTS). Grandpa poured many hours of preparation into this project. Prof. Hanko

THE EARLY YEARS

came to Singapore for six months to assist in organizing the curriculum. There was a room in Basement 1 of First Evangelical Reformed Church that was set aside for the classroom and library of ARTS. The instructors prepared detailed outlines of their lectures and also made CDs of the outlines, so their work continues to be available for future use. ARTS is set up so that the courses can be taught in Singapore but also in other countries. An endowment fund for ARTS was set up in the PRC, and the interest from this fund is available to meet the operational expenses of the school.

In 2002, Grandpa completed ten years as minister-on-loan. He would soon retire from the active ministry, so Hope PRC began the calling process for a replacement minister-on-loan.

Pastor denHartog accepted the call to go once again to Singapore to labor among the churches there. He arrived in January 2002, and we returned to the USA in September 2002, so Grandpa and Pastor denHartog had several months that they were able to work together. In 2005, after serving for three years in Singapore, Pastor denHartog accepted a call from Southwest PRC in Grandville, MI.

In 2003 we had the opportunity to return to Singapore for three months so that Grandpa could teach some courses at ARTS. Then we returned again in September 2005, due to the death of CERC's pastor, Cheah Fook Meng. CERC asked Grandpa to officiate at the wakes and funeral of Pastor Cheah and also provide them with much-needed assistance for a few months' time. The Lord willing, we will return to the USA on March 29, 2006.

We can only commit the future to the Lord. At the present time, the two churches, FERC and CERC, are going through a difficult time as they deal with the issue of divorce and remarriage. It remains to be seen how this will affect the congregations.

December 2005

Chapter 2

OUR FIRST SINGAPORE EXPERIENCE

The Protestant Reformed Churches in America (PRCA) have a sister-church relationship with the Evangelical Reformed Churches in Singapore (ERCS). While Pastor Arie denHartog labored as missionary in Singapore from 1979 to 1987, two congregations were organized: First Evangelical Reformed Church (FERC) and Covenant Evangelical Reformed Church (CERC). Pastor Lau Chin Kwee was the pastor of FERC and Pastor Jai Mahtani of CERC. Both Pastor Lau and Pastor Mahtani received their theological training at the PRC Seminary.

It was in the summer of 1991 that the contact committee of the Protestant Reformed Churches approached Grandpa about going to Singapore for a period of six months. The council of Grandville PRC, where Grandpa was serving as pastor, agreed that he could leave for that period of time since Grandville, being in the Grand Rapids area, would have no difficulty getting pulpit supply and other help as needed. Going to another country for that length of time required some preparation on our part. We had to fill out lengthy forms to apply for employment and dependent passes, called Green Cards. After that was all approved, we were able to leave for Singapore on August 28, 1991.

We had tried to find out as much as we could about Singapore before going, and that was helpful alright, but we were still in for quite a culture shock. You really don't understand a place until you live there and experience it firsthand. You must learn about the culture of the people and understand how they do things. Singaporeans are mainly Chinese, Indian, and Malay, and each race has its own

OUR FIRST SINGAPORE EXPERIENCE

culture. You must feel the heat and humidity, use public transport, taste their foods, identify the smells, etc. Singapore has many holidays. The country declares a national holiday for two religious days of each belief. The holidays for the Christians are Good Friday and Christmas. It seemed strange to us that not only the Christians, but everyone, called it "Good Friday." Before going to Singapore, we had been gone from home for two months at one go, but this would be the longest period of time that we would be separated from our family.

The only people we knew in Singapore were the ministers. It's true that we had met some other members of the ERCS before, but our memory in those cases had to be refreshed. Already in the airport, the congregations very warmly received us. As we had experienced before when going to a new place, you quickly establish friendships when you are united in faith. Background, race, and culture never stand in the way when you know and love the Lord. They are all our dear brothers and sisters in Christ.

We knew the Mahtani family the best because they had been members of Grandville PRC while he was studying in the seminary. They were very happy to see us again, and the very first day we were there, Pastor Mahtani took us to see Mount Faber. My maiden name being Faber, he thought we should see Mount Faber right away. The Mahtanis drove a church van, which was convenient for their family, but also had the added advantage of being able to go places that you cannot easily reach with public transport.

For those six months we lived in an HDB flat (Housing Development Board). These are high-rise buildings with many apartments that are subsidized by the government. The locals refer to them as "pigeon holes." The flat we lived in was on the seventh floor. Our unit did not have window grills, which actually is quite scary because you frequently read of people accidentally falling or committing suicide by jumping from high floors. Some of the church members, especially those with young children, did not like to visit in homes that did not have window grills.

The second day we were there was a holiday in Singapore. Our landlady had off from work and wanted to show us around. It was a kind gesture on her part, but as she drove from one place to another, it really didn't make a bit of sense to us as we didn't have a clue yet as to where we were living in relationship to where she took us. The holiday was Election Day. The People's Action Party (PAP) is the ruling political party, and although this is a democratic society and there is an opposition party, the opposition hardly has a chance in Singapore. Prime Minister Lee Kuan Yew was stepping down and he would become the senior prime minister. Goh Chok Tong was the PAP nominee to become the next prime minister. As we recall, he received around 90+ percent of the votes, but still he wondered if he should carry on since the opposition had received a larger percentage of votes than it had previously received. To us this was nothing short of a landslide victory.

When Pastor denHartog labored in Singapore, the ERCS members were mostly young people. I believe he officiated at some of their weddings. By the time we appeared on the scene, there were many young couples, and the second generation of Christians was being born into the church. As a result, the ERCS was experiencing some internal growth, as well as continued external growth when others joined the church, as they came to faith later in their life.

Grandpa had to get right to work at CERC. The congregation was going through a difficult time and needed much help. Pastor Mahtani is a very energetic pastor and also has a pleasing personality. He worked hard in CERC, he introduced them to two Sunday services, he preached faithfully, and he was leading the congregation in becoming a solid Reformed church. Problems arose within the church when changes were made too quickly. The congregation held a feedback session during which the members were encouraged to express how they felt. Feedback sessions can tend to become a free-for-all, and things are often said without sensitivity. The outcome of that feedback session was a vote of "no confidence" for their pastor.

Following this, many session meetings were held, there were meetings with individuals, and there were meetings with the Mahtanis, in

OUR FIRST SINGAPORE EXPERIENCE

order to try to get the full picture and to obtain some direction for the church. It was finally resolved with Pastor Mahtani being released from the ministry in CERC. This was a very sad time for CERC as some of the members agreed with Pastor Mahtani and were very hurt and upset with what had happened. An elder described the situation as "the people feeling beaten," and he wondered if they would have to dissolve the congregation and return to FERC instead of having two churches. However, through it all the Lord was with them, and again CERC had renewed hope for the future.

God's grace certainly carried the Mahtani family through this difficult time. They came faithfully to church, stayed active in the activities, didn't harbor ill feelings, and remained confident that the Lord would certainly have a place for them somewhere and sometime, according to his perfect will. As you know, the Mahtani family eventually moved to the USA, and the Lord did indeed give them a place of service again as they took up their work in the PRC and continue to be a blessing to many. This whole situation within CERC made up the bulk of Grandpa's work while we were in Singapore for those six months.

With Pastor Mahtani no longer preaching in Singapore, Grandpa preached in CERC twice each Lord's day. Occasionally, once a month or so, Pastor Lau and Grandpa would exchange pulpits, with Pastor Lau preaching in CERC and Grandpa preaching in FERC. FERC did not have their own church building at that time, so they rented an auditorium in the Regional English Language Centre (RELC). The rooms in this building were rented out to various church groups on Sunday. FERC was only able to hold one service each Sunday as their time slot was from 1:00 to 2:30 p.m. Some church members of FERC lived near us, and they would pick us up when Grandpa had to preach in FERC.

Grandpa also gave several series of lectures, which were held on Thursday evenings. Some of the lecture series went for six weeks, while others went for four weeks. The lectures were held in CERC's church building. Ee Ming from FERC enthusiastically and faithfully made videos of all the lectures. In addition to that, Grandpa gave the Reformation Day lecture in early November. This lecture was held in a public auditorium somewhere in town.

Those six months were strenuous, and there seemed to be no end to all the work Grandpa was called to do. Besides dealing with the difficulties in CERC and ministering to all the needs and concerns of its members, there was preaching every Sunday, visitations, and the making and giving of a public lecture each week. Grandpa also felt a bit crippled with having to use a very old computer and printer. All the work finally took its toll on Grandpa, and he became quite ill. He had a severe bout of Crohn's, and his heart palpitations were frequent (almost constant), so that going to the doctor became a regular activity. Pastor Mahtani brought Grandpa to their family doctor, an Indian doctor with the name Vaswani. Dr. Vaswani said Grandpa's heart condition was serious and that Grandpa should have complete bed rest for about five days.

This was during the monsoon season, so it rained, and rained, and rained. Usually the rain would bring welcome relief from the heat, but for Grandpa, it was very chilly and gloomy. Slowly on he began to feel better, and he longed to get out of the house and have a change of scenery. He suggested an easy outing to Chinese Gardens where we would be able to take our time and stroll through the park, but we soon learned that he didn't have much strength at all; we did a lot more sitting than walking.

The plan was to stay in Singapore until the end of February 1992. Since that time was drawing near, and my birthday was coming up on February 13, Grandpa wanted to take me to someplace special for dinner. We decided on high tea at the Westin Hotel, 72nd floor, where you can overlook Singapore, the financial district, the bay with all the ships, etc. It was our first time there, and we were impressed. It was pretty high-class in comparison to anything we knew and the food was delish! But…what we talked about that day nearly blew my mind!

During our six-month stay in Singapore, the ERCS was asking the PRC to loan them a senior pastor who could help them in their

OUR FIRST SINGAPORE EXPERIENCE

beginning efforts in mission work and theological training. Mission work has always had a soft spot in Grandpa's heart, so it wasn't surprising that Grandpa would be thinking very seriously about that possibility. We talked and talked and talked. His health had improved by this time, but he realized that if he were to return to Singapore, he would need to seek medical advice when we returned to the States. If he would receive the call to become that minister-onloan (M.O.L.), and if he would receive a clean bill of health, and if, and if, and if, then that might be the Lord's indication that he should take up the call to Singapore. Wow, what a shocker!

I didn't sleep a wink that whole night! And Grandpa was sleeping soundly. I can even remember breaking out in tears as I thought upon it—what about our family, our kids and our grandkids, how would that ever go? I couldn't stand the thought of leaving them.

Just as an aside, it's interesting that the very same thing happened when we were in Northern Ireland. Grandpa had used an evening out for dinner to discuss the possibility of going to Northern Ireland, and that had been a sleepless night as well. When we returned to the States from Singapore, Grandpa received two calls: Northern Ireland and Singapore. Now what? Suddenly Northern Ireland looked attractive and struck me as the place to go: similar culture, etc., but Grandpa felt the call to Singapore, as the need there seemed to be greater.

While in Singapore for six months, I had to find things to do. For one thing, I got myself quite absorbed with books from the library and read books by local authors and also books on culture. The culture is so different and fascinating that I just wanted to understand more and more of it. Thursday morning was my letterwriting time for the family. We had borrowed an electric typewriter, and I would stand by the kitchen counter to type. The counter was quite high in that house, so it worked fine to type while standing up and being able to look down on my letter as I was writing.

We bought a secondhand fax machine, so after the letter was written, I would fax it to a gas station in Byron Center, Michigan, and they would call Aunt Lori to let her know a letter was there for her. Aunt Lori would go down there in a jiffy to collect it, and then she would make copies for all her sisters. Those were the days before email, and telephone calls were expensive. I remember Uncle Barry and Aunt Lori calling us at Christmas. It was just so exciting to hear each other's voices once again, but in a way it was funny too. The conversation went something like this: "Hi, how are you? We're thinking about you and wish you a blessed Christmas. We'll keep this short because it's so expensive. Love you. Bye." Wouldn't it be fun to know how much that call actually cost?

I tried to be of help to Grandpa in any way I could, and that gave me the job of errand girl, sometimes walking and sometimes on the bus. If it meant going to town for something or other, it could easily eat up a half day. There was a small provision shop about four blocks away from where we lived that did copy work; I would take Grandpa's detailed outlines down there to be copied, go back again the next day to pick them up, and then take them home and collate and staple them together so they were ready for his lecture.

Getting the groceries was quite an ordeal—I couldn't find things I wanted, and many items were so strange that I wouldn't even know how to use them. I was forced to be a bit more innovative and also to get along with whatever cooking utensils were in the kitchen.

There wasn't a lot of interaction with FERC. We did meet the people at the church service once a month, but that wasn't enough to really get to know them. A few families did take us out to different places. One family from CERC took us to Haw Par Villa soon after we came to Singapore. Although we enjoyed the fellowship with this family, we were not impressed with Haw Par Villa as it was all about Chinese mythology, and we thought it was rather weird. One section had the twenty stages of hell, and it was gruesome. We didn't care for it at all. Haw Par Villa finally had to close down because they were not getting enough tourists visiting there—not surprising.

An FERC family brought us to the Chinese Lantern Festival. It was the last night of the festival, so it was the last opportunity to see it, but it was on a Saturday night of all things. The festival was so

OUR FIRST SINGAPORE EXPERIENCE

jam-packed with people that we could only take a step forward when the person ahead of us took a step forward.

Wee Beng and Siew Kiong (Siew Kiong was Aunt Lori's pen pal for years) took us out for a whole day. They showed us some different things that you would never see when taking the bus and also took us to some temples, etc. The Mahtani family treated us very well: took us different places, had us over to their home several times, and included us with some of their extended family activities, and were very hospitable and kind. I guess the amount of activities we enjoyed were about as much as Grandpa could handle in addition to all of his work.

There still remained one more bridge for us to cross. In late January or early February, we received a form from the Inland Revenue Authority of Singapore (IRAS) for income tax. I just so confidently said to Grandpa, "Shall I just throw it away? We certainly don't have to pay any income tax here." His wise reply was that we should at least call them, explain the situation, and get their okay on it. I called, and to say the least, I was shocked with what they told me. We were responsible for income tax!

The reasoning was that while we were working in Singapore, we were earning money. Regardless of where the money came from, it was made while we were in Singapore and consequently was subject to Singapore income tax. This included our wages, the rental value of the flat we were living in, the utilities if they had been paid for by the church, and the little bit of interest on bank accounts in the USA and Singapore. There were no allowable deductions and besides that, if you are in Singapore for less than six months in a calendar year, you are taxed straight across the board at 16 percent. We were in Singapore for four months in 1991 and for two months in 1992, hence we were required to pay the 16 percent.

I went down to the IRAS to plead our case (which was a bit embarrassing for Grandpa), but I had to give it my best shot since it just seemed so unreasonable. Guess who won. We didn't even have that kind of money with us in order to pay it. They finally agreed that we could charge it on our Visa card, and the PRC generously reimbursed us for it when we returned. Live and learn. The ERCS had no idea of these laws either, so they were as surprised as we were.

I can't remember if we thought those six months went by quickly or not. I just know we were happy and eager to get back home and be with the family. The weather in Singapore is much the same every day: hot and hotter. It always rains somewhere on the island, so you take an umbrella with you all the time. It's summer all twelve months of the year.

We were introduced to many new, and sometimes strange, foods. I think in that department, Grandpa is more adventurous than I am; he dared to try anything and everything, while I was a bit choosier. How does soup with chicken feet sound to you? How about Pig Organs Soup (chunks of blood, intestines, stomach, etc.); just the name is enough to turn one's stomach upside down.

All in all, that first stay in Singapore was quite an eye-opening and enriching experience for us. We loved God's people there, and it was a thrill to worship with them as they were learning to sing the Psalter numbers and were growing in their understanding. The members of the ERCS appreciated Grandpa's work and leadership, and we experienced the Lord's blessing too in the work not only, but also in his sustaining grace and care in our lives.

Part Two

Personal Conversion Accounts

The Good Shepherd

The Lord my Shepherd holds me
Within His tender care,
And with His flock He folds me,
No want shall find me there.
In pastures green He feeds me,
With plenty I am blest;
By quiet streams He leads me
And makes me safely rest.

Whatever ill betides me,
He will restore and bless;
For His Name's sake He guides me
In paths of righteousness.
Thy rod and staff shall cheer me
In death's dark vale and shade,
For Thou wilt then be near me:
I shall not be afraid.

My food Thou dost appoint me,
Supplied before my foes;
With oil Thou dost anoint me,
My cup of bliss o'erflows.
Thy goodness, Lord, shall guide me,
Thy mercy cheer my way;
A home Thou wilt provide me
Within Thy house for aye.*

---

* No. 55, in *The Psalter with Doctrinal Standards, Liturgy, Church Order, and added Chorale Section*, reprinted and revised edition of the 1912 United Presbyterian Psalter (Grand Rapids, MI: Wm. B. Eerdmans Publishing Co., 1927; rev. ed. 1995).

Chapter 3

IT WAS ONLY A PICTURE

Amazing grace! How sweet the sound
That saved a wretch like me!
I once was lost, but now am found;
Was blind, but now I see.

'Twas grace that taught my heart to fear,
And grace my fears relieved;
How precious did that grace appear
The hour I first believed!

The Lord has promised good to me,
His Word my hope secures;
He will my shield and portion be,
As long as life endures.

Yea, when this flesh and heart shall fail,
And mortal life shall cease,
I shall possess, within the veil,
A life of joy and peace.[*]

*A*mazing grace! This story is unique in many ways, and amazing! The story covers many years, and the details are as I recall them. You will enjoy reading the story of a young girl named Poh Li.

Our first introduction to Poh Li was when Karen, a member of Covenant Evangelical Reformed Church, brought her to church one Sunday morning. I'm not sure of the year, but it must have been somewhere around 1995. Poh Li was only twelve years old at the time. According to God's sovereign will, Poh Li was in a store one day,

---

[*] John Newton (1779).

looking at pictures, and the one she was studying at the time was a picture of Christ. Karen walked up to her and asked, "Do you know who that is in the picture?" The answer from Poh Li was, "No, I don't."

Karen started to explain to her about Christ, and then Karen asked her if she would like to learn more. Poh Li responded positively, so they agreed to meet at a certain time in the void deck of Poh Li's flat so that Karen could tell her more. (The void deck is the ground level of a high-rise apartment building. It's an open area, and it can be used for various activities or social gatherings.) They had several such meetings at the void deck, and then Karen invited Poh Li to come along to church; that was when we met her. Poh Li loved to come to church, and she continued to do so.

Poh Li's mother was not happy; she didn't want her young daughter to be going to church. Just as we bring up our children to know and love the Lord, and it would be very sad and heartbreaking for us to see our children depart from the ways of the Lord, so they do not like their children to depart from the religion in which they were brought up and embrace Christianity. You have to understand also that having their child attend church is very threatening for the Buddhist, as well as those of other pagan religions, because they believe in ancestor worship. After a parent has departed from this life, their children and grandchildren must continually worship them so that the parent can enjoy a good life in hell. These parents have been faithfully worshiping their ancestors; and now, if their child should become a Christian, who is going to be there to worship them when they die? That's the big question in their minds.

Poh Li suffered persecution. She did not dress up to come to church but instead left home in jeans and a T-shirt, just as she would dress if she were going any other place. When she returned home and her mother inquired as to where she had been, she would truthfully tell her mother that she had gone to church. Her mother would be so very angry with her for going to church that she would cane her daughter on the back of her legs. This caning is not something insignificant—it hurts and hurts badly, so much so that marks would be left on the skin and the skin would even sometimes break and bleed. Poh Li once showed us the welts on the back of her legs a whole week after the canings had taken place.

Can you imagine how Poh Li felt when she would come to church again, knowing full well that a caning was in store for her as soon as she returned home? The young girl finally resorted to lying; she told her mother that she was going shopping with her friends when actually she was going to church. Her mother was pleased with this change in her daughter. I'm sure she thought the canings had accomplished what she wanted, since her daughter was no longer going to church, or so she thought. However, as a Christian, it is wrong to lie, and Poh Li had to be taught that lesson as well.

The session of CERC wrestled with this problem, and they finally had to advise this young girl that for the time being, it would be better if she did not come to church. She was still very young, and she should not try to lie her way out of persecution as lying is not good Christian testimony. It was arranged that, in the meantime, Karen would continue a weekly Bible study with her, trusting that the Lord would, in due time, work things out so that she would be allowed to come to church. Although you do not encourage one to stay away from church, you must take into consideration that there are cases where that would be advised, and in making that decision, you must consider what the difficulty is.

There was another case where, because his wife was not converted, a man was advised to go slowly, even to the point of staying away from church for a while and then to come only occasionally. His going to church brought difficulty into the home as Sunday was a family day, a day in which they could do things together, and now by going to church, he was denying his family that activity. Our reaction would be clear and simple, obedience to the Lord regardless of the outcome. But would you still say that if the result would be a divorce? He had to learn how to live with an unbelieving spouse. He did not give up on God, but he patiently waited for the Lord's leading in his life, and now he is able to attend church faithfully each week.

This went on for some time with Poh Li, but it was surprising how quickly things turned around and Poh Li was back in church. Although we don't know what went on in the home, I think it's safe to assume that Poh Li shared with her mother what she was learning and her desire to attend church.

12. For the eyes of the Lord are over the righteous, and his ears are open unto their prayers: but the face of the Lord is against them that do evil.
13. And who is he that will harm you, if ye be followers of that which is good?
14. But and if ye suffer for righteousness' sake, happy are ye: and be not afraid of their terror, neither be troubled;
15. But sanctify the Lord God in your hearts: and be ready always to give an answer to every man that asketh you a reason of the hope that is in you with meekness and fear:
16. Having a good conscience; that, whereas they speak evil of you, as of evildoers, they may be ashamed that falsely accuse your good conversation in Christ.
17. For it is better, if the will of God be so, that ye suffer for well doing, than for evil doing.
18. For Christ also hath once suffered for sins, the just for the unjust, that he might bring us to God, being put to death in the flesh, but quickened by the Spirit. (1 Pet. 3:12–18)

After that we didn't see Poh Li for a long time, many years in fact, and it wasn't because she quit going to CERC or that she was a backslider. The Lord was certainly working in the heart of this young Christian. It was around that time that Grandpa became the minister at FERC and Pastor Lau went to CERC, so there was a change in the church that we attended.

Our next contact with Poh Li was at the Reformation Day Conference when she was eighteen years old. The lectures that year were held in the sanctuary of FERC. As we were visiting among the people after the lecture, a young lady came up to us and said, "Do you remember me?" Oh boy, when someone says that, you immediately feel somewhat embarrassed; you don't like to admit that you can't make the connection. She said, "I'm Poh Li." Wow, what a surprise that was! We were so happy to catch up with her and find out how she was doing.

She was so eager to tell us that both her father and mother had been converted, and she was attending Chinese worship services with them since her parents do not understand the English language. She told us that their home is such a different place now, and she is so very happy and thankful that the Lord has worked in the hearts of her parents as well. The biggest change was in her father. He had been a typical Chinese father before his conversion; he provided for the family but had very little involvement with them. He gambled, smoked, was an alcoholic, and used bad language. Now he is entirely different. In the morning before he goes to work, he reads the Bible and prays; he comes home after work and has fellowship and devotions with the family. He has given up gambling, smoking, and drinking, and his speech is no longer accentuated with cuss words. He now speaks as one who knows and loves the Lord. *Amazing grace!*

Poh Li is a registered nurse now. She would never boast about anything she does, so it was from someone else that we learned that she faithfully witnesses of her Lord. As a nurse, she has contact with many other nurses and has brought many of them to church with her. Her spiritual life bubbles over in all her contacts, and she continues to be used of the Lord in this way.

Karen did not know and certainly did not expect that the Lord would use her simple little remark to kindle a flame in Poh Li's heart and that later the flame would be spread abroad into the lives of so many others. It is God's work alone that calls his children out of darkness into his marvelous light, but there are means through which he works. May we all be faithful witnesses of the glorious truth that he has revealed to us in his word. Not everyone has such a dramatic conversion story to tell, but God's saving grace is just as marvelous in every Christian's life, and our prayer is that we may always be thankful to God for the gift of salvation in Jesus Christ, our Lord.

You might wonder what became of Karen. Karen married a man from Malaysia who belonged to the Reformed Baptist Church, so she joined that church along with her husband. They lived in Penang for several years but later moved to Singapore. Karen is a sincere Christian mother of three young children.

Chapter 4

CHRIST, THE LORD OF ROMANCE

'Tis not that I did choose Thee,
For, Lord, that could not be;
This heart would still refuse Thee,
Hadst Thou not chosen me.
Thou from the sin that stained me
Hast cleansed and set me free;
Of old Thou hast ordained me,
That I should live to Thee.
'Twas sovereign mercy called me
And taught my opening mind;
The world had else enthralled me,
To heav'nly glories blind.
My heart owns none before Thee,
For Thy rich grace I thirst;
This knowing, if I love Thee,
Thou must have loved me first.[*]

We first met Siew Hua in late 1992 or early 1993. One Sunday evening when Grandpa was preaching in CERC, a newcomer walked in just before the service began. There wasn't time for introductions before the service, so we had to wait until afterward to find out something about this young girl.

After the service was over, Siew Hua came up to Grandpa with

---

[*] Josiah Conder, 1836.

this question, "Can you help me to become a Christian?" (That in itself was surprising, as it's quite unusual for someone to ask that out of the blue.)

Siew Hua was a young girl in her early twenties at that time. She had just returned from a trip to Australia, where she had met Anton Suurmond, a young man from the Netherlands who was also vacationing in Australia. The two young people had taken a shine to each other, but Anton had said to her, "I can't even consider having you for a girlfriend unless you become a Christian, and not only that, you must become a Reformed Christian." This girl was a Buddhist through and through and didn't have a clue what he meant by all of that.

Anton told her that when she returned to Singapore, she should look in the yellow pages of the telephone book under churches and then find Reformed churches. She followed through with his advice and found that CERC was the only Reformed church listed, so that was what occasioned her coming that Sunday evening. She was very interested in having Anton for her boyfriend, so naturally, caution came to our minds: is she doing this just to have him? Time would tell.

Grandpa agreed to meet with her on Saturday mornings if she could come to our apartment at Happy Mansion, 9C Happy Avenue. She was a working girl and Saturday was the most convenient for her. At first Grandpa had to get to know her a little better in order to understand where she was at. Her religion was the Chinese religion, a combination of Buddhism, Taoism, and Confucianism. She was very knowledgeable and knew what she believed. As Grandpa would find out, she could tell him many things about the Chinese religions. She was quite involved in Chinese art and one time brought along a large book of Chinese drawings from her collection and explained to Grandpa what some of the things meant. She was very insistent that the book was for Grandpa and that he was to keep it. Besides her having a difficult family relationship, the thought of getting out of Singapore and being free from the hectic lifestyle looked attractive to her.

As it turned out, for approximately two years Siew Hua came faithfully to our house every Saturday morning to receive instruction.

CHRIST, THE LORD OF ROMANCE

In teaching her, Grandpa made use of a book on the Heidelberg Catechism, written by Rev. Norman Jones. Rev. Jones is from the Reformed Church, Eureka Classis. His book treats the questions and answers of the Heidelberg Catechism from the viewpoint, "What is necessary for us to know that we may live and die happily?" Grandpa also found the book helpful as it contains much explanation on each question and worksheets are included in it.

It was interesting to watch the relationship of Anton and Siew Hua develop. Anton would come to Singapore occasionally to check up on her progress. I guess that's not saying it quite right; he came to spend time with Siew Hua, but her progress in becoming a Christian was also very important to him. Siew Hua also made a few trips to the Netherlands to see Anton, meet his family, and learn about the culture and living conditions in the country that would eventually become her home.

It was simply amazing how Siew Hua grew in knowledge not only, but also in her love for Christ and in her personal assurance that her sins are covered by his precious blood. It's always a marvel how God brings two young people together, but it's an even greater marvel how he calls one of his precious own out of the darkness of heathendom into his marvelous light. Siew Hua became a sincere Christian and faithfully attended both services at CERC while she lived in Singapore.

Along with her instruction in understanding the Scriptures, Grandpa also counseled her in the handling of relationships, especially with her family. Being a Christian with Buddhist parents has a great responsibility. It's not our choice as to whether we should obey and honor our parents, but it is God's command to us to do so. The witness must always be that when a person becomes a Christian, they are also a better son or daughter than what they were before their conversion.

Anton belonged to the Liberated Church in the Netherlands. Here was Siew Hua, an infant Christian, who was going to marry Anton, migrate to the Netherlands, and join the Liberated Church. How ironic that the first convert Grandpa could lead to Christ would become Liberated and not evangelical Reformed. It wouldn't be right to add confusion to this young Christian by telling her how the Liberated Church is wrong in their theology. What Grandpa taught her was the truth that we believe in the Protestant Reformed Churches (PRC). If she would have theological questions in her new church, the pastor there would have to explain the view they hold to. We have to see that the church universal is larger than the PRC, and God has his children in other churches as well.

Siew Hua had faithfully studied her lessons, was having her devotions daily, and now had come to the point where she desired church membership. After confessing her faith at a session meeting of CERC, she had adult baptism and confession of faith during a Sunday morning service. That is always a time of great rejoicing in the church. Most of the church members are first-generation Christians who easily recall what a big step it was for them at their baptism, so they quickly identify with the immense feelings of the person being baptized and truly rejoice with them.

Then the time came for the marriage of Anton and Siew Hua. Anton's family came to Singapore for the wedding. Grandpa gave the message at the ceremony, and Pastor Lau officiated as he was licensed in Singapore to perform marriages. They were married in the Zion Bible Presbyterian Church because, at that time, the ERCS did not have a suitable building for a wedding. The wedding reception was held at a social hall of the condo where her brother and sister-in-law lived. By this time we knew Siew Hua very well, so you can understand that this wedding also meant a lot to us.

She moved to the Netherlands with Anton, but that didn't stop our involvement with her. There were problems, not with Anton thankfully, but with other issues. You can only begin to imagine what it meant for a Chinese girl to move into a Dutch culture. Her in-laws could not speak English, people at church seemed to avoid her (racial prejudice?), she had trouble with grocery shopping when they didn't have the foods she was accustomed to, and the list went on and on.

Grandpa suggested that she enroll in a class to learn the Dutch language; this would give her something to work on and would also help her to adjust to the Netherlands. Trusting that advice, she quickly applied herself to doing that. Then the next thing was that the church wanted her to make public confession of faith again. She couldn't understand why. She had made confession of faith once; was it necessary to do that again? She wrote, "Will you write to my pastor and tell him what we did in Singapore and the confession I made?" Letters between Grandpa and the pastor were exchanged, but I don't recall how it was resolved.

Siew Hua learned Dutch. In addition to speaking Mandarin and various dialects, she had mastered the English language, and now she was living in the Netherlands with a whole new culture and speaking Dutch. She would send us postcards with her beginning efforts in the Dutch language. Talk about determination; she had it.

After a couple years, they made a trip to Singapore along with their first daughter, named Anna. It was delightful to have them stop by so that we could have a time of reconnecting and learn that Siew Hua was slowly but steadily adjusting to her new life. We found it so cute that their little girl was carrying an alphabet book in the Dutch language. Later on, they made another trip to Singapore, this time with two daughters, and we were able to have a visit with them again. On their last trip to Singapore, we were in the United States for our annual visit so we didn't get to see them, but they did leave a large tin of Wilhelmina peppermints for us at the church.

They would love to have us visit them sometime in the Netherlands, and I'm sure that would be a delightful experience for us. If we ever get to the Netherlands, we would certainly try to do that, but right now that seems quite unlikely.

We still do keep in touch occasionally, once or twice a year. I wrote to them in September 2005, and we were surprised to get an email back from them so quickly. She wrote in part,

Dear Mrs. and Pastor Kortering,

Counting back, it's nearly twelve years that I've left Singapore. Every reflection of the place is a mixed cocktail of emotion. The reason of your return to Singapore is indeed a painful one. My brief encounter of Pastor Cheah is an impression of a sincere man. He would have made a big influence in CERC. The Lord has his purpose; I remember very clearly Pastor Kortering's words that we may feel lost in chaos but turning the picture around then we'll see the whole embroidery.

As for me, I'm becoming to accept the real me. Since I've become a Christian, I've been trying to fit in. There's a part of me that I can't ignore. Before becoming a Christian, I was active in the arts-circle in S'pore. I've lost contacts since my interest in the Bible. I've realized I'm not good in anything only in drawing and painting and working with my hands. I've been producing works again and sold a few and participated in a few exhibitions.

Motherhood doesn't come as naturally as I would expect. Marriage and parenting comes with a lot of commitment. I'm grateful the Lord has brought us together and given us three healthy girls. An is becoming nine in two weeks. Luka is turning six in a month. And Feye is two and a half.

Congratulations with the birth of your first great grandson, Derek Lee. I'm full of admiration that you are still so active in traveling and adapting to all sorts of new situations. May our Lord continue to keep you both in good health so that you'll continue to make a difference to lives; you have certainly made an impact on mine.

Groetjes uit Den Helder,
Anton, Siew, An, Luka en Feye Suurmond.

And so life goes on for a dear struggling saint. It hasn't been an easy life for her, but that's not what the Lord promises us either. Each one has their own pilgrimage and we're thankful that the Lord never forsakes his own. I will write her soon again, encouraging her in her Christian walk with the Lord as she serves him in her calling as wife to Anton and mother to three young daughters. Our prayer is that the Lord will sustain and strengthen her throughout her life on earth till the time he calls her to her heavenly home to be with him in glory.

Chapter 5

MY SISTER WAS GIVEN AWAY

> Not unto us, O Lord of heaven,
> But unto Thee be glory given;
> In love and truth Thou dost fulfill
> The counsels of Thy sovereign will;
> Though nations fail Thy power to own,
> Yet Thou dost reign, and Thou alone.
>   The idol gods of heathen lands
>   Are but the work of human hands;
>   They cannot see, they cannot speak,
>   Their ears are deaf, their hands are weak;
>   Like them shall be all those who hold
>   To gods of silver and of gold.
> The heavens are God's since time began,
> But He hath given the earth to man;
> The dead praise not the living God,
> But we will sound His praise abroad,
> Yea, we will ever bless His Name;
> Praise ye the Lord, His praise proclaim.[*]

I have a good friend who was willing to share with me some of her background and also some life experiences. What we really want to see through this account is that she is an elect child of God, chosen from all eternity. As you read, keep in mind what she went through

---

[*] No. 308:1-2, 5, in *The Psalter*.

in her lifetime with little introductions to Christianity during her youth. You will see how the Lord worked faith in her heart when she was a teenager, and what a change this brought in her life. We can truly magnify God when we see his great work of conversion, calling one of his own out of darkness into his marvelous light. This story comes as a first-person account, a bit complicated at times, but it is very interesting.

My name is Cheng and at the present time I am in my late forties. I'm from a family of twelve children, seven sons and five daughters. The second daughter was given away (I'll explain that later), so there are eleven of us.

My grandmother was married at the age of sixteen or eighteen and her husband was from China. The husband was kind of a lone ranger: he was in Singapore alone without parents or other relatives. In those days when couples married, they would generally stay with the husband's family, but since he did not have family in Singapore, the young couple stayed with my grandmother's family. To that union one child was born, who is my father.

While in Singapore, my grandfather became sick with tuberculosis and returned to China for treatment. Something happened along the way that he passed away; how, where, or under what circumstances no one knows. He might even have died on the ship. My grandmother was then a widow with a young son and living with her parents. A younger brother, probably eight to ten years her junior, did not receive this well; to him it was an intrusion. He insisted that his sister and the child should not live with them: "A daughter must be out of the house when she is married." He, being a son, wanted his rightful place in the family.

My grandmother had no way to support herself and her child, so the only answer was to get her another husband, and her parents arranged a match-made marriage for her. With the second husband, my grandma had three more sons. There was an agreement that the stepson (my father) would retain his surname and receive an education. My father's relationship with his stepfather and stepbrothers was very good.

MY SISTER WAS GIVEN AWAY

One time Grandma made a trip to China, and she brought along the second and third sons. In China, the second husband's brother had a family of four daughters. The brother-in-law reasoned that something was wrong here: why did one have three boys and the other four girls? It must be because the grandfather's coffin was not situated correctly. When Grandma reached China, they discussed whether the coffin should be dug up. Grandma was against it; the casket could be rotted by this time, and besides that, if they didn't get it situated correctly the second time, it could bring bad luck to them. Grandma's solution was, "Why don't you give me one of your daughters, and I will leave one of my sons with you?" Sounded reasonable enough to that family, so that's exactly what happened.

Son number three was left in China with the aunt and uncle, and Grandma went back to Singapore with one boy and one girl. The son left behind was three or four years old at the time, and Grandma did not see him again for at least forty or fifty years. It was hard on Grandma; she wanted to go back to China in her old age and live with her son and die there. The family in Singapore discouraged that: "Grandma, you don't even know him." Personally, I could not stand the thought of my grandma leaving, as we knew her so well and loved her. Finally it was arranged that the son would come to Singapore to see her; he didn't even know his real mother. They cried together when they met but did not harbor ill feelings toward each other.

The son who was left behind in China (my uncle) was like a king in his new family there. Sons mean everything and daughters are of little value. Being the only son, he was very spoiled. He became a great gambler and even drove his wife to commit suicide. On the other hand, the girl whom Grandma brought to Singapore (my aunt by adoption) was very well treated and accepted in Singapore as she was the only daughter in the family. Grandma died in 1984 at eighty-four years of age. She was considered to be very generous in that she was willing to give away a son. Give away a girl? Why not? But give away a boy? Never! Later with communism and the one-child rule, many in China would kill their daughters by burying them alive and wait for a son.

My father had a store near the Singapore River, and his business was that of selling wood for burning. At that time, wood was used for cooking. The kitchens were at the back of the house; there was a hole in the floor in which they would place the wood, and then the wok or pots and pans would be placed over the fire. During World War II, the Japanese bombed my father's store so he was left with nothing. After that, he got enough money together to purchase a lorry (truck) for providing services in transporting goods. He would hang around at the godowns (warehouses) and take whatever jobs he could, or sometimes he would help someone with shifting house.

My father needed help with all the lifting and carrying of goods, so my eldest brother had to leave school after his primary education and help our father. When my brother was old enough and got his driver's license, my stepgrandfather (from now on called grandfather) bought another lorry so they could have two lorries for the business. My father was a gambler and would often play cards with his friends. He would park his lorry at the godowns while waiting for business, and someone would come and want him to do some work and he would say, "Oh, don't bother me." He'd forget about his business and continue his gambling.

My grandfather helped to provide lodging for the family so we didn't have to pay rent; we could live with him. He provided the main bulk of the food. In those days you could go to the market to get rice and other groceries; this would be recorded and the bill would be paid at the end of the month. My father provided food from the market, fish and vegetables. My grandpa especially loved the granddaughters and my eldest brother and gave us pocket money.

My father was the eldest son in his family, the second son was a bachelor until the age of about fifty, the third son was the one traded off in China, and the fourth son also married late. My father and mother gave Grandfather eleven grandchildren. Grandchildren are a great blessing, so Grandpa was happy. In that way my father benefited. But my father was angry because Grandpa often scolded him for not providing well for the family. My grandpa did quite well; he had bumboats that he rented out. Grandpa was financially strong, he loaned money to relatives, and then the relatives were good to our family in return by giving vegetables.

My father did not discipline. My seven brothers take after their father—they do not discipline either. My mother disciplined, but Grandma was the great disciplinarian master. Grandma was a small woman so she would make the child go on all fours and she would sit on their back and cane their butt; otherwise, they could run away from her and she would not be able to catch them. The eldest brother received the most discipline. Brothers two and three didn't give any trouble. The fourth brother was truant, so my third brother would help to catch him and get him back to school.

My mother was so busy with all the children that she didn't have time for discipline, and moreover, she pampered her sons. Sons are special, and she loved them and treated them more special than the daughters. That was so much a part of her that today it is still the same way, but then you also have to understand some of my mom's background.

My maternal grandfather's first wife was not able to conceive. At the time when they married, a maid also came along with the wife. Since there were no children, my grandpa took the maid for his second wife. (Reminds you of Abraham and Hagar.) My mother is the daughter of the maid, the second wife. Later another daughter was born, but the baby died soon afterward and then wife number two (my real grandmother) also died. Now there was only the first wife and my mother.

Grandpa left wife number one and my mother in China, and he came to Singapore and married a third wife, who bore him three sons and one daughter. Later on, he sent to China to have wife number one and my mother come to Singapore. They all lived together in the same house, but wife number three bullied wife number one: "You can't conceive," "You didn't contribute anything to this family." By the time Grandfather took wife number four, wife number one had died, and wife number four was several years younger than his eldest daughter (my mother). The fourth wife bore him seven daughters and two sons.

They had a large shophouse with a business downstairs and living quarters upstairs. Grandpa was considered a "small millionaire"; he had a car and a chauffeur. He had a pig farm and could provide for the family, but he could not keep his own assets in order. Wife number four's father helped Grandpa by arranging the purchase of other homes in Singapore but never put Grandpa's name with it, so Grandpa was bilked of his money by his own father-in-law.

I am number eleven in my family. First there were three sons. The fourth child was a daughter. The fifth child also was a daughter, and she is the one who was given away. She was given away unintentionally; my mother wasn't planning to do this. My mom went with the baby to visit her family. A relative, not a close relative, was also visiting there. My sister at that time was about three months old, a nice chubby little girl. The woman commented on the beautiful child, and my mother being so modest said, "So ugly, if you want to have her, you may." My mother did not mean this of course, but the other woman had taken it seriously.

In the end, my mom felt that it might not be so bad; this couple did not have any children, they were quite well-to-do, and it might be better for her daughter as she would be the eldest in this family rather than number five in her own family where the income was not stable. (In those days when you gave away a child, you would have to give condensed milk, which was a supplement for breast milk, because there was no formula then. Not the other way around, that the couple receiving the child would pay you something. You had to give condensed milk because you were "giving them a burden.") My father didn't have a real bonding or affection for the daughter, so it really didn't matter to him that the baby was given away, and my grandfather didn't make an issue of it either, since there were three sons and a daughter already and this was another girl.

The couple who received my sister did not keep the baby for themselves. She had a sister-in-law who also did not have any children and had been married for several years so she gave the baby to her. This couple did not live near my parents. They lived in Sembawang in Singapore, which in those days was considered very far away. Singapore is a small country; nothing is far away nowadays, but before they had all the public transport, it was difficult to get to some areas. They gave my sister away without informing my parents about it, and my mother didn't follow through to check up on the baby, so they actually lost contact with their child.

The couple in whose home my sister grew up later had children of their own. Whether my sister had difficulty with school or whether she was needed to help with the family, she was only given two years of education. The family had a farm, and she helped with the work on the farm and looked after the younger children. She knew she had been adopted; she knew who her real parents were and even maintained that surname, but she was never allowed to have contact with them.

When my sister was around eighteen and had a boyfriend, the boyfriend encouraged her to find out about her real family, and since they were some distant relatives, she was able to do this. She was very, very bitter about her situation. She learned that the rest of the family had some education and she had only two years of school. Quite naturally she felt that her mother did not love her since she could give her own daughter away so casually.

When the government of Singapore started building the Housing Development Board (HDB) flats, the family who adopted my sister had to leave their farm as the land would be used for the building of high-rise apartment buildings. Consequently, at that time, my sister had no choice but to work for a construction company, carrying stones and cement. She married at age nineteen and had two daughters and one son.

At first her husband was a good family man and cared for his family, but there were problems. The husband felt that my sister overdid her affection for the son, resulting in the son not showing respect for his father. He had also lost his job, and my sister, in order to earn some money, took some work of collecting illegal betting that she would then turn over to an illegal booker. After about ten years, the marriage deteriorated to the point of divorce. My sister felt that her husband betrayed her by informing the police of her activities, and she was eventually sentenced to three months in jail.

After the divorce, my sister left the family. The children at that time stayed with their father in the family home. My sister was destitute and needed a place to stay. By that time, the adoptive parents had already passed away. My sister is not a Christian, but she reached out to me to see if the family could help her. I encouraged my parents to take her in because we had an extra room in the house where she would be able to stay. My mother's reply was, "Yes, she's my daughter," but my father said, "No, she already was given away." My mother did have the feeling that probably my sister would be taking problems with her into the home, so she didn't object to my father's opinion. It was very difficult for me to explain to my sister that she was not welcome to live with us.

There was a time when we would see her on special occasions and with the Chinese New Year, but since the divorce, she does not wish to have contact anymore. Her two daughters are married now and sad to say, the son is not filial. I do feel very sorry for her; she had a difficult childhood, some good years in her marriage, but then a difficult life again after that.

When my grandfather passed away, we did send for her to come to the funeral. She came but then left immediately afterward. She is very angry and refuses to speak with our mother, but she will still speak with our eldest sister.

Our family was not strictly Buddhist in that we worshiped only Buddha. We weren't really Taoist either. I would say we were more pagan worshipers with many gods and idols. There was the monkey god, the kitchen god, etc. Before I was even old enough to go to school, I would follow my grandmother to the temple to chant because my grandma was very devout. I don't know what the chants meant because I was too young to understand, but it was easy to learn as it was very repetitious. Using beads, you would say the same thing over and over again; same concept as the rosary in the Roman Catholic Church. None of my family was exposed to Christianity, so we just followed along.

We had an altar in our home and worshiped our ancestors and would offer joss sticks. Our parents did this daily, and we children would do it on special occasions, like with our grandparents' birthdays, Chinese New Year, on the gods' birthdays, seventh lunar month, etc. There were many occasions for mini-celebrations when this would be done. The Chinese pagan worshipers believe that during the seventh lunar month, spirits of the deceased roam the earth. These are spirits (guards who receive the dead when they die) and they must be worshiped during this month.

At one time my mother was behaving strangely after visiting the temple and they thought she was possessed with an evil spirit. They consulted a medium, who advised my mother to move out of the family home and live in a hut for a time. Since I was one of the younger children, I went along with her.

My first exposure to Christianity was in Primary 2. My form teacher was a Christian and she is now the principal of the school my son goes to. She was a neighbor to us in the kampong and brought me to church. I don't remember the worship service, but I do remember the Sunday school and I liked going there because we would receive something for attendance. I remember one little song that we sang.

> Clean hands, dirty hands
> Brown eyes or blue
> Short hair or curly
> Jesus loves you.

My parents didn't stop me from going to church. They knew the broad term Christianity but could not distinguish that from Roman Catholic. To them it was just another place to go and it didn't worry them at all. They more than likely didn't expect me to believe, and maybe because I was a girl, it didn't matter to them what religion I had. My brothers and sisters were not exposed to Christianity at an early age as I was.

During primary school days, life was simple. I just walked to school and walked home afterward and then would play on my own, pretending to be a teacher. There was no TV and we didn't have toys. Many times we would just hang around our dad's lorry and play together. We would play cooking, using the old pots and pans our mother gave us. Grandmother was the mother-in-law, so she didn't do any of the work in the home. My mother was the one who did all the work, the cooking and washing. Grandma would entertain the children and bring them to the park.

For various reasons, the children in our family did not complete their education. Some had to leave school after Primary 6 and others went through their O-levels (tenth grade). Although there was a kindergarten in my day, I was not able to go because the family was too poor. I did have a lot of freedom during my growing-up years and could join games at school. Besides being illiterate, my mother was very busy with her large family, so she would not be concerned if I had studied, and my father was busy with his gambling. My eldest sister, ten years my senior, was like a second mummy to me. She always would check to make sure my school assignments were complete and that I was ready for tests.

I was very privileged; after Primary 3, I improved tremendously in my grades so when I reached Primary 6, I was first in my standard. My teacher said, "Your results have been quite good and consistent since Primary 3. I think you should be able to go to Raffles Girls' School," the top secondary school in Singapore. I was very simple; whatever my teacher said, I followed. When I came to RGS, there were bright girls from all over Singapore at that school, and I thought, "Oh, dear, now what?" but I tried not to let it bother me. I must say in school days, I was more for fun than studies.

It was in Secondary 1 or 2 that I went along for Youth for Christ.

MY SISTER WAS GIVEN AWAY

There was a house next to the school where a Christian family lived, and they would let us use their house once a week for the YFC meeting. They would have singing and a story, and it was fun, so why not join them? So I went for YFC, but I did not believe. My parents didn't make an issue of it. I would tell my sister about it but really, we didn't talk much about such things. In Secondary 3, a present church member witnessed to me of the gospel. I was a hard nut to crack. She told me how sin entered this world, and I would question and question her until she couldn't answer, and then I said to her, "You can't convince me."

During my secondary school years, our family lived in an HDB and we got enough money to buy a black and white TV and a radio. I joined the police cadet course so I would be busy with foot drill. My weekends were spent with ECA (extracurricular activities). My parents didn't have any objection to anything we did—what shows we watched on TV, what music we listened to on the radio; we just did whatever we wanted. My father was not involved in discipline at all. My mother did teach us things like hygiene, be courteous, respect your elders, girls should not behave in such a way as to invite trouble.

We were poor so could not choose our own clothing. There were hand-me-downs, and once in a while my sister or cousin would sew for us. We didn't have McDonald's at that time, but I longed to go to A&W after a game; the root beer was such a treat. Other entertainment was occasionally going to a Chinese movie show. We didn't go to the English shows, as they were hard to understand because they talked so fast, so it was always the Chinese shows. My eldest sister went on dates, and it was common then to take a younger brother or sister along on a date, so I frequently tagged along with her and her boyfriend. RGS girls were not to hang around in shopping centers with their uniform on. Some of my friends had branded goods because they came from rich families, but they did not brag about the things they had or wore. The only drug at that time was opium.

I went to Hwa Chong for junior college (grades 11 and 12). It was there that I was approached by Campus Crusade. You're familiar with the Four Spiritual Laws, right? After someone met with me, I suddenly wanted to believe and accept the Lord Jesus. For a time the Campus Crusade followed up with me. It was also about this time that one of my friends from RGS introduced me to GLTD (Gospel Literature and Tract Department). Pastor Lau Chin Kwee was leading this group in a Bible study on Saturdays, going through the books of the Bible. He was quite straightforward; "Hair is a crowning glory and God does not intend that we should cut our hair short." I was quite a tomboy and had short hair. All the girls there had long hair and I was the only one with short hair. I felt embarrassed but carried on just the same.

My family was very terrible in religious worship. They are neither Buddhist nor Taoist, but besides having so many idols, they even seek the medium's help. The medium would be in a trance in the spirit of one of the gods, and they will seek some kind of divine help. When I was sick, my mother would go to the medium, come back and burn some special paper with red writing, put it in water, and give it to me to drink three times a day. Rather than seeking a doctor's help, they would go to the medium. My mother would go to the medium not only for medical reasons but also if she was worried for the children when taking a very important exam or if my brothers were going for their driving test. In this way my mother gave us a blessing. I didn't think there was anything wrong with that until I became a Christian.

I remember when my grandfather passed away and they wondered how he was getting along in hell, they got a medium to come in. The medium came and said, "Now look at your grandfather's spirit. Your grandfather's spirit will come into this woman, and she will behave like your grandfather now and tell you what happened." Not only that, but this woman, who was a complete stranger, could also tell us who we were and other things about ourselves. I wondered how that could ever be. My grandfather, through the medium, said he was okay; he was very rich in hell because my grandma burned big paper ships, paper houses, and lots of paper money for him. He didn't need anything, so my grandpa didn't have any complaint.

MY SISTER WAS GIVEN AWAY

But another spirit tried to enter this woman, and that was the spirit of my true grandmother who died in China. That grandma said nothing was good for her because no one was praying for her. It was true, we had all forgotten about her. So my mother started worshiping her ancestors, praying to her mother and offering joss sticks. She became very devout and believed this was the true god; whenever she had any worries or concerns, she would go to the medium.

My mother also consulted with a fortune-teller and was told that I should be given away, with the reason being that the family was big. Yes, the family was big alright, there were eleven children (my younger brother was born already by that time) and I was a girl besides. There was a family that wanted to adopt me; they were thinking of me as a child bride. I would live with them, care for the needs of their grandson while I was growing up, and then eventually I would marry him. Funny thing is, this family also went to a fortune-teller. They were told that I would not be a good match for their grandson; they had checked the date of my birth and it wasn't auspicious. Perhaps I could not give them children or something, or perhaps I would be too independent, so they didn't want me anymore. I look at this as a blessing.

There was another family who wanted to adopt me; they already had three girls and a couple boys. I only came to know about this family at the time of my maternal grandfather's death. This particular family was some relative of my grandparents, so they were at the funeral. The lady remarked, "Oh, this is the girl that I was supposed to have." The reason I was not given to them is because about that time my father won a large amount of money from the lottery, and since this was the first time he won, they considered me to be a lucky child.

It's truly amazing how the Lord preserved me throughout my youth. I did burn joss sticks when I was young, but that was before I became a Christian and I didn't know the Lord. When I came to know the Lord, it made such a big difference in my life. When I was in secondary school, I read a book of Charles Darwin's theory of evolution and was very much impressed. But when I started reading the Bible and came to know the Lord, I thought what foolishness to believe in evolution; creation meant much more to me.

I also saw the foolishness of idol worship. One of the idols that is worshiped was a general in China. Although he didn't consider himself to be a god, he is worshiped because of a particular experience in his life. The story is that many years ago, a battle was fought with bows and arrows. The general was struck by one of these arrows, which had poison in it. They had to cut away some flesh because of the poison, and this general was so great that the flesh could be cut without using any anesthetic, and his mind was still so clear that he could play chess. Somewhat superhuman, he is considered to be a great hero and is worshiped yet to this day. Especially the policemen will worship this god because he was a warrior. You will see a photo or an idol of this person in many of the police stations in Singapore.

There is a story of the monkey god that goes something like this: The monkey god, a pig, and a monk go with an abbot (chief monk) on a journey to get the scriptures and travel along the Silk Road to Nepal. The monkey god was naughty and made havoc in heaven. He could become a fly and go in and out of a body and make trouble. At the time I was very much taken in by these stories, but I had a teacher at RGS who I don't believe was a Christian, and she told me the real meaning behind the story. She said it had to do with the political situation in China at the time, perhaps communism. Someone wanted to criticize the situation in China, but he could not do this openly and use the real names or he would get himself in trouble; so instead, he fabricated a story that was supposed to convey what was going on there. There are many variations of the story now, but people took it seriously and still believe it to this day; you can read about it in books.

When I became a Christian, all of this was completely foolish. You wonder how people can believe all this stuff; it's only because God has not opened their eyes and worked in their hearts. It was not a concern at all to my family when I started going to church. The same thing was true when I was going to be baptized, although my mom did caution me; she said, "You might want to wait with being baptized until you have a life partner. What if you would marry a nonChristian?" But I went ahead and was baptized.

I was a very unforgiving person who would carry grudges. My brother one time offended me with something he said when I was in junior college. I didn't talk to him for ten years. Family and friends would say to me, "You're a Christian now, why do you behave like that?" Whatever you do, they watch how you behave and what you say. Even after becoming a Christian, it took time for me to have a forgiving spirit.

After leaving college, we would have house parties where we would just get together to play games and chit-chat. When I first became a Christian, I was not very pious; I was not reading my Bible enough. I even backslid for a time. I told one of the sisters, who was also my classmate in RGS, that I wanted to quit church. The elders of the church were trying to reach out to me but I would tell them to leave me alone, that they could better spend their time on the new members who were coming to the church. At the time I was depressed but couldn't share this with anyone; it had to be worked out with God alone.

There were a couple reasons for my depression. I was attending the U (university) and my family was very happy about this since none of the other children went to the U. Because I was in the first batch to attend classes in Kent Ridge campus (it was new and out of the way), I was lonely there. By nature, I am a very outgoing person, and I found school to be very boring and miserable without my friends around. The subject I feared most was commercial law because it just didn't sink in. Another subject I had was accounting, which I thought I would fail. I wanted desperately to quit, but the family wanted me to continue. Finally my grandma, being so tired of hearing all the complaining, said, "Why don't you just quit then?" Great! I would take that advice, so I quit within my first two months there. I took a job and tried to convince myself that I would not regret having quit the U. Another upsetting thing in my life was the breakup with my boyfriend. He was a Christian and I went with him to his church sometimes, the Church of Christ. No one knew of my difficulties; my family didn't even know about my boyfriend.

The GLTD was meeting in a kampong at River Valley Road. A ladies fellowship met on Saturday, which I enjoyed, and I continued going back there each week. They would sing, study Scripture, and pray for the needs of each other, and I found this to be encouraging. Still, no one knew what I was going through. This went on for two or three months, and I would just cry every night. I knew it would be wrong for me to commit suicide, so when I came home at night, I would walk down the middle of the road and hope that a car would hit me in the dark, and then it would be all over.

There were ups and downs in my working life. I was putting all the blame on God for the difficulties in my life, and I didn't go back to church. I kept questioning God and it seemed God did not answer my prayers. I think it was about a half year that I didn't go to church. At the point of giving up entirely, it was only God who could turn my life around.

Finally, when I did go back to GLTD, I found the messages to be too long and too dry. So, for a time, I tried other churches: Lutheran Church, Queenstown Methodist. The messages there were shorter, but they did not bring peace to me. Then I went back to GLTD and haven't moved since. I could never have peace until I was back in God's house. It was God who worked in me. It would have been hopeless if it were left up to me. I will never leave the church again; I love my Lord so much. He has carried me through; I want to always stay faithful to him.

My family accepts me and does not persecute me. It's interesting that anyone in the family who has problems prefers to talk it over with me. My brother went through a time of depression and asked me to pray to my God for him. A couple years after my dad passed away, my mom was diagnosed with cancer. She understood that my God is powerful, and she asked, "Can you please pray with me to your God?" She asked the same thing of my cousin who is a Christian, so I was becoming hopeful that now she would desire to learn more of Christianity, but after the hospital stay, she went to live by my sister and things changed again as my sister is Buddhist.

In the Psalms, David says we are conceived and born in sin. That is me too. But I also believe that from the day I was born, God had chosen me to be one of his children. When my mother was pregnant with me, she even drank Chinese herbs in order to abort me since she had so many children, but that did not work. It was the Lord who kept my life. He preserved me in my younger days so I did not get caught up in materialism, sinful temptations, etc. A person's faith in the Lord will only be strengthened with a personal walk with God. The Lord has molded me. If there's anything in my life, I will never give up on God.

My father-in-law is a Catholic, but he only became Catholic when my husband was a teenager, so my husband never joined the Catholic church but he did follow his father for a time. The Lord has given us a son, and through the son has taught me to be a patient person. I have a sister who became Catholic when she married her husband. This is confusing to my family; they say, "You are both Christians. She can carry joss sticks and you don't. Her mother-in-law consults a medium even when she's Catholic but you don't." My mom says, "You're a bit too strict; the other one is easier to understand." To them, if there's a cross, that means Christian.

The family doesn't have the peace that we experience. When it comes to death, they are fearful. For now they are caught up with greed. They believe the idols are the ones who can fulfill their needs for health and wealth, and if they don't get as much as they want, they resign it all to fate. They will also go to a fortune-teller to change fate.

When a child is born, they will check out the year, the date, and the time. In the Chinese Zodiac calendar there is a cycle of twelve animals; you could be born in the year of the rat, ox, tiger, rabbit, dragon, snake, horse, goat, monkey, cockerel, dog, or pig. For example, if a child is born in the year of the tiger, and beside that if he is born at night, that would be very good because that would mean the child will be ambitious; the tiger hunts for prey at night. They believe the personality of a child is according to the year they are born. If the year had something to do with fire, the baby would probably be given a name that has to do with water in the Chinese language, like the word for river, stream, or rain.

My parents didn't pay much attention to this. In their generation, they thought more of geomancy. A person might ask what the best day to shift house is; one day would be more auspicious than another day. A geomancer would tell new homebuyers to get a pineapple and before going into the house, throw the pineapple in. When you speak this word in the Hokkien dialect, it sounds like prosperity, so you would throw the pineapple in and leave it for seven days, which would mean prosperity will come in.

Recently in our home, we were singing Psalter 308. To me this is so very real and I took the time to carefully explain it to our son. "The idol gods of heathen lands are but the work of human hands; / They cannot see, they cannot speak, their ears are deaf, their hands are weak; / Like them shall be all those who hold to gods of silver and of gold" (stanza 2). My brother prays to the idol to win the lottery. He was very angry when he did not win; he came home, went to the idol, and scolded him. In pagan worship there are many gods and supposedly each god has its own certain powers.

My grandmother did become a Christian. There was a real change in her life; she loved to talk about it and asked many questions. She would sit in her chair with her eyes closed and pray out loud. It was so meaningful and precious to witness that. I do speak to my mother about the gospel and have taken her to the Chinese worship service, but she is not expressive. I would like her to talk more.

Chapter 6

THEY TORE UP MY BIBLE

> Jesus is all the world to me,
> My life, my joy, my all;
> He is my strength from day to day,
> Without him I would fall:
> When I am sad, to him I go,
> No other one can cheer me so;
> When I am sad, he makes me glad,
> He's my friend.
>
> Jesus is all the world to me,
> I want no better friend;
> I trust him now, I'll trust him when
> Life's fleeting days shall end:
> Beautiful life with such a friend,
> Beautiful life that has no end;
> Eternal life, eternal joy,
> He's my friend.[*]

Dorin is a member of FERC, along with her husband and their three daughters. When Dorin was young, primary school age, her parents, with their seven children, were poor. Her father was very sickly and unable to work. Everyone had to pitch in as much as possible to help the family meet the day-to-day expenses. The older children had some work but were not able to bring in enough money.

---

[*] Will L. Thompson (1904).

Dorin had to help her mother in her "bread business." Her mother would get bread from the bakery and bring it home in a cart. When Dorin came home from school, she would help by "cutting the skin off" (in Singapore you can buy white bread without crust), slicing the bread, wrapping it in "butter paper," and stapling it shut. Then they would go around and sell the bread to the neighbors. This didn't bring in much money, but they had to do whatever work they could find—every little bit helped.

Due to the father's sickness and the mother working, the discipline of the children was mostly left to the eldest brother (six or seven years her senior) and the eldest sister. The brother could tell the children what to do and administer the caning if they didn't obey. Her older sister cooked food for the family every day, and it would be left there for everyone to help themselves whenever they were hungry.

Dorin shared this background with us, and what follows is the religious activity of the family and what her life was like when she became a Christian. She tells her own story.

We had ancestral altars in our home. My parents prayed to their ancestors every day and burned joss sticks; they believed this was their duty.

I often wondered, so I asked Dorin, "What is their prayer like? What do they say?"

They always pray for good health, family to be okay, more money, prosperity, lotteries to be won, good luck; just pray for themselves, that's all. Their prayer to the kitchen god is for rice every day, sugar, food—not a stingy amount, but bountifully, so you always have enough food.

You said your family was poor. Did you ever lack for food?

Thank God, we always had enough to eat. We could always eat the leftover bread.

My parents would pray every day, and on the first and fifteenth of the month they would burn incense paper to the dead, to their ancestors, to their gods. My parents were staunch about this. They taught us children to do this as well; we had to burn the joss sticks and pray. My parents would furnish the altar with little cups of wine or tea before they prayed, and afterward they would just leave the wine or tea there until the next time and then throw it out and start over fresh. Occasionally they had to clean the altar, not every day, but the joss sticks and incense made the altar quite dusty, so it must be cleaned up. Every year they would change the frame around the altar and have a special prayer. In this activity, we children just followed the example of our parents.

The Chinese New Year celebration in our family was quite simple. As others marry into the family, different dialects and customs are brought in. My husband is Hokkien dialect, and his family is not as superstitious as my family is. Both of my parents are Hainanese. There were many superstitions in our family; for example, you cannot use a broom on certain days. For them, they were praying for good luck, so you must not sweep it away. This is a very common practice with Chinese New Year, but different families have different customs. For my family, the broom was always put out of sight, and we replaced the brooms regularly.

In Secondary 1, we had a Christian teacher by the name of Mr. Goh. He was very devoted to God, and during recess time (we called it tea break), he would invite the students to come to the science lab, where he would have a short Bible study with them. I was quite curious as to what was going on there behind the school hall. He had the students pass out pamphlets and tracts to others, so it soon became known that they were holding a Bible study along with a time of singing. I was not attracted to the Bible study; it was the songs that attracted me, so I went there to sing. I love to sing.

I knew my family was very opposed to Christianity, so I was determined to take a stand and thought, "No, I'll just go there to listen, will not get involved, just go there to sing." The leader, Mr. Goh, was also my science teacher. When the Bible stories were told, I really didn't react to them at all. I would say to myself, "No, I cannot do it because my family will definitely object; they may push me away." All I can say is I know it was the Lord's working in my heart that I was converted. I don't know exactly when I was saved, but I realized I needed a Savior to save me from my sins, and I believed the Word of God. I was given a Bible and some worksheets to do at home and would secretly keep them in my bag so the family would not know.

I faithfully attended the twenty-minute meetings at school each recess time. Later on, I became more involved in the group and went to school early in order to help them distribute tracts, but I didn't tell my parents about it. If they found out what I was doing, there would be a stop to it immediately. As time went on, I realized I had to tell my family. I had to make a stand for the Lord Jesus, so I went home, and I openly read my Bible. I was around fourteen years old at the time. My brother went to the same secondary school and was aware that there were some group meetings at school, and he slowly put it together that that was what I had become involved in. He went to school and complained to the principal about these group meetings.

At that time I was very enthusiastic for Christ's sake. I had to spend time in my family with the work, and I also wanted to go to church. On Saturday morning there was the GLTD meeting at Life Bible Presbyterian Church that I wanted to attend, so I tried to sneak out of the house when I should have been working. When my eldest brother came to know of it, he was so furious with me.

That's when the real persecution began. He said, "Your God is so powerful? I can stop you!" and he locked all the doors. They also scolded me, but I was stubborn and still carried on, and then they would just come back with more punishment.

What kind of punishment?

He would beat me. I was given a choice: did I want them to use a broom, a wire, or a stick to whip me on my legs? He would run around chasing me and beating me. Really you know, it was very bad, leaving caning scars behind.

And you were at such a tender age; I think of kids who are fourteen years old now.

But I always felt the Lord strengthened me. The Bible says, Blessed are ye when you are persecuted for Jesus' sake, so that verse kept me going; you are blessed because you are persecuted. This news spread to the Bible study group at school, and they encouraged me and prayed for me. I don't remember if Mr. Goh actually talked with my brother or not when he complained to the school.

I was always keen to go for the Bible studies. They also had camp outings, and I was keen for that as well.

Were you able to do that?

I just told my family I'm going off, and zoom, there I go. Of course when I returned, they were very angry. The camp outings were usually one or two days. The students' parents had to give their permission for their son or daughter to attend by signing a form. That was something I could not ask my parents to do; they would not sign such a form. The leaders of the camp, knowing my situation, allowed me to go without parental permission. I know it wasn't right to do, but I wanted so much to go.

I had to endure a lot of persecution when I came back. My family members tore up my Bible and anything that had to do with Bible study; they ripped it all up. That was when I realized I had to memorize God's Word; I didn't have my own Bible anymore, so I tried memorizing everything I learned. It is so comforting; I can still remember God's Word, so marvelous, "I will never leave thee, nor forsake thee" (Heb. 13:5). These verses always come back to me and give me strength as I go through so many years already.

My brother continued to be very strict. He still scolded, still punished; in fact, the whole family was involved in scolding me. And then he would warn my sister (I have a younger sister who was also in secondary school): "Don't you ever become a Christian." I did bring her along to the Bible study, but she had seen all that I went through; it was so terrifying that she dared not come.

The Lord gave you strength; it's amazing.

It's tremendous.

When they gave me food to eat, I'd always say grace. My family would taunt me, "This food has been offered to idols."

Did they offer the food to the idols every day?

Not every day, occasionally, maybe once or twice a week. They offered everything, the food and the drink. They would set the table, place all the food on the altar and pray, and then eat. On those days, I would go without food. They would say to me, "Okay, you think your God is so great, he can provide anything." I told them, "I am a Christian, and I don't take food that is offered to idols." In the Bible we read, "As concerning therefore the eating of those things that are offered in sacrifice unto idols, we know that an idol is nothing in the world, and that there is none other God but one" (1 Cor. 8:4). I knew I could eat that food, nothing was changed, but my family didn't believe that; and so I could not eat with them.

Would you have to go completely without food, or could you go to the kitchen and get something?

My mother was very kind and would keep something, bread or something, for me. The Lord will always make a way. My mother isn't a Christian, but she pitied me, she didn't like to see her daughter suffering, so she would secretly pass me food so I could survive to the next day. I knew roughly when there would be food again; I would be going to school the next day, and during tea break, I could eat till I was full.

Our family home was one room and one hall (living room) in an HDB flat; all the family members lived there, nine of us. We slept in the living room; there was no privacy at all, no place where I could go and be by myself. Everything we did, the family knew. When I would pray, they would come and disturb me, knock on my head and say, "Hey, what are you doing?" Then I would go in the toilet[*] to have some quiet time, and they would say, "Why are you taking so long time in the toilet?" Soon I thought of ways to have my Bible study and devotions outside instead of at home. When I would say grace before eating, I would always hold on to my food; otherwise, it would disappear! It looked so funny, but I said, "Lord, I have to do it. I have to give thanks. I have to stand as a Christian."

---

[*] In Singapore they use the word "toilet" for bathroom.

The Lord carried me through. So *wonderful!* Each time as I stand for him, I become stronger, and the Lord brought me through all these many trials. I thank God. Without all this, I would just be a weak Christian. So things change; the Lord is good.

After you became a Christian, did they still want you to go to the temple and burn joss sticks?

Oh, yes, they did not leave me alone. They still forced me to pray to the gods; they still insisted that I must pray to the ancestors and carry joss sticks. When I was young, we went to the large temple in Waterloo Street where there is the Goddess of Mercy. In my primary days, I would pop by the temple and pray before I went home every day. When I was young, I would do that.

We were taught how to pray and throw the charms or something like that (some temples use sticks, others have small wooden semicircles). If you throw right and open like that, your answer is successful. If it opens another way, it's not successful. Every time before my exams would begin, I would go and pray, "God, please give me good grades." Throw, and if it's right, I'm so happy. Otherwise I'll keep praying and throwing until the thing comes right.

My family reminded me of those days and said, "Go back to the temple like you used to do. What you are doing now will not make you happy, so do not follow Christianity." My brother tried to think of ways and means to stop me from being a Christian. They were definitely trying to break me down. They physically forced me all the way to the temple, so I had no choice but to say in my heart, "God, what am I going to do? Give me thy Spirit." So I went with them, but my heart was not in it. Then I told them, "I am not praying to your god," and again, they became so very angry with me.

The Word of God just kept me. The songs that we used to sing, "The Lord's My Shepherd," "What a Friend We Have in Jesus," "I Have a Friend in Jesus, He's Everything to Me," they are so encouraging; I sing them over and over. I realize the Lord gives sufficient grace to go through. Finally, when there was absolutely no way they could stop me, they left me alone. When I was in Secondary 4 (grade

10) and went to work and brought home some income, they became more relaxed. My faith still carried on, and I went to church, but I was like an outcast of the family.*

I was not at home when my father passed away. I was at either a camp meeting or another church activity. I believe it was on a Saturday, one of the times when I had snuck out of the house. That day it was raining, very heavy, so I couldn't come home right away. My father had been hospitalized for a year, and during that time, my mother was so very busy with her bread business and going down to see him.

My father always liked it when I would come to visit him. I had opportunity to witness to my father, and other members of the church also came to visit and witness to him. Sometimes his eyes would tear, but he could not respond, although he did shake his head. My father loved me. God made a way that I could spend time with my father and talk with him and pray with him. I said to my father, "Believe on the Lord Jesus Christ, and thou shalt be saved, and thy house" (Acts 16:31). I claimed that promise to God. I don't know if he became a Christian, but he heard the Word of God. I've no confirmation, because he was gone just like that. I claim this, "Lord, you gave this to me, I leave it to you." Each time I talked to him, he just listened. He didn't respond much.

Like I said, the day he died, I was away at church activities. When I made my way home, I remembered that was the day they would be offering the food to the idols. I found it to be different; the house was so dark when I reached home, and otherwise it was so lively. My brother had left a note: "Father has passed away." That was all he wrote. Poor me; I was only in Secondary 2, fifteen years old. I didn't know where he was; all the family was away.

---

* Her comment about being forced to go to the temple reminded me of what we read in 2 Kings 5:18: "In this thing the Lord pardon thy servant, that when my master goeth into the house of Rimmon to worship there, and he leaneth on my hand, and I bow myself in the house of Rimmon: when I bow down myself in the house of Rimmon, the Lord pardon thy servant in this thing."

I thought the procession (funeral wake) would be by our house. Here it was six something already; they should certainly be setting it up by this time, but my father was not put there. He was put in a funeral parlor because my mother was thinking: "We do this business; it's a bad omen to have a dead body there, so we cannot put it by the house." It was so terrible. I was crying away and didn't know what to do. I didn't have a phone at that time, didn't know how to contact anyone, so terrible. Later, my brother came home, and first thing he did was, BOOM, he hit me. He inquired, "Where have you been?"

In those days, after they put the body in the casket, you would not see it again, so the family was waiting for me. All the family members are expected to be there at the time of death. They have a superstition that the coffin must be closed at a certain appointed time for the good of the people living. It was so terrible. The coffin was closed already, and I never got a chance to see my father again. I'm not supposed to kneel down to him, but I had no choice. When I got to the funeral home, I was forced to kneel down and crawl to the coffin. I felt so broken. I said, "Lord, I have no choice."

The wake for my father was for seven days. Then when they had the Buddhist procession, I was so weak and couldn't take it anymore; I said, "Lord, you know my heart." Some of the members of GLTD came and supported me.

After forty-nine days, the family must go to the tomb (he was buried, not cremated) to show their respect, and then one week after that, they must worship the ancestor. They believe that on the fourteenth day, the spirit of the dead person will come back to the house. The altar is set up with food; everyone will hide, and the main door will be open. I was very curious, and I heard tap, tap, tap, like that. (Weren't your brothers and sisters making that noise?) No, everyone was in the room, so I believe the evil spirit came. The food wasn't gone, only we heard the sound. Everyone was very quiet, and then when it was silent, we could come out. My brother queried me, "Father's spirit came back; how do you explain that?" I didn't know how to answer. I believed it was an evil spirit, but I couldn't tell my brother that, so I just kept quiet and thought upon God's Word.

My wedding was so different from my siblings'. Again, I must stand for the Lord and have a wedding in a Christian manner. In the Chinese culture, you must worship your ancestors, kneel down before your parents, and serve tea. (Did you do this?) No, we didn't. (I think I heard that some couples did have this tea serving ceremony.) Yes, with certain families it's a must to kneel down to show respect. I did have a tea ceremony but not bowing down to all the idols and all these things. My family prayed to their gods and ancestors for me. They would say, my daughter is getting married, this son-in-law is getting married, give them good health, productivity, prosperity, all these things. All I could do was just sit there quietly. I had to make a firm stand for the Lord; no bowing down, have the wedding in a church service, which they don't have; they go to the temple.

My family did come to the church wedding. My father had already passed away by this time, so I was quite worried that my brother would not give me away; he's quite staunch in what he believes, so I then had a good talk with him, and he relented and gave me away. He doesn't like to go to church. With my wedding, the whole family supported me. Thank God, it's always the working hand of the Lord.

Now the attitude of my family has changed. They know where I stand; they know that I am a Christian, that I will not carry joss sticks. Every year they will go to my father's tomb for Qingming. He is still buried; his grave has not been exhumed. Every year I'm out; I don't go with them to the tomb; this is a testimony that Christians do not worship the dead. It's not that I wouldn't go with them, but I won't participate in worshiping the dead or carry the joss sticks, so they know that Christianity is this way.

Does this result in your not being close to the family? Are your other siblings closer to each other?

No, I am close to them because I take good responsibility for my family. My mother is quite ill; she had a fall. Sometimes she will not stay over in Selegie (her home) but will stay at my brother's place or my younger sister's place. I always do my part by bringing her to the hospital for her check-ups and going to visit her, so the Christian testimony of taking care is there.

Do they include you for family gatherings?

Yes, they do, and I usually do the cooking for them and things like that; but when it comes to anything with religion, they know I will not participate. Yes, I'm still very close to them. All of them, when they have problems, I give them a listening ear, and they talk to me. So I'm not totally cut off. My mother still says till today, "Being a Christian is very good," because I bring her to the doctor and things like that.

Your conduct is a real testimony to the family.

My family can see the difference. Even my little children can see the difference, so the testimony is there.

(Here she shares some of her spiritual journey and her evaluation of where the church is today.)

Each individual Christian is different. You must walk close to God, but many of us fail in this area. We become so involved with home, children's activities, and work, it seems that spirituality is lacking in our homes. Unless we really have a God-centered home, instructing our children, knowing our calling as mothers, being a good example for younger women in our church, and teaching the important calling regarding motherhood; if we don't sense that calling, then our future generation will suffer in the sense that they really do not have the Word of God in them and cherish it. We must also prepare them for leadership as a wife or as head of the family; we still must prepare them, you see. But if you don't see that goal, the future generation will deteriorate.

In your life there was such a contrast between heathen worship and then God-centered living. It's a great blessing that your children are brought up in the line of the covenant from early youth, but we must have that same urgency and desire to instruct and teach them in the ways of the Lord.

Yes, we must have that. If you don't have the calling to instruct, you will never have that interest. You must have the conviction and calling to be a mother at home.

The hectic lifestyle of Singapore, we must have that because we are living in this country, but we must know our boundaries; we are just strangers in this land. We must be wise in what we do, have our priorities in order, be God-centered; this is my view.

After my husband and I were married, my family didn't bother me anymore about being a Christian. I married out of the family, so it was okay with them for me to believe as I wanted. But there was still another crisis in my life, and that was being childless. I went through many operations because I couldn't conceive. I tried fertility treatment, and we even considered adoption. Finally we gave that all up; I had to surrender myself to the will of God. I cried so much, Why is it this way with me? but finally, I had to switch off and say, "God, it is in your hands." I learned that through this, God was helping me to be a better witness so I could encourage others who were going through this difficulty.

We went on a trip to Bali, and I didn't know at the time that I was expecting; upon our return, I found I was pregnant. I was so happy. My first pregnancy resulted in a miscarriage in our fifth year of marriage. Two and a half years later, we had our first child. There were complications; I was bedridden for six months each time I was pregnant, and all three children were born by cesarean section.

I can see through my life that the Lord gave me many trials, but the Lord mercifully carried me through. I don't know what the next stage will be, but I know the Lord will carry me through. All these things help me to grow in trust and to really experience his presence, especially the peace that he will not leave me. For our church and all the children, we also have to build them up with the Word of God.

With the lifestyle in Singapore, they don't suffer poverty and trials. They may say, "Oh, my parents are Christians," but this may be very dangerous. We must sink the Word of God in them. What we lack is communication with our children. To establish communication, we must spend more time with them. Now we may not see; but slowly, when the children are getting older, communication will get less and less if that pattern is not established.

A parent being committed in serving the Lord is also very important. You can see how this reflects in the children. What I would say for the next generation in our church is very simple, "Trust and Obey." As parents, our lives must always be a good example for our children; it takes God's grace to live consistently.

"Whoso is wise, and will observe these things, even they shall understand the lovingkindness of the LORD" (Ps. 107:43).

Chapter 7

MY YOUNG DAYS WERE FULL OF DANGER

> I've found a Friend, O such a Friend!
> He loved me ere I knew Him;
> He drew me with the cords of love,
> And thus He bound me to Him;
> And round my heart still closely twine
> Those ties which naught can sever,
> For I am His, and He is mine,
> Forever and forever.
>
> I've found a Friend, O such a Friend!
> So kind and true and tender,
> So wise a counsellor and guide,
> So mighty a defender!
> From Him who loves me now so well,
> What power my soul shall sever?
> Shall life or death, shall earth or hell?
> No! I am His forever.[*]

When I interviewed Peng Lan, the amazing thing about her story was that even though she was brought up in an ungodly home, witnessed so much idol worship, and was exposed to so many wicked behaviors, the Lord protected her from being absorbed in all of this and in her teen years brought her to a saving knowledge of Christ. The text that immediately came to mind was

---

[*] James G. Small (1866).

MY YOUNG DAYS WERE FULL OF DANGER

Isaiah 43:1: "I have redeemed thee, I have called thee by thy name; thou art mine."

I think it's best that she tells it all her own way, so what follows is what she told me.

I came from a pagan home. My mother is a very staunch Buddhist. I have a grandmother who actually confessed when she was young that she trusts in the Lord. It was through the Girls Brigade that the Lord spoke to my grandmother. However, she did backslide, and so she did not go to church. She was the main force behind me for the faith. In fact, I was miraculously put into the Methodist Girls' School (MGS). Now to get into this school, you must be a Christian and must show your baptism certificate for registration in Primary 1. When my mother went to register me on that date, the principal told her she would have to come back later because we did not have a baptism cert. As she left the principal's office, she met a very distant relative, who worked as a cleaner at the school. He asked my mother why she was there, and she told him it was to register me, but that the principal had asked her to come back the next day. He offered to help her, and my mother was able to register me without the baptism cert. The Lord helped me in this way to be exposed to the faith when I was very young. I have a very interesting background because we lived in the slums. My family was very, very poor. We had to get our rice from my father's boss, my mother had to work in the factory, and my grandmother had to take care of my younger brother and me, and I had to help her. Since my grandmother took care of me from youth, I became very close to her. My brother was very close to our grandfather. These were my father's parents; we stayed with them, which is the way our Chinese culture is.

My family is poor; probably you wouldn't say it is a slum where we lived, but it's a flat in a shophouse where many families lived together. The shophouse belonged to my father's boss, the warehouse was downstairs, and they provided the upstairs shophouse for all the workers. We shared the kitchen and bathroom with the other families, and the toilet was the bucket system; men would have to come each day to collect it. The kitchen was large, so each family had their own little space for cooking and we had our own dining table. There were four or five families living there, and our family had three of the rooms.

We did have fun with so many families living together under the same roof. I followed my grandmother around. My grandmother liked to gamble and often went to her friend's gambling den. I went along with her and sometimes I was so tired, I would just lie down there and sleep. The room was filled with smoke, and all the people were engrossed in gambling. After school I would mix with the kids in the back lanes. I had a friend whose mother was actually a prostitute, and another mother worked in an opium den, and I followed them sometimes. I still remember seeing the addicts take morphine. It's like a piece of chalk. They would put it into powder form, mix it with water, and then use a syringe to inject it into their bodies. As a child I witnessed all that. My young days were very colorful, and it was full of danger, but the Lord kept me throughout and I was oblivious of the many snares. This was the lifestyle, and I was not warned to stay away from it.

My mother said I was condemned because I always followed my grandmother and followed this group of friends. I made a resolution not to go down when my friends called, but it's very difficult, it's just like an addiction, I have to go down to join my friends. All this happened up to Primary 5. I had friends who later became prostitutes themselves. In those days, Bugis Street was a night market; it has all been demolished, and now the place is called Bugis Junction. Back then, the sailors would come in during the nighttime, and my friend would meet up with them, make them drunk, and then steal their wallet and throw it to her mother who would be waiting nearby. The mother would empty it of all the U.S. dollars and throw it back to her daughter, and then my friend would put the wallet back.

When I came to Primary 6 (about twelve years of age), the Lord really intervened, miraculously. I was preparing for PSLE (Primary School Leaving Examinations), and I don't know why but I stopped hanging out with the kids and concentrated on my studies. I continued my secondary education in MGS (secondary education is comparable to the American grades 7–10).

At MGS I was in a very protected environment; most of my classmates came from Christian homes. At MGS we had a badge that was very, very important, and many times I was forgetful and would lose the badge. That badge, I always remember, cost about thirty cents, and in those days thirty cents was a big deal. When I lost the badge, I would have to buy another, and I didn't have the money to buy it. And so whenever I lost the badge, I would panic and pray to Jesus Christ and to the Goddess of Mercy. I would ask both of them to help me get back the badge. When the badge was found, I would thank both of them. Our punishment when we lost the badge was to sit on a pail.

Basically I am a very proud person. I came from a poor family; we tell ourselves that we must work very hard. It's also our culture, our destiny; you work hard, you will be successful. So I have that mentality, and I told myself I must get out of poverty.

When I did my O-levels (examinations after Secondary 4, grade 10, before going on to junior college), the Lord had to handle me and break my pride. I passed all my subjects except for English, and that set me off. I could not take it, because first of all, my family expected me to pass, and second, those who were not doing as well as I was managed to pass their English. If I had passed my English, I would have been qualified to go to the best junior college. After that I told myself, I will prove to God that I can do it.

Every Monday morning at MGS, we had chapel where I did hear about who Christ is, but I did not know him personally. It was after I failed the English that I came to know Yoke Sim. Yoke Sim reached out to me, tried to speak to me about the Lord, and then brought me to Gospel Literature and Tract Department at Life BP Church. At first I did not want to go with her to the meetings because of pride. I could not repeat Secondary 4 because it was only the English that I failed. My family could not afford to send me for private lessons;

I had nowhere to go, and so at age seventeen I began giving tuition (extra tutoring for students). I could save some money and also help the family. Because of my pride, I ostracized myself, cut myself off from all my former classmates.

By the time I was going for my A-levels (after JC 2, equivalent of our grade 12), I thought, Oh dear, I'm so alone, I should go to church and meet other people. During this time, Yoke Sim was very patient with me; even my mother says she is a patient person. It was in 1974 that I started to go to church at GLTD to make some friends. So the Lord handled me until I told the Lord, I give up, if you want me to pass, I will do my part without expecting anything.

The Lord brought me through university, and I know it is all of the Lord. The thing is, I did not have enough funds to go through school. When I was in my final year of secondary school, I became good friends with another church sister because of our failures. We both had to repeat the final year of our secondary education. We became good friends because we understood one another. But to be very honest, her results were definitely better than mine. Her family was also very poor, she could not afford to go to university, and because of her family situation, she had to find work.

The Lord opened the way for me to go to the U. Throughout the years I had been giving tuition, but in my university days I could not give as many tuition sessions, and consequently, by the time I came to my second or third year I did not have enough money to pay the fees of $600. I was faced with a big problem and nearly had to stop my education. My family gave me $50 a month but that was not enough. My dear friend soon came to know about it, and she loaned me the $600 because she had worked for a year and had saved up some money, thus enabling me to complete my university degree. We remain the best of friends even till today.

I remained with the GLTD and then the ERCS all this time. I remember when Pastor Goh Seng Fong returned from the States and had his different Baptist views; it was very upsetting at the time.

Do you think at that time you were able to understand the issues that were involved and you could make decisions based on what the Scriptures taught?

I think at that time I was upset because I was still very new, and I did not know what was going on.

So what did you do? Did you just follow friends, or did you try to evaluate the issue yourself?

First of all, at that time I was very busy completing my university and I had to work, so I just attended church and then went back. I knew that there was this issue going on, but I didn't know what it was all about. Then we had Prof. Hoeksema come down and then eventually Pastor denHartog came, and the Reformed faith was introduced. The Lord kept me through all this. But quite a number of the pioneers, the leaders, left because they are all from Arminian backgrounds, and they could not accept the doctrines of election and reprobation and all that.

How did your family accept your going to church? Was there any persecution?

Yoke Sim brought me to GLTD and two or three years later, I requested to be baptized at GLTS (GLTD became GLTS—Department became Society). At that time Pastor denHartog was not here yet. When I desired to be baptized, my mother was very, very furious to the extent that she threatened to sever the motherdaughter relationship and she threatened to break Yoke Sim's leg when she would see Yoke Sim again.

The thing is this, my mother is a very staunch Buddhist, and she has high expectations of me to carry on the ancestral worship upon her death. So she was very angry when I told her I was going to be baptized; but with my grandmother, I have a backing, which only made my mother to be angry with my grandmother as well. My mother felt that because of my grandmother's support, I became very bold. There was always quarreling between my mother and grandmother because of this, so we left the house whenever my mother was at home because we did not want to repeat the cycle. She was so angry; she threatened to throw the ancestral tablet and took a chair to throw at it. So it caused a great stir. My father is passive; he really doesn't bother. My father does not believe in anything, but my mother is different, she is a very staunch Buddhist and very superstitious whereas my grandma is more inclined to the Christian faith. That was a very rough patch of my life, but the Lord mercifully gave me the strength to carry on, otherwise I don't know how I could survive through.

Much later my mother told me, "You are behaving very well." I told her, it's not my own merit; it's my Lord who has transformed me. When I look back on my life, I'm really amazed how the Lord kept me throughout, even when I was not aware of it, and kept me from many dangers. I had one friend whose husband was a gangster, sold drugs, and was in prison; they have a baby. I no longer have contact with them. My mother says, "You are different from them." I told her, "No, it is actually my God who has kept, transformed, and preserved me. Left to my own, I perish."

Did all this give her the desire to know more about God?

No, in fact, there is a church group that tried to witness to her every week, and at first she welcomed them for my sake but she is not interested. Unless the Lord really works in her heart, she will not believe. I brought her to the gospel meeting at church; sometimes she just goes along, but she has not come to faith in Jesus Christ.

It was eighteen and a half years ago that I started teaching. Things were entirely different at that time. The students were more respectful and were easier to teach. In fact, I was teaching religious knowledge, Bible Knowledge. Our government wanted to inculcate good character through religions, so we had Confucianism, Islam, Bible Knowledge, and Buddhist Studies taught in the schools.

I was teaching in Presbyterian High School, a Christian mission school, so every student had to take one of these religious studies, that is our MOE's (Ministry of Education) policy. Because I was from Presbyterian High School, I was assigned to teach Bible Knowledge. We had some students from other schools come together with my own students at Presbyterian High. We were supposed to teach the four gospels; actually it is very humanistic, to inculcate good values through religion. Other teachers instructed in Confucianism, Islam, and Buddhism. The government wanted all the students taught to be morally upright.

One time when I was teaching Bible Knowledge, by God's grace, I taught against purgatory in my class. There were Christians from many denominations in the class, Catholics, charismatic, Pentecostal, and some were not even Christians at all but were just interested. In the class I taught them that we should not worship Mary and I hit against purgatory, and I told them also that God doesn't love everyone. So there was a lot of argument between the students and myself, especially the Catholics; they are very outspoken. In the Catholic churches, the children are taught catechism when they are very young, and my teaching contradicted what they had learned. They were very bold and would argue with me. Not only that, they brought up a complaint to my principal and way up to the MOE.

In fact, I received a call from a father of one of the students who told me over the phone, "Miss Liem, you cannot teach all this. God is a loving God. He loves everyone. How can you say God only loves certain people and not everyone? You are a Christian; I am a Christian also. The Bible says God is a God of love." So we had a bit of argument over that.

The interesting part is that in this Presbyterian High School, we have what you call a chaplain; he is a Presbyterian pastor, very liberal and Arminian. I went to see him about this, and he told me, "I take salt more than you take rice," something like that (an expression meaning he is older and more experienced, so he knows better). I told him, I know you are a pastor and I am just a young teacher.

The worst part came one day when my principal told me, "Miss Liem, there is a curriculum specialist coming down to observe you in your Bible Knowledge class." At that point, I didn't know there were complaints to the MOE. This specialist is supposed to be a Christian. So I told my principal that my Bible class was scheduled from 12:00 to 1:00 p.m. The next day I went to school and began my Bible class teaching at 12:00. 12:30, 12:45 passed and no one came, so I just continued to teach; God really gave me the boldness to teach. At 1:00, the bell rang. I went down, and there I met the principal and the specialist standing by the door. We looked at one another and were shocked.

My principal said, "Miss Liem, I was told that you were on MC" (medical leave for which a Medical Certificate is required). I said, "No, I am not on MC, and I was waiting for both of you." She said, "Miss Sim is here, we checked the attendance register, and it indicated that you were on MC, so we have been talking for one hour because I thought you had no class." She proceeded to look at the attendance register where the teachers signed in. What happened was, the teacher whose name is before mine was on MC, and I was not on MC, but they saw it wrongly; they see that I'm on MC, but it's my colleague who is, so I was spared of scrutiny that day. The specialist said, "I am very busy, I cannot come down anymore."

I am thankful that the Lord kept me; otherwise, I could get into trouble and even lose my job or be under discipline. Strictly, we were not supposed to teach that Christ is the truth, the way, and the light, even in those days. God used that ministry over there and also the Girls Brigade that I was involved in to bring some PHS students to our church. Later on they closed the Religious Knowledge Classes—the MOE stopped the whole thing, and now they have introduced Civics and Moral Education. Actually, I was spared from teaching Civics and Moral Education over all these years.

I just received notice that I must teach a course on Religious Harmony next year, meaning that all religions lead to the same God. This will be very difficult as we are restricted from promoting our own religion. I don't know how, I just pray that God will open the way. I must also be a teacher counselor where the students come to me for counsel, and when they send Malay girls to me, I am not supposed to share the gospel; I am not supposed to mention the Scripture at all. In fact, when I counsel the girls, I must be very diplomatic, worldly wise, and philosophical.

Next year is going to be a very difficult year. My principal and vice-principal are both Christians, but they are very diplomatic. They promote our government policy; they promote religious harmony; they have to say all religions lead to the same god. There must be mutual respect for all religions. The policy is that we must inculcate in the students that we must have religious harmony; we have to, and especially after September 11. We cannot promote any religion at the expense of another religion, otherwise we are considered as extremists, like the terrorists. All religions stand on equal footing.

We have so many young people in our church. You think of the camp this week, there are about seventy-five young people attending. All these kids are in these schools. Are they going to have all this instruction, and how do you think they will handle it? Will they be affected with it, or will they just take it and shake it off? Is this a subject that they will be tested on?

CME (Civics Moral Education) is tested, and there is a grade, so they will be required to give the answers that are expected of them.

How much are our kids influenced by this?

A lot. That is actually my concern. Even if you send a child to ACSI (AngloChinese School Independent) or Methodist Girls' School, it makes no difference. In fact it's worse, it's very liberal. The instruction our children receive in the home and church is so very important. They must be grounded in the truth, know what they believe, and defend it.

In school, besides the Civics Moral Education, the education system instructs the kids that their destiny is in their own hand; they must work very hard for the good of their own future. We call it positive thinking. So this is what is inculcated in the kids: you have to depend on yourself. It's just like God helps me when I help myself. This philosophy is ingrained in the kids.

The streaming system in the schools is very, very bad. A mother told me that the children in Primary 2 are given a test and on the results of the test are streamed before Primary 4. Primary 6 we stream again, and Sec 2 we stream again, and Sec 4 we stream again. When

God's people are in this streaming system, can you imagine how easily pride is puffed up, and God hates pride. The whole thing is unhealthy spiritually. The world we can understand; they have no hope, but this is very unhealthy for Christians. This is happening in our own church, and the kids feel it. Parents must be very careful not to get caught up in this mentality and put that kind of pressure on their children.

In the home, we must instruct our children in the Word of God; instruct them in the Heidelberg Catechism, make them strong in God's Word; so when they go to school, they will be able by God's grace to discern truth and error, and God will keep them. It's also important to pay attention to what our children are learning in school, go over their lessons, and give them the biblical view. This is the antithesis; the world gave you this view, but God's Word gives you this view.

We are a peculiar people; our convictions are different from the world. When you study hard, you study hard for the glory of God. When they study hard, they study hard for themselves—to achieve success and to pursue after wealth, but we ought to study hard for the glory of God and for his kingdom. We can't blame it on the education system in Singapore; we can't stand before God one day and say, God, this is the Singapore system, I cannot help it.

To be a single is not easy. We have our struggles too; we all have the desire to be married. Even at our age, sometimes we are still affected; we still hope to get married. We have a tough time to struggle through, especially in our twenties and thirties. I think for us, we must be very thankful to God that God provides sisters as friends so that we can share with one another, can pray with one another, and when we are affected, we can call one another. We can understand each other. We also have some friends who have left us because of being unequally yoked, and all those who are unequally yoked seem outwardly to be happy, but spiritually they know that it's better to be single than be unequally yoked. We often visit the other singles, we tell them we have gone through similar struggles and tears, and we try to encourage them.

Chapter 8

BAPTISM WAS A BIG ISSUE

> In sweet communion, Lord, with Thee
> I constantly abide;
> My hand Thou holdest in Thy own
> To keep me near Thy side.
>
> Though flesh and heart should faint and fail,
> The Lord will ever be
> The strength and portion of my heart,
> My God eternally.
>
> To live apart from God is death,
> 'Tis good His face to seek;
> My refuge is the living God,
> His praise I long to speak.*

This will be the story of Huey Min (not her real name). It's not going to be her whole life history, but the main focus will be on her spiritual development. She became a school teacher after completing university, so some of those teaching experiences will enter in as well. Huey Min has only one sibling, a younger brother, who was actually adopted from her aunt, her father's sister. Both her parents had full-time jobs, so a cousin cared for the children; but as she grew older, she was left pretty much on her own. There was very little communication in the home, and the family members hardly spoke with each other. When she returned home from school, the only

---

* No. 203:1, 4-5, in *The Psalter*.

question her father would ask is, "Have you taken dinner?" (This is the equivalent of our greeting of "How are you?").

She liked to ask questions when she was young, and her mom would calm her down and say, "Ask no more." Her mother either didn't know the answers or found the questions to be too much of a bother. From very young, the parents took care of all the children's needs physically. Her father would tell her she was old enough to decide things for herself; she could do however she thought was right, so there was hardly any guidance given to the children. Huey Min had lots of free time, which she used in reading books and studying.

Huey Min managed to get into Raffles Girls' School, which is one of the elite schools in Singapore. It was in Secondary 3 (grade 9 and about fifteen years old) that a classmate regularly shared the gospel with her. There was a fellowship outside the school that was sponsored by Campus Crusade, and this classmate brought her there. Ministers from all denominations in Singapore came to speak to the group. With this little introduction, we'll let Huey Min take over in telling her story.

From a young age, my mother brought me to the temple with all those frightening idols, and I didn't like it; so when I heard about the Christian faith, I quickly embraced the gospel. After that I was keen to attend church and went to several small churches. One was Moulmein Revival Church. They regularly had people coming to our housing estate to share the gospel, so it was quite natural that I would go there.

When I started going to church and my mother found out that I was interested in Christianity, she was very, very upset with me. To her, I am her only real child. Her thinking would be, if she dies, nobody will mourn for her, no one will take care of her burial, and to her, if any child becomes a Christian, it is like being given to a Western religion and a loss to the family; so she was very upset about my going to church. The persecution I experienced was of a different nature; I was not beaten, but my mother would be crying and sobbing so much that after some time I could not stand her sorrowful state any longer, and after going to church for a year or so, I stopped attending. After a while, whenever friends invited me to meetings, I would go along, so I have visited a number of churches here and there. I remember that I was keen to seek out more and wanting to go back to church, but each time it was interrupted with her crying.

My father was one who did not want to impose anything; I could have the right to choose my own faith. My father said he also went to church when he was young through the Boys Brigade, so he had heard the gospel, and Christianity is a good religion. But he did not embrace it himself because that would upset my mother, and he wanted peace in the family. My father would not go to the temple, but if my mother needed to pray at certain festivals, he would help to lay the table for her, so he would be very supportive of my mom in her activities. During the seventh-month celebrations in the neighborhood, he would also join in. For the peace of the family, he just goes along with my mother. My mother was one who just followed tradition. She was born into this; this is what was expected of her, and all the relatives were aware of the religion she followed.

We did have a few idols in our home, and we had ancestral worship of my father's mother. My mom felt it was her duty as a daughter-inlaw to pay respect. If they do this for their ancestors, then hopefully they also will receive this kind of treatment from the next generation. When I was younger, I followed my mother to the temple and carried joss sticks, but once I started attending church and professed that I am a Christian, I refused to take joss sticks so there were some conflicts.

I always desired to attend church more regularly, and another church that had a big impact on my life was Harvester Baptist Church, which I attended for quite a few years. Harvester Baptist claims to be very conservative and doctrinal, and they have a lot of preaching. I attended very zealously over there and was even baptized at Harvester (I was probably about twenty years old at the time). When I told my parents I wanted to be baptized, my mother said she wanted to disown me, and again there was all her crying. To her (by this time), if I wanted to go to church, it was alright as long as

I didn't get baptized. The moment I would be baptized, I would no longer belong to her.

In Harvester Baptist I also faced problems in the sense that they baptized people over and over again. They stressed very much on repentance and faith and that a Christian must regularly examine their life, and if they find that their life is not as godly as it should be, according to the standards of Scripture, then perhaps they are not saved. They often cast this kind of doubt on the people, even among the elders and the church workers, who lived godly lives. Many times when we attended a church meeting, a longtime Christian would just stand up and say, "God just spoke to me that I'm not a Christian. I realize that I must repent, and now I know that I am saved." Then that person would be baptized again.

That upset me very much and caused a lot of self-examination, so much that sometimes, in the evenings, I would be crying out to the Lord: "God, am I really saved?" "Do I really know you?" "Have I measured up to what a Christian ought to be?" I would get very troubled like that in the night. They also had altar calls. Very often I would feel, "Oh, I'm still so sinful," or, "Oh, I do not measure up." Many times I would go up to the front and pray, "Oh, God, forgive me and save me." I wanted to be sure I was a Christian. I was never rebaptized. I did have the impression that the church was doctrinally sound, but it was sad that many members did not have the assurance of their salvation.

They also emphasized that we should not leave the church and based this on 1 John 2:19, "They went out from us, but they were not of us; for if they had been of us, they would no doubt have continued with us: but they went out, that they might be made manifest that they were not all of us." So we also had the fear that we are not supposed to leave the church because otherwise we are not one of the true children of God; like reprobates, only they did not use that term. I was brought to Harvester Baptist by a RGS friend who attended that church. I worshiped at Harvester for about four years.

Another RGS friend introduced me to River Valley Outreach

BAPTISM WAS A BIG ISSUE

(RVO) around 1978. (This friend has since left GLTD and is attending Life Bible Presbyterian.) At first we attended meetings at Life BP and then at River Valley. I was there shortly before Pastor denHartog came. All along I was only familiar with the Arminian way of the gospel that God has made salvation possible and it is by your own human will that you have to accept Christ to be your personal Savior in order to be a Christian. I attended all the various lectures Pastor denHartog gave to explain the Reformed faith, and that was the first time I got to hear the five points of Calvinism, election, predestination, sovereign grace, and other biblical doctrines. Then there was Pastor Goh Seng Fong and Pastor Lau, and they held forums, and we sat and listened to all the different arguments, so it was quite a struggle to come to understand.

Now I can understand when new converts come and we try to explain the Reformed faith. They question, "Could this be a cult? Are they introducing something new to the gospel?" I can understand that kind of resistance when someone first hears about the Reformed faith. When we say we treasure the Reformed faith, they say, "No, you must treasure the Bible." I read all the materials and asked many questions of Pastor denHartog. Then there was the question of the necessity of infant baptism, which was all new too, so we had to go through and analyze the two views and come to our own conviction of what is the teaching of Scripture. I hardly talked with my family members, but I found friends in church, one of whom was quite inquisitive and would ask questions, so that forced me to start thinking and talking. We lived in the same area, so we could spend a lot of time together and talk and talk and talk about all these things.

My family lived in a three-room flat. From youth I shared a bedroom with my brother, but then as we became older, it was awkward having a room with him. I went to Nanyang University to do a Bachelor in Commerce degree, and for those three years of university, I lived in the hostel there. I was used to having my own freedom and living apart from the family, so after my schooling, I did not go back to live at home anymore.

Since I became a Christian, I very much wanted to share the gospel with my parents and cousins about Christ dying on the cross, about his blood being able to cleanse us from our sins, so I would try to share with them, but they would usually turn it off. They would say, "Don't tell me about it. Christianity is a Western religion. We have to continue with the worship of ancestors. Don't you be so silly to believe what the preacher tells you." They would come with their point of view and say, "I don't believe a thing that you say."

They would bring up things like, "See, your auntie is a Christian, she is a regular churchgoer, and look at what happened. She married late to a Christian husband, and the husband died of cancer. What's so good about your Christianity?" Or they would say, "Look, you have another auntie, she is so old, she is not married. You also claim to be very faithful. I think you are going to be like her because you insist on looking for a Christian husband, but I think you will be old and will not be able to find a Christian husband. If you are so strict about being a Christian and choosing a Christian husband, I think you will end up like your auntie." Another reply would be, "What's so good? You go to church; they don't even have a cup of drink for you. I go to the temple; wow, they have so much to eat." My father's response to me was, "Do not disturb the peace; you cannot have two religions in the family. If you want to believe, alright, you have the right to believe, but do not raise this issue to cause your mother to be upset and cause her to have reason to nag more."

The opposition was mostly in my school days. Immediately after my university days, they take it that I'm serious in the faith, they can't change me, and above all, I'm over twenty-one, so they just leave it to me. Then my cousins told my mother, "Don't worry, you lost a daughter, we are like your daughters," so my mother became closer to my cousins. My mother likes to adopt goddaughters, so she made two of my cousins her goddaughters; she lost me but she still has goddaughters.

It was only when my dad was struck with a stroke and became bedridden that he didn't shut me off. I had more opportunity to visit

BAPTISM WAS A BIG ISSUE

with him and bring up the urgency that he should trust in Christ, that we are sinful and cannot come to God by our own merits, and that we have to look to Christ, so it was only when he was sick that he became more open. When he was mobile, he would cut it short to maintain the peace of the family, but now he would listen. He wrote on a notebook, "I believe in Jesus." That was a great comfort to me, and then I asked the pastors to visit with him as well.

I really don't know if he became a Christian, but I have to commit that to the Lord. Soon he was so paralyzed that he was not able to talk or to express himself, so what went on within his heart, I really don't know. He would just listen to whatever I said to him and nod his head. I did ask him, if you say that you believe, would you like to be baptized? His answer was no.

What was your mother's reaction when your father listened to the gospel?

She said, "It's not fair, your father is not in a right state of mind. Even if you share with him and he nods his head, that doesn't mean that he agrees." She asked that I not share with him, but I just ignored her. My father knew English; my mother doesn't understand English. I spoke with my father in English, so my mother knew I was visiting with him, but she didn't know what I was talking about. I pointed out to my mother that all these things that she believes are of the devil, and she became very angry with me. "How do you dare say that? My god is just as powerful as your God."

My mother would often go to the temple to consult about different things, like in moving house, "Is this the right house?" Or, if someone is trying to matchmake, she would go to the temple to consult, "Is this person good for my daughter?" It was my mother's practice to visit the temple regularly to find out answers about what is right or what is wrong. Also in regard to my father's death, she went to find out whether my father would die soon or if his life would be lengthened. That is what they do in the temple: they will ask, and then they have those sticks, shake them, and one stick drops off. They take that stick to a man, and he will have all kinds of papers, and he will match a slip of paper to the stick and then he will interpret. He will ask, "What is it that you are asking about?" Your husband, your children, your house, or whatever, so they have a hint from her what she wants to know, and then they will interpret the outcome.

Do they ever get an answer that they don't like?

Whatever the answer, they will say that it is very true. They receive quite a general answer, so whatever way it goes, it will follow up somewhat. She likes to consult all these fortune-tellers and temple mediums. When I was young, she also consulted a fortune-teller as to whether I would get married or not. The fortune-teller told her that this daughter will get married when she is very old, and she will marry somebody whom she has known for a long time. So my mother believes that.

From time to time, she will still try to matchmake, especially among her colleagues. They will say, "Oh, you have a daughter, how old is she? Is she married? I know of this person, would your daughter consider this person?" Then my mother will bring it up to me: "Hey, there's this person, what do you think?" In the initial stage I told her I only want to marry a Christian. Then later on she said, "Oh, there is this Christian, he goes to church very regularly, but he has been divorced and he has a son, ten years old. Very nice, don't you think so? After all, you're also of age. It's difficult to have a young child to bring up. This person is really enthusiastic about his Christianity. In fact, I introduced him to your cousin who is not a Christian, but they have nothing in common to talk about. I think he will be the best for you." From time to time she would bring this up to me, but I would say, "No, No, No," and so I have turned down many offers of matchmaking.

My parents just follow family traditions, more Taoist than Buddhist, but they don't study the scriptures; it is more of ancestral worship. Many things are done from pride; like when my dad died, my mother kept thinking that he would be going to this certain place. She believes that for those who have died and are in this place,

BAPTISM WAS A BIG ISSUE

people who are living must provide for them, supply them with things that they may need, otherwise they might be hungry or be a poor person there. This place is where the spirits are, and whether or not the things that are provided actually go there, it does not matter. People say you can burn all these paper houses, and cars, and money, and all that, and who knows? Who can actually tell you whether the dead receive it? But as for the living, we do our part for him, so that at least he won't come and bug us in our dreams that we did not care for him when he died. So my mother finds that it is worth spending a sum of money to have all kinds of rites, rituals, and chanting done by the priest, and also to burn those paper houses, cars, and whatnot.

They call that money "hell money." Do they believe that the people or spirits are in hell?

They never claim that they will go to heaven; just that they go somewhere, but most likely it is to hell. They believe in different levels of hell depending on how good a life one has lived. And, of course, they believe in reincarnation. If you do well in your life, you might be reborn into a richer family or be in a better state of life in your rebirth. If you do wicked things in life, you may be reborn as a cockroach or a lizard. That was the motivation to live right and abstain from things that are evil, so in the next life they would be better than in the present.

They do have moral values, like lying and stealing are wrong, gambling for fun is okay, but gambling and losing your house and all your money is wrong. They stress a lot on filial piety; you take care of your parents, do good to them, then you have done well. So my mother just wants to do her little part for my father with no assurance whether or not he receives it, but at least she has done her part to keep him rested. That is the only kind of hope that she has.

Didn't you ask your mother what your father would think if he knew he had a funeral like this because he said he believes?

I did tell her that Father said he was a Christian so it is better for him to have a Christian funeral. Then she said, "No, he's not in his proper state of mind to say that, and moreover, who is going to manage the funeral arrangements? I have the support of your cousins; they will run the whole funeral for me." So she insisted that he should not have a Christian funeral and that I should have no part in it. She will manage it the way she wants it to be because all the relatives recognized him as a Taoist, since he has joined them all his life in the Taoist kind of worship. My brother went along and did his part to carry on all the rites as prompted by the relatives. We had the Buddhists chanting because my mother joined a temple association in Moulmein and paid a sum of money to them, so she is assured that there is a place to hold their ashes in the temple upon their death. She also joined the association for my father, so at the time of his death, they provided this kind of service. *(This is difficult to go through as a daughter, but here we must just bow before God's sovereignty. If your father was a Christian, even if there is a Buddhist funeral, that doesn't frustrate the Lord; it is all in his hands.)*

I have a couple of Christian aunties, my mother's sisters, who still keep in contact and share the gospel with her. They invited my mother to come along to a church camp, and she went with them because it was in Malaysia—she went along more for the scenery than to listen.

In my workplace, I don't get to teach Bible Knowledge. I teach Accounts, 1-T, so it is very neutral. It's only from time to time that I try to share the gospel with students, and I find over the years that there are fewer and fewer students who are interested in the Christian faith. When I started teaching, I was keen to set up a Bible study group, so I tried to ask among the students whether they were interested in having a Bible study. In the earlier batches of students, there would be one or two who would express interest. I actually had one group where we had Bible study for quite some time, and recently they met me and said, "We want to meet up with you. You are the one who shared the gospel with us, and we had such a good time of study together."

Did they become Christians?

Yes, a few of them did. This coming Saturday they are having a gathering, and they wanted me to join them. In fact, through a friend, they asked, "Do you know a teacher called Huey Min?" I started the Bible study group with them twenty years ago, and they remember me for that.

Occasionally there would be a little time at the end of a lesson when the students could ask some questions. It was in times like that in personal conversation with students that I tried to impress upon them the gospel. Sometimes we discussed about religion as a whole, and they would say, "Oh, you are a Christian. What is it that you hold to in your faith?" These were the little pockets of opportunity to share the gospel with them. It still is acceptable, if someone asks a question, that we may answer it.

Last year there was this boy who is really a rascal. He is very corrupt in his mind, and he would come to school and say, "Hey, I come to school to look for girls. Do you have any to introduce to me?" I told him it is not right for him to have these kinds of thoughts. Marriage is honorable, and one man should only have one wife. He claims he is a playboy and flirts around with girls, and he is so frank and outspoken. He was infiltrating the minds of the others, so I tried to stop him. He also used the name of God lightly, and I had to tell him off. He would laugh at me and say, "Oh, you're a Christian; you're in a different world from me." When I tried to correct him, he would turn it around and make a joke of it; he would say, "You don't understand people like us who need to rough it out in our life; we have to be tough."

From time to time he still emails me, but he emails all kinds of porno, so now I just delete them. I told him not to send that stuff; I don't appreciate it, I'm a Christian and I don't like all these things, but he would continue to flood my emails with all this porno stuff. I try to persuade him: you cannot live this way, you're not respecting women, and God is not pleased with this kind of lifestyle. Well, I believe I should share God's Word liberally at every opportunity and trust that he would have mercy on whom he would have mercy in his own timing.

As a Christian living among many unbelievers, I am conscious of the need to live godly in Christ Jesus. They are looking more at our walk and are not so interested in our talk. Whenever we did anything wrong or we seemed to get depressed over things, they would question, "Is this what your religion teaches you? Why are you suffering all these, if, as you say, God is good to you?" When we expressed the hope of eternal life, they would jeer at us: "You think that only you Christians have the right to go to heaven? That is ridiculous. All who do good in their life will be rewarded when they die. Some Christians have done terrible things, how can they be in heaven?"

As I learn more concerning the sovereign grace of God, I am deeply grateful that no matter how wretched I am, it is of the Lord's mercy that I am saved from the power and bondage of my sins. Now in this earthly life, I experience the joy and comfort of belonging to Jesus and being led by his Word and by his Spirit. And one day, at my death or at his coming, I will inherit eternal life and enjoy heaven's glory.

Chapter 9

I WAS DELIVERED FROM DEMONS

Marvelous grace of our loving Lord,
Grace that exceeds our sin and our guilt!
Yonder on Calvary's mount out-poured
There where the blood of the Lamb was spilt.

Grace, grace, God's grace,
Grace that will pardon and cleanse within;
Grace, grace, God's grace,
Grace that is greater than all our sin![*]

*P*astor Willy Ng and his wife Kim, along with their two sons, became good friends of ours while we were living in Singapore from 1991 to 2002. God mightily used the pastor and members of a local Bible Presbyterian Church when Willy Ng was delivered from the power of the devil. He subsequently studied for the ministry and was ordained at Grace BPC and functioned there as associate pastor. Pastor Ng later left Grace Church and was instrumental in the organization of Criswell Tabernacle, an independent Reformed church in the eastern part of the island of Singapore.

Criswell is a small congregation, and as they grow in their understanding of the Word of God, they are also growing numerically. At Criswell Tabernacle, Pastor Ng uses catechism books and Sunday school materials from our churches, and he is also a regular subscriber to The Standard Bearer. Interestingly, Pastor Ng wrote his theses on divorce

---

[*] Julia H. Johnston (1910).

and remarriage, and his position is not only no remarriage, but also no divorce.
What follows is his story the way he shared it with us.

My grandparents were involved in Chinese witchcraft. In ancient China, there were many branches of witchcraft, and my grandparents followed one of them. And now, speaking from hindsight and not having the ability to demonstrate to you, you might not believe some of the things I have seen. Locally we eat a lot of fishes; everything, bone and head and all that. Very frequently we will have neighbors, and even ourselves, getting a bone stuck in the throat. Nowadays you may go to the hospital to remove the bone, but if my father was around at home, people would come and say, "Look, I have a bone here and very painful, can you please help?" At twelve noon, he would go to the house with a bowl of water, say a chant, and then draw in Chinese the word for fish, and before all of us (we were still children then) would ask the person to drink. The person would drink, and surprisingly, the fish bone got washed out.

    I don't know how to explain it, but in those days you have people cutting a lot of things. Our knives are not like the American knives, our knives are cleavers. We use a lot of choppers, and oftentimes a finger gets cut. The nearest clinic is so far away, and it's so expensive. When there was an injury, people would run to my house and say, "Uncle, can you please help?" My father would go to the kitchen and take a leaf from a vegetable; it didn't matter which vegetable, he would just pluck a leaf off. He would draw on it the Chinese character for the word *tiger*, chant on the face of it, hold it on the injured finger, and in a moment's time, the cut was healed, and even the scar was gone.

    Now you may think that I am telling you a story, but actually before our very eyes, we have seen not once but many times people sticking out their tongue and cutting it into two pieces; we saw this in a Chinese temple. We know it isn't magic because the guy would open his mouth, and half the tongue is gone. He would be holding the other half and would put that on a small plate. After that, he would take a Chinese paintbrush (you know those kinds that they use for calligraphy), and he would write the chant on a piece of yellow paper, and then he would burn it and put it into a glass of water. He would put the piece of tongue back into his mouth, and the tongue would suddenly be whole again. How do you explain that?

One guy actually took half of his tongue out, put it into a bowl, put the bowl in a plastic pail and got someone to cover it, and he went around and everyone could see it; it was not bleeding. You could touch his tongue, but they would not allow you to use any finger but the left finger. Half of the tongue was gone; you could see inside there.

At that time I was in primary school or junior school. I was always very fascinated by this and thought it was magic, you see. I went to my father, as I didn't think a father would lie to his son. I asked my father, "How did they do it?" And my father said, "You don't try it. This is not magic, okay? We are talking about a real thing; the knife is sharp. You go and see. Is the knife sharp? We are talking about a real thing, son, you had better not try it."

And once, no not once, twice, I can recall it from my mind. Have you ever seen a Chinese dried, salted fish? Have you seen it in Chinatown? It's dead, it's definitely dead, and it's even salted. Normally, in our kampong, you would hang it in the doorpost in the sun and leave it there. This man would say, "Go and take one. Go to any of the houses nearby, take one." The guy isn't even near my father; he isn't near the plastic container, when he instructed us, "You can put it inside there. Okay. You quickly go and fetch a pail of water. Okay. You cover it." And they will go there and chant and they'll say, "Okay, you go and open it," and you find the fish is alive, swimming! Where is the dead fish?

I used to go there and think it must be someone hiding underground to change it, but it cannot be for it is a plastic pail. You do not cut a plastic pail at the bottom; it's water, you know. How do you explain that?

So when I was converted, I shared this with some of the local pastors and they said I was deceived; I was demonized, and that's why I saw all these things. That was the beginning of my denial, and I didn't want to talk to people because they thought I was lying, and second, they thought I was mad. A senior pastor in my denomination actually said that I was mad, so I did not dare say, "Look, this is my experience, and here you're claiming to be Christian and even claim to be some sort of Reformed man, and you tell me it's not true?"

Am I supposed to insist that it is my personal experience? I cannot deny myself. Or am I supposed to deny myself and accept what they are saying? In the beginning of my Christian life, that was my problem. I denied myself; I told myself that it's not true. It's all nonsense, I was deceived, I was demonized, it never happened before.

Then what happened was, after having been a Christian for four or five years, I went to Bible school. One day, shortly before my grandmother passed away, I went back to the village, and there, behold, they were doing it again; the same thing. The salted fish was alive again, so I told myself, "Look, I am not possessed. I'm a Christian. The fish is still fish, what do you want me to say?"

So it was a very big struggle. I read a book by Walter Chantry about the signs of the apostles and things like that, and he kept saying there's no such thing as demon possession and casting out demons in the first place. So I became depressed. Now who is Willy? Why did the Lord allow me to be in this situation? Am I a Christian? Am I mad? This is my experience. And then there was a group of people, Christians, who cast out the demon, and now I read this book that says if you are Reformed, you cannot believe in demon casting. Then where do I fit in with all these things?

It was only in 1989 that I went to London to study and I came to a period where I felt very much at peace with God. After I shared with one of my teachers, he said, "Willy, see, this man Walter Chantry and others, they are all school men. It is true they have studied the Word of God without all these missionary experiences. It is true they came to such conclusions and are very dogmatic about it." But he said, "Willy, in your case you are not mad; you are just someone, a first-generation Christian, saved from heathendom, and these things did happen to you. So you are not mad; you must come to terms that this is your experience. The Lord is merciful to you, but don't use this to attract attention to yourself because you must glorify the Lord, not yourself."

But at least, thanks be to God, I could accept myself that I'm not mad. I cannot deny that such things happened. During the Hindu festival of Thaipusum, people can see we are not talking about tiny needles, we are talking about needles that are so big and they poke these through the skin, and after Thaipusum you go and examine it, and there's no sign of any needle marks. So if that kind of thing can happen publicly, even screened on television, you tell me that mine doesn't exist? It's only as I mature in age that I realize, Look, these people were very kind but very dogmatic.

You see, my father was that way, but when we grew up, we became Thai Buddhists. We have been involved in chanting from a very young age; all the sutras, we've been taught how to chant and what to do. One day, someone in the village who belonged to a different sect threw some charms at my family, and we knew about it. You may not believe it, but into a pail, a clean pail of water, a pail that had never been used before, they poured water and threw flowers inside; I don't know what kind of flowers, but they were white and very pretty and fragrant (maybe jasmine). They threw the flowers in and chanted. You wouldn't believe, but you can see people's images inside.

So we knew that something bad was happening, and furthermore, we had what we would call "a little ghost." "Little ghost" is a small glass bottle with a cap on; inside there is a statue of a naked woman and a naked man kissing one another. This piece of wood that is used to carve the idol is actually taken from dead bones, people's dead bones; they go and dig up graves and take the bones back. And it is filled up with oil, but it's not fragrant oil. What they do is, when a man dies in Thailand, they will remove the corpse, and then they make the dead person sit up, and a candle will be lit beneath a portion of the jaw, and as it burns, the body oil will drip. They collect the oil and then go and chant and pour the oil into that container with the idol, and then it becomes a living spirit.

You wouldn't believe this, but if you keep it in your pocket and then you are in trouble, you just knock on the table and call the spirit: "Brother, younger brother." You say, "Younger brother, younger brother, your older brother needs help," and it will come whether day or night and whisper into your ear. I still remember that initially I used to slap my ear because I thought it was strange and ticklish, but it kept on talking. In Chinese we call our older brother "Ah Kor." The spirit would say, "Ah Kor, I'm here, I'm here." At night in the village, when the dog saw us, the dog would howl, and we knew that someone was following us. When we looked back, there's nobody following us, but yet the dog howled. Even as I'm talking to you, you can see my hairs are standing up. It's over twenty years ago, and you can still see what effect it has on me when I talk about it. It's a spirit, and if you carry it along, the spirit will come and talk to you.

We could say, "We want to know something about a particular person. This person lives where, where, where?" In order to get things going, I must have a part of the person, maybe a hair, or a shirt, or whatever, and I'll say, "This is part of him, go and find the person who owns this hair," and the spirit will be gone; it could be days, or sometimes two or three hours, but when it returns, it will tell you things about this person.

But now on hindsight, I realize that the spirit cannot tell you what's going to happen but only what happened before. Very strange, it can tell you what happened in the past but nothing about the future. Is it real? I don't know, it's up to you to think, but I can only tell you this is my experience. I came from that kind of background.

I am going to relate this true story to you. Once a man threw a charm on our family—a black magic spell. What happened was, he had gone to the graveyard, a freshly dug grave where the Muslims bury the dead (they bury the dead mummified with a piece of white cloth). Usually a practitioner of black magic will go and cut a piece of the cloth and bring it home. He will write his victim's name and address and ask the spirit to go and visit that person. There would be chanting, and the spirit would even threaten that person; that's what a charm is, and the intention was to kill my parents. That is what happened.

One day when I was twelve years old, it had been raining the whole night, and in the morning it was still raining. I woke up and saw my mother behaving in a weird manner. My mother was a very nice lady, but here she was wearing sunglasses, and it was raining, no sun at all. When she took off her sunglasses, we were all shocked: all black. We thought that maybe my father and mother had a fight in the night or she fell from the bed, but when my father came back from the coffee shop, he said, "What happened to you? Why is your face like that? So black?" We knew there were no fights and it couldn't be that she fell from the bed, because my father didn't even know.

About 12:00, my mother grabbed my hand; I still remember, this hand, and she started to walk very fast. I was trying to keep up with her and I said, "Mummy, Mummy, where are you bringing me?" My mother smiled and said, "I'm bringing you to a place where there will be many bicycles." At that point of about twelve years old, I was crazy about bicycles, and we had many friends nearby, neighbors, who had new bicycles, and I was asking for one. "I'm getting you a bicycle so you can play."

I felt funny; why is she pulling me and saying that? So I said, "I am not going with you. Where are you going?" She said, "This is the place where we are going, and in order to go there, I'm going to throw you down, and then I am going to jump after you." I didn't know about this throwing down and jumping, but again there was a voice. I don't know if from here or from there, but the voice chanted in Chinese, "Don't go, don't go, don't go, don't go, don't go, don't go," and as we approached the nearest high-rise, the voice became very loud and very disturbing to me. I said, "I'm not going," and surprisingly I managed to pull myself off my mother's grip.

My mother stood in front of this big tree; I still remember, that big tree is still there. My mother said, "If you don't follow me, I'm going to a happy place, and you won't see me again." I said, "Mummy, you wait here. You wait here while I run home and tell Father and Auntie about it. I'm coming back, you wait for me here," and I ran back. When I told my father, he said, "You crazy fella, your mother is just frightening you. You are a naughty boy, isn't it? She's just frightening you; she'll come back shortly, she always will." And so I thought, "Ah, oh, what a relief."

Two hours later, the police came and said, "A lady staying here, this clothing, this bag?" She had jumped from the eighth floor, and when the body landed on the ground, it landed in the drain. The face was all caved in, one of her hands flew about fifty meters away, and both the legs twisted the other way around. We were brought to identify the body, and there she was.

Now and then, it's already over twenty years, I will still have nightmares. Because why? After they found the body, they moved the body to the hospital mortuary for identification. And then it is the Chinese custom that being the eldest son, I must feed my parents for the last time. So with a bowl of rice and vegetables and with chopsticks, they puuuuuushed me to the edge of the coffin, and there she was, supposedly my mother, but the face is gone. They forced me that I must feed my mother; if I don't feed her, she will come back again and be a hungry ghost. That's why sometimes I wake up and sweat and, ohhhh, it's very terrible. I'm talking here about my own mother, not someone else's mother, but my own mother.

So from then on, my father says we must take revenge. To a Chinese, taking revenge is a duty of the children. If someone attacks your family, you must take revenge. My parents belonged to the old school, so I was sent to the talisman to learn chanting. The old man has died now, but he was one of the chief Thai monks in Singapore, and he taught us all of this chanting. I was involved in all this nonsense for many, many years.

We made people giddy. You know the car tire? We squeeze the

charm into the car tire; when the car moves, the person goes giddy. The whole day the person will be very sick and cannot work. The car goes again, the person becomes giddy again. When the car stops, then okay. Come to think about it, it is quite funny, but it's quite terrible.

If we want someone to have pain over the body, we will make with our own hand, out of wax, an image of a person and say who that person is. Then after chanting and calling the spirit to come into this person, we go and bury it nearby, probably at the bus stop; in those days the bus stop was all sand so that was easy to do. Then when people step on it, pain all over, and the whole day the person can feel it, like life is horrible and you're very frustrated with yourself. That kind of thing we were able to do.

But the time came, when I was eighteen, that I decided to be a Thai monk. I told myself this is a sick world. "Look, there are many mothers in the world. Why must it be my mother?"

That year was a horrible year. After my mother died, my youngest brother also died; he was only two years old. You tell me, how can a two-year-old suddenly die? We brought him to the hospital, and we didn't see him anymore. My family says, and this is a Chinese belief, if your child dies so young, you cannot perform any funeral rites for the person, so we just left him at the hospital, and I don't know how they disposed of my brother.

Then a few months later, my father was involved in a serious accident; as he was trying to cross the road, a bus stopped to pick up a passenger, another bus came along, and as my father was trying to cross from the back of the bus, the second bus did not stop and banged into him. He was crushed between two buses, so he was in the hospital for six months in a coma. (I am the eldest of the family, one younger sister, two younger brothers, but the youngest brother died.)

The bus driver, nobody went to scold him, no one reprimanded him, everyone was frightened of him, we were even brought up to be afraid of him: "He did that to your parent, he can do it to you too." My Thai monk said, "You go and learn from this. You must destroy that person," so from very young, we learned. But before we could do anything, the man died. Everybody knew that he was a horrible man, but nobody dared to say anything because he had this special power. So I was looking forward to being a talisman in Thailand and forgetting about life.

I came from a mission school. Every Friday when we would be brought to the chapel, there would be singing. One of the songs was "Give Me Oil in My Lamp," and I would sing, "Give me hate in my heart, keep me hating, hating, hating." I hated life; I hated people. I had no friends; people avoided us in the kampong because they saw what happened to me. I hated everything. I wanted to leave this sick world, you know? But Singapore has a law that if you want to be a priest, or a monk, or whatever, you must do your national service; you must go to the army first. So I was very frustrated with this stupid rule; it's so stupid, I'm going to kill somebody.

But it was at this point that the Lord started to touch my life. My own grandmother, who had been looking after us since my mother passed away and my father's injury, was in the hospital. I went there, and I was very depressed because there was no one else in the world who I loved but my grandmother. She loved me; she understood me. When my mother died, I cried on the bed. I was sleeping with her for many, many months; she was such a wonderful, wonderful grandmother. The doctor said we cannot help it; she is already over seventy years, she has this lung problem, she will die soon.

So I went back and prayed to the idols. We believe, "Look, you take a few years off my life and then transfer it to my grandmother. Make my life shorter so my grandmother's life can be longer." For once there was no response. (There would be a knock to show response, but I waited and waited and there was no response.) I thought, "Why is it like that? Are they serious?"

I went to visit my grandmother every day. There was a nurse working in that hospital who was my long-lost cousin, my father's sister's daughter, but we didn't like that family because that family all became Christians. We didn't want to have anything to do with that family; they didn't visit us, we didn't visit them. But this cousin works in the hospital, so she would come and visit my grandmother. She would come and talk to my grandma and say, "Believe on the Lord Jesus Christ. Repent of your sins. You are old, you must have hope if you want to be in heaven and be with the Lord."

Every time I went to see my grandmother, I would be very angry with my cousin. I don't know if you have ever been that angry, but there was just this fuming, hot fire rising from inside me, so hot and so angry. I said to her, "You go to hell. You want to eat potatoes, you go and eat potatoes. You leave my grandmother alone." (Eat potatoes is the Chinese way of saying if you want to be a Westerner, go and be one.) "My grandmother will die a Chinese" (Chinese means Buddhist). "You leave her alone."

My cousin is very zealous, she's Mary, you know? Salem and Mary in our church? She can verify everything I say. She is a small person, but she was very brave. She pointed her finger at me and said, "You are a worshiper of the devil. I know what you do; you do all that chanting and all those terrible things. I know what you do, but there is a God in heaven who cares. If you are so powerful, I challenge you" (and from her bag she took out the gospel of John in paperback and handed it to me), "I challenge you, young man, to read the Bible." I said, "I'll read it and come back and tell you what I think of your Bible."

I took the Bible and I went home. I came from a Catholic school, but that was the first time in my life that I saw a Bible; I didn't know what it was. When reading the Bible, the two verses that sort of jumped out and smacked at me were about how the Lord Jesus Christ is the resurrection and the life. You see, this is the problem with me. When my mother died, we went to the crematorium, and that was where I wanted to go. The Buddhist monk, after burning my mother, prayed over it and said my mother in her next life is a duck. What kind of comfort is that, that my mother has become a duck? So, from that point on till today, sorry to tell you this, I hope I don't stumble you, but I don't eat duck. Not because if I eat duck, I might eat my mother. I used to believe that; that accidentally I might eat my own mother. It's a very bad taste, so I won't eat duck today.

So I went to ask all the monks and anyone who is religious. I asked them, "What happened to my mother?" They said, "What did the monk say?" I answered, "That she became a duck." Their reply was, "Then she became a duck." Then I asked, what will happen to us? No one could give an answer that gave me peace. I have no peace, that's why I hate the world; there is no meaning in life.

Deep inside me, I was longing for meaning and purpose, and so there it was in the Bible. I saw that if I wanted to know what happens to anyone when they die, I must ask this man, because he died before. If anyone knows about death, he must be the one who has been there before. Now Buddha died; he founded Buddhism before he died, he can say whatever he likes, he never came back to verify it. Mohammed studied Islam before he died; he can say whatever he likes, he never came back to verify it either. Jesus Christ, he died, he came back, he verified, so that was the breakthrough for me, spiritually speaking. Isn't this what I had wanted to look for?

Another verse that really stuck out was, "Greater love hath no man than this, that a man lay down his life for his friends" (John 15:13). That really struck me, for in the practice of black magic, you must be stronger than the other person, the devil must be stronger; if not they will come and attack you. The moment you stop offering them what they dictate to you, the moment you stop serving them, they abandon you right there to yourself. But here I read about the loveliness of the Lord Jesus Christ that he came to love sinners, and so loving was he that he gave his own life to save. You tell me, if you know my background, where I was coming from, and I really came to a point where my heart was, my soul was just broken.

I went back to my cousin; I called her up and said, "Look, I need to talk to you." So she met with me. I went to her house and said, "I never knew that there is a God of love. All I had known from youth is I miss my mother, there is no such thing as God, there is only revenge, hatred, and be more powerful and more successful than other people. But here, is this true?" She told me, "I am not educated enough in the Bible. How about letting me bring you to my pastor."

I WAS DELIVERED FROM DEMONS

So I went to the church. The pastor talked to me further and told me that we are all sinners. "You have been worshiping the devil; you must confess your sins." The moment I confessed Christ, I blacked out. The moment I woke up, I could see the pastor's face; I knew where he was, but there were so many faces everywhere and all speaking different things. They tied me down; I didn't know why I was tied down. They used clean bedsheets to tie my legs and hands. I said, "What are you doing to me?" They said, "You are very violent, you are very strong, we have to tie you down."

And then I saw myself, my leg is going up on its own, and we're talking about three or four young men holding me down, and I lifted them up. I was frightened because I saw my lifting these people up, tearing the bedsheets up like that. They were shocked, they were trying their best to pin me down, and I was shocked too with what I was doing. My legs and my hands were out of my control. How to explain that, I don't know.

For a week, they were praying for me, reading the Bible to me, and then finally I got well. In the name of the Lord Jesus Christ, they commanded the evil spirit to come out of me. This is what happened, and then my heart stopped. They panicked; if somebody died in the church, what were they going to tell the Buddhists? My heart stopped, nothing, no pulse. They told me that the pastor, for the first time, panicked, and then I came back again, so then he knew, "Oh, this is terrible." This all happened in about five minutes' time. The entire struggle lasted a week.

After I got well, they still took care of me. I stayed in the church for a few weeks; they locked me up, they thought I might take my own life, but I did not want to take my own life. I went back to my cousin's place; she stayed in an eleventh floor apartment, and there was a voice that kept telling me, "Jump, jump, jump, jump," so I told my cousin, "The voice keeps telling me to jump. It's very loud." It made me very disoriented and very frustrated. It's just like, in order to get rid of it, I wanted to jump, and it was bugging me. It's like, you know, you just don't want to leave the house. I felt like jumping but they told me, "No, don't do that."

There were some doctors in the church; they gave me sleeping pills. They asked me to take one, and then they said, "Willy, we like to sleep too, can you please sleep?" So they gave me one more, then one more. Finally the doctor said, "No, I can't give you more, you already took twelve. You should be fast asleep already, and you keep staring at us. What is happening?" I said, "I don't know what is happening, I just can't sleep."

Was there a clear indication when the demons finally left you?

My experience is that suddenly you don't find any frustration anymore. Suddenly you just feel that you become very light and just free. If not, you just feel very congested. I don't know about other people but that is how I felt. How do you explain it, I don't know. As I told you, I'm not here to tell you a story and have a collection, but since you want to know, this is what I tell you, and if you ask me, "Do I believe in demons?" I don't know. All I know is this is how I was delivered.

Maybe the people who helped me, the pastors and all, they are not Reformed and doing things properly, but God in his mercy delivered me. I am not the only one, I know of others, here and there. I don't care about charismatic churches; they cast out demons day and night. Well, we don't believe in that kind. I know of another man who became a Christian. He was also demon possessed, and he was delivered. You have things like that, but it is very rare.

(*He wonders at this point if we are able to understand what he is talking about.*)

We watch so much David Copperfield magic and all that, we may think there is no such thing, and if you grow up in a Christian family, you may think that the Lord Jesus Christ is just a topic or a subject for study. In my ministry I have spoken to many old folks; many of them came to Christ, crying all their way. Why? Because for the first time in all their life, they heard about someone who loved them, loved them enough to die for them. Never before did they know such a Savior in all their religious life. Here we have a Savior who took our place; when we should die, he died for us. So we should appreciate that the gospel of our Lord Jesus Christ is really a deliverance from sin; it is salvation.

Someone who also was seeking for meaning in life but died could not verify whatever theory he formulated. How do we know there is reincarnation? He never came back. Now if really death is the biggest question that we all must come to terms with, shouldn't we ask someone who has that practical experience? If you ever want to know about Singapore, you are foolish if you ask someone who has never been to Singapore. You ask someone who has the experience, someone who has been here. You go to Mohammed, you go to Buddha, you go to all the gurus, you are a foolish person. Go to the one who has been there before. There is only one in the history of mankind who has been there before, the Lord Jesus Christ.

That is the thing that has held me together to this day. Why am I a Christian? Why am I a pastor? Well, for this single fact, I serve someone who knows the meaning of life and can verify it; the only one with credentials and qualifications, nobody else in the world. That is why I believe with all Reformed men that the resurrection of our Lord Jesus Christ is what stands and holds Christianity together. If Christ be not risen, we are all in our sins, we are nothing. But Christ is alive. That is why we as Christians are full of hope. That is why martyrs were willing to be burned at the stakes. Why? Because they knew what they were doing, and they knew where they were going.

Long before I became a Christian, and long before my parents died, I still remember, we had a very large house in the village so we rented out some of the smaller rooms, and there was this Indian family. They came and wanted to rent a room, and so my grandmother graciously rented a room to them for a few months while they were waiting for their apartment to be ready. They came in, and they had all their Hindu altars and gods and elephant gods, and someone gave them a Roman Catholic picture of the Lord Jesus Christ, so they put it right on top. As a young person, I was wondering, "Why do you want to put the Western God right on top?" They say, "If we put it below, when we pray, our god will not hear. That God is bigger."

I didn't believe that Jesus Christ is bigger than other gods; I was fed up with that, so I went and asked my grandmother. I said, Grandma, the fellow said like that; isn't it nonsensible? My grandma and my father said, "Look, I am telling you, Jesus is actually a bigger God than all of us." I said, "What! Is that true?" He said, "Look, the rationale is like this. Jesus is like the emperor in the palace in Beijing, okay? He's the biggest, but you see, not all of us can see the emperor. If we really want to get things done, we go and ask the corrupted officials in the palace to help us; that's why we must have all our gods." He said, "You cannot ask the emperor to help you with the lottery; the emperor will have no time for that, so you go and ask the officials."

This is what they say. And this is true because with Chinese New Year, one week before the Chinese New Year begins, the Chinese people will send off their household gods back to heaven. Once a year the household gods will go back to heaven and report the happenings of the family, what sin they committed, whatever they do, the household god will go to heaven to report. In order to prevent your household god from reporting bad things about you, all of them will prepare what you call a sticky cake. You can still buy it, you know the sticky cake? They offer the sticky cake to the god with this in mind, that when the god eats the sticky cake and then goes to heaven, his mouth is stuck, and he cannot speak properly, and because he cannot speak properly, he dare not open his mouth or he will offend the emperor in heaven.

There is rationale behind all the things they do. I have a relative over fifty years of age, a very nice man; he told me that he will never be a believer. I asked why. He said, "You people, you worship a pure God. You cannot gamble; I like to gamble. I like to go to the nightclub. I like to go to prostitutes. Your God will never allow me." I said, "That's sin, you should repent of your sins." He said, "I'm not willing; I really enjoy exactly what I'm doing. Don't bother me with your pure God." So I said, "We are not holy, we are also sinners. It's the Lord Jesus Christ who saved us."

What a marvel that God chose you out of your family.

I am the only Christian in my family. I'm an outcast today; they do not like me, worse yet my becoming a pastor.

How about your sister, is she a Christian?

She belongs to a cult.

Isn't she the one who takes care of your children?

Mary, the cousin, takes care of the children. She's a cousin-sister. She is Salem's wife, she's retired, she's over fifty years, and she has no children. Salem said, "You stay at home, so boring," so now she takes care of the children; she comes over every morning and stays the whole day while Salem is at work.

What cult is your sister in?

She goes to True Jesus Church. You know True Jesus Church? They call themselves the True Jesus Church because they say they are the only people on earth who worship the true Jesus. Other churches worship a false Jesus. If you are not a member of their church, you go to hell because you are following a false Jesus. She came to me once, many years ago, when she first became a member, and said, "You are a pastor. I'm telling you, you better be a member of my church because you are going to hell if you do not become a member of my church." And they have weird practices. They say the proper mode of baptism is neither immersion nor sprinkling; the proper mode is stand before the pastor and bow your head three times. You ask them, "Why?" They say, "How did the Lord Jesus die? He did not pass away lying down, he did not pass away kneeling down, he passed away hung on the cross with his head bowed."

How about your father? Has he passed away by this time?

Yes, he passed away four years ago. He was cremated and his remains are placed beside my mother in the earth.

This ends our session with Pastor Willy Ng, and then he took us to see the burial place of his parents.

Chapter 10

THIS TIME IT WAS A STORY

Not what my hands have done
Can save my guilty soul;
Not what my toiling flesh has borne
Can make my spirit whole.
Not what I feel or do
Can give me peace with God;
Not all my prayers and sighs and tears
Can bear my awful load.

Thy work alone, O Christ,
Can ease this weight of sin;
Thy blood alone, O Lamb of God,
Can give me peace within.
Thy love to me, O God,
Not mine, O Lord, to Thee,
Can rid me of this dark unrest,
And set my spirit free.

Thy grace alone, O God,
To me can pardon speak;
Thy power alone, O Son of God,
Can this sore bondage break.
I bless the Christ of God;
I rest on love divine;
And with unfaltering lip and heart
I call this Savior mine.[*]

---

[*] Horatius Bonar (1864).

THIS TIME IT WAS A STORY

*T*here is a very special dimension in the life of a first-generation Christian; they love to speak of their conversion, when God by his grace worked in their hearts, delivering them from the shackles of sin, and gave them the gift of salvation in Christ. Their hearts overflowed with joy, they were filled with zeal for the Lord, and they had the desire to reach out to their relatives and friends with the gospel.

What's neat to notice is that the Lord may be pleased to use just a simple witness or testimony as the drawing power to bring an elect child to him. It's not how much education a person has, how well he or she may speak, or the fear of not knowing what to say, but it's a matter of the heart. Is our heart overflowing with thanksgiving so we desire to tell others, or are we content just keeping it all inside? That is the question.

Pilgrim is a young woman in the church who was brought up by her godparents for thirteen years. It was necessary for Pilgrim's mother to work, so she stayed with her godparents during the day and at home with her mother at night. The godparents were strong believers in Taoism and ancestral worship, and she was influenced by them a lot. She remembers that when she was young, Christians would come occasionally to the doorstep to evangelize. Here is her story.

My nanny would not be rude to the Christians to their face, but she would brush them off, and then behind their back, she would say, "These people are like pests. They intrude into our religion." So she influenced me. You know, really, I am saved by grace. Nothing can save me except that God really touches me. Otherwise I cannot. I really disliked these people from my heart, although I didn't verbalize it. I told myself, these people are really pests. Why are they going around trying to force people to believe what they believe? I was really indoctrinated by my godparents. When you're young, your mind is like a sponge, but thank God, God sifted it out.

At ten years of age, during one of our family gatherings at my grandmother's place, my cousin called me and another cousin into a room. She said she wanted to tell us a story. So just the three of us were in the room sitting on the floor; I will never forget the setting.

She told us the story of the garden of Eden. My cousin was someone we looked up to, so when she called us to tell us a story, I was just filled with curiosity at the garden of Eden. Until now, I really cannot imagine why, because it was just a story, not really just a story, but nothing so miraculous like God healing the ten lepers or restoring sight. Probably then I would have reason to marvel, but it was just like a new place where two humans existed. She told us about the serpent tempting Eve and the fall into sin. My heart was very moved.

After telling us the story, she asked if we would like to come to church. It's very indirect, you know. If it were something like those evangelists out there, I would not listen. But God really sent my cousin in another setting, in a place that I was very familiar with, and she sat down and told us the gospel. That's why I say, it can never happen except that the Lord ordained it. Also, I am not the only one who listened to the story, the other cousin listened too. The other cousin did not become a Christian.

I wanted to go to church very much. My mom encouraged my cousin to take me to church because she had a good impression of Christians. She felt my cousin had a good Christian testimony, and she felt safe to entrust me in her hands, believing this religion will teach me to be good and not go astray. Being a single parent, she may have found it very difficult to raise us up, so if others could help with good moral values, she received it. I thank God, in this way there was no objection, and I was brought to church.

My mom would say, "Just go and listen, don't dwell on it." So when I was baptized, that was another story. She did not object vehemently, but she just asked me not to dwell on it. This is just something you can go and listen to, and then the next day, you can forget about it.

Usually at the age of twenty-one, a young girl is given a key chain or a cross. For a non-Christian, it would be a key chain that symbolizes you could make your own decisions and come and go as you please, but a Christian would receive a cross. My mother had told me that she would never buy me a cross; you must have a key chain.

THIS TIME IT WAS A STORY

When I was baptized at age seventeen or eighteen, my mother did buy me a pendant cross, for which I thank God. It was a wonderful time when I was baptized. In fact, I got dizzy when I went on the stage to be baptized; I was so excited. Before my baptism, I started evangelism myself, but I was very careful, because from youth I had the impression that those Christians who do tracting usually push too hard. Instead of the impression of helping others, you lose them, so that taught me to be very careful.

I abstained from those foods that were offered to the idols. It just came very naturally. My mother would say, "This food is offered to the idols; this food is not offered, so this is set for you." Sometimes my godparent's children, my siblings, poked fun of me. When I would pray grace at the table, they would say my prayer as if I am praying, like jesting. Then when I was finished they would say, "You think your God gave you all this food?" Every time they would have something like that to say. I would reply, "If God doesn't give you sunshine and energy and health, do you think you can have the energy to work? An invisible hand guides everything that you don't get to see, but that doesn't mean that you can just take it for granted."

Would they believe that their god is in control of everything?

Their feeling to their god is not like our feeling to God—ours is of reverence, theirs is of fear, fear of what is going to come to them if they don't perform. They fear punishment, whereas we say chastisement because God still loves us. They believe in punishment, so when they go to their god to ask for something, they have to give their offering, give money and make their request at the same time. We don't have to do that. And talking about peace, they wouldn't share with you that they have peace. This is how they manifest themselves. If they really had peace, they wouldn't have to go from god to god. Some of them have just one god, but they manifest their anxiety in other ways, like their anger.

Taoists have more gods, and they will visit from one god to another. In case this god doesn't listen to my prayer, I can go to another, this kind of thing. They actually show their disbelief in their god when they go from god to god. They go to their god to supply their needs, and then they seek other means, like the lottery.

Those two cousins are quite close to each other to this day, and both are members of the church. The Lord also used the cousin in the conversion of her parents. The father became a Christian first, and toward the end of his life as he lingered on, the pastors and elders of the church would minister to him in the home. The mother would just stay in the background during this time, uninterested. The father passed away, and there was a Christian funeral. The Lord also worked in the heart of the mother some time after that, so that she started to attend the Chinese worship service at FERC and has been baptized.

Thanks be to God for his saving grace in the lives of his dear children!

Chapter 11

SUFFERING FOR THE REFORMED FAITH

> Before Thy people I confess
> The wonders of Thy righteousness;
> Thou knowest, Lord, that I have made
> Thy great salvation known,
> Thy truth and faithfulness displayed,
> Thy lovingkindness shown.
>
> Let all who seek to see Thy face
> Be glad and joyful in Thy grace;
> Let those who Thy salvation love
> For evermore proclaim,
> O praise the Lord Who dwells above,
> And magnify his Name.
>
> Although I poor and needy be,
> The Lord in love takes thought for me;
> Thou art my help in time of need,
> My Saviour, Lord, art Thou;
> Then, O my God, I pray, I plead,
> Stay not, but save me now.[*]

This chapter will acquaint you with Rev. Titus San Ceu Luai from Yangon, Myanmar. We don't know much about Rev. Titus' younger years except that he is from a town in Irawaddi Division called Kyangin Town, Myanmar. We have met his parents, his

---

[*] No. 112:1, 3, 4, in *The Psalter*.

brothers, and his sister. His brother Timothy, along with his wife and two children, attends the church that Rev. Titus pastors in Yangon.

Titus had some training for the ministry in Myanmar. His uncle Rev. Thawm Luai is the principal/administrator of the Far Eastern Fundamental Bible College (FEFBC) in Yangon, which is an extension of the Far Eastern Bible College (FEBC) in Singapore and is sponsored by the Bible Presbyterian Church. The uncle planned for Titus to be a professor in the school in Myanmar, so Titus was sent to Singapore for the purpose of earning a degree, which would qualify him for that position. This was sometime in the mid-1990s. Titus was married to his wife Cer Te at that time, and they had one daughter, Jemima.

While studying in Singapore, Rev. Titus attended the Reformation Day lectures sponsored by the Evangelical Reformed Churches in Singapore; he was invited by a fellow student who was then a member of the ERCS. The speaker that year was Ian Murray from the Banner of Truth Trust. At that time (1994), Allen Brummel was in Singapore, doing his internship for the PRC seminary, and he had occasion to speak with Titus after the lecture. Allen was impressed with the sincerity of Titus and the interest he showed by inquiring more, so he took the time to introduce Titus to Grandpa. That was the beginning of a meaningful and fruitful relationship, which is very precious to all involved.

Titus was going through a period of real soul-searching around that time; he had thought FEBC was a Reformed school, and he was very disappointed to learn that it was not. On the first day of the lectures in FEBC, the instructor, Rev. Timothy Tow, drew a picture of a scale and said that for salvation, man was 50 percent and God 50 percent. "Then I found myself, I am going to spend three or so years wasting my time in this non-Reformed school. I thought to go back many, many times, but the Lord kept me for another purpose. Homesick, culture shock, different living and standard, my mind could not think properly." That is how Titus came to the lecture, with real confusion in his mind. This is how Titus tells his story in a letter he wrote to us.

"Then I changed my plan of going back, and you made me a very different person. Now, I become like this. The reason is none other than the Lord brought me to you. Too wonderful. I never think of, never enter in even my single thought. Thanks for all your instructions and guidance and friendship and support and advice all the way till today. I can never stop giving thanks to our covenant Lord as well, who brought me to you and learn and love the truth. Even if I cannot leave any inheritance to my children, I am happy to die because I can leave with them the knowledge of our covenant view and belief and confessions. Now they know God is our covenant Lord and we are his covenant children, our family is in his covenant care.

"Before I met you, one thing happened in my life. It was in FEBC's library that I found a SB magazine [Standard Bearer] in his providence. None of the students ever read them, but I read and found the truth there. So I wrote to them, 'I want to study more about the truth,' and before I received their replied letter, I met you. And when I received their reply letter, in that letter they said that I should meet Rev. Kortering, their minister-on-loan to Singapore, and mentioned your address, but I met you already. How wonderful is his providence guide.

"Before I met you I have a very few knowledge about Reformed truth. That also wonderful. I read through some of your little tracts at FEFBC, my former school in Myanmar. The head-master of that school, Rev. Thawm Luai, my uncle, went to Singapore FEBC in 1986 and received quite a number of books and tracts. Among them some are from the PRCA, like 'Calvinism the Truth and Arminianism the Lie.' So, I know the five points of Calvinism. That is all I know, but in my mind, there are many more to learn. So I came to Singapore FEBC, but I did not get at that school, but I get the truth from you. So, the reason the PRCM is in this country is from beginning to till today, the hand of God, very clear. Not because of me, but because God wants that way. Humbly I am serving him, following where he leads me."

The ERCS was already working in Myanmar prior to this time. They were working with a Pastor Moses from the United Reformed

Churches of Myanmar (URCM), and the occasion of our first trip to Myanmar was for Grandpa to conduct a seminar for URCM men. Rev. Titus was studying in Singapore at the time, so he asked that we go to the FEFBC in Yangon and meet his uncle, Rev. Thawm Luai, as well as Cer Te and Jemima. Cer Te, Jemima, and Cer Te's mother were living on the campus of the school while Titus studied in Singapore. Rev. Luai invited Grandpa to speak for the chapel exercises, which he did. Cer Te and her mother could not speak English, so we communicated as best we could with gestures and smiles, but that was about all we could do at that time.

Rev. Titus was very keen to learn and understand more of the Reformed faith, and he asked if Grandpa could give him some instruction. Rev. Titus came faithfully to our home, two afternoons a week, for a couple of years. He would sit at the kitchen table with Grandpa and drink in all the instruction he possibly could. The studies continued year round, except while we took our furloughs. Grandpa and Titus went through Rev. Herman Hoeksema's *Reformed Dogmatics*.

Titus really took hold of the doctrine of the covenant; it was all completely new to him. He was just amazed how it pulled everything together, and he could understand so much better the teachings of Scripture, how doctrine and life are intertwined, and the importance of family and the instruction of children. He loved it with all his heart, and Grandpa said he was the most delightful person he ever taught. He always came well prepared, having read all the assigned reading, and he was always eager to absorb more.

They also studied the confessions and Reformed church government, which was completely foreign to Titus. The Myanmar churches were used to church government with one-man rule, which caused much trouble, mainly that of submitting to dictatorship and jealousy among the preachers. Titus would get all excited as he was learning, and he couldn't wait to go back to his country and start teaching the people that there is another way and that it is biblical.

There are many food courts in Singapore, and Titus always looked forward to going out for some dinner after his class was finished.

Sometimes we would eat at home, if Grandpa had other commitments for the evening, but if we had the time, Titus would enjoy our taking him to the hawkers, where his favorite meal was a piece of steak. After the meal, he would catch his bus to go back to school.

When you have a student from a poor country, you wonder if he will be completely spoiled after seeing all the wealth in a prosperous country. We were concerned about that with Titus too, and we would talk about it with him. He assured us that his heart was in Myanmar, and his burden was for his own people to hear more of the truth of God's Word. He was used to poverty, and that was exactly what he wanted to go back to. Truly, that was the Lord's working in his heart, and that continues to be the case. Titus has been back in Myanmar now for quite a number of years, and he is content in the Lord's provision for their needs. He never speaks of the luxuries he had while in Singapore.

I think it was between Titus' second and third year of studying in Singapore that he was able to take a short break and go back home to see his family. It was at that time that their second child was conceived. I'm sure it wasn't easy for Titus to be away from home so long during his wife's pregnancy; there was always the concern of how she was doing. Finally, on September 10, 1996 he had the happy news that they had a newborn son, whom they named Josiah, and both mother and child were doing well. If I recall correctly, a fellow student at FEBC paid for a trip for Titus to go home for a few days to be with his family and to see their new son.

Finally Titus' training at FEBC was drawing to a close, but during those years, a big change had come in his life. He now embraced all the teachings of the Reformed faith, and he hadn't come across anything that he wasn't in agreement with. He often remarked that he was learning more with Grandpa than he learned in all those years in FEBC. This put him in a difficult position; his beliefs had changed so that he no longer was Arminian and premillennial, but instead, he now was Reformed. How could he go back and be a professor in the FEFBC?

Grandpa advised him that he must be honest and upfront, so together they decided that he should inform his uncle that he no longer believed as they did, but that he was still willing to teach in the school if they would have him (FEBC had covered all the cost of his education and living expenses), and he could teach whatever subjects they chose. The uncle felt he had to inform FEBC of this development, and when FEBC learned of this, they immediately expelled him from the school. Titus was about two weeks away from graduation and receiving his M.Div. degree, but he did not back down. The degree was much less important to him than having the truth.

Informing the FEBC of his change in beliefs also had consequences in Myanmar—FEFBC informed Cer Te that the family would have to move out of the school premises. Titus was informed that he would be excommunicated from the denomination of which he was a member. Titus felt relieved and very happy. He was so convinced of the truth and was willing to submit to however the Lord would lead him. His trust was strong that God did not bring him to this point without a purpose. He moved over to our house for a few weeks. The immediate need was to get some money to Myanmar so that Cer Te could arrange to rent a home; rent in Myanmar is paid in advance by the year.

Finally the time came for Titus to go back to Myanmar. Once back, he met with his home church that he had pastored before all this took place. The session there agreed with his position and decided to uphold his ministerial status. He took up his residence in Yangon and started to organize a church there, which was under the supervision of the session of the home church. Titus loved the truth as taught in the Protestant Reformed Churches in America and chose to name the new denomination, which he began, the Protestant Reformed Churches in Myanmar or PRCM.

When the ERCS went to Myanmar to conduct seminars, generally for three weeks at a time, the PRCM joined with the URCM in attending the seminars. These seminars would be given by one of the

ERCS ministers or by the PRC minister-on-loan to the ERCS. The lectures were given in English, Titus would translate into the Burmese language, and another pastor would translate into the Chin dialect.

Titus has been supplied with books at various stages along the way; he receives the *Standard Bearer*, and he is on the book member list of the RFPA. He has a computer with a Burmese keyboard, which he uses in the extensive translation work he has been involved in since his return to Myanmar. He publishes a *Standard Bearer* in Burmese, in which he writes his own editorials and also translates some articles from the *Standard Bearer* of the PRC. He has translated the three forms of unity: Heidelberg Catechism, Canons of Dordt, and Belgic Confession. He continues to work on books published by the RFPA.

In addition to translation work, he has had opportunity to teach seminary courses in other seminaries in Myanmar. He preaches and teaches catechism classes in his own church and conducts seminars for the pastors in the PRCM. These pastors come down to Yangon for a couple weeks at a time, live in with Titus' family, eat at their table, and attend the classes. He occasionally travels to Kale or Falam for seminars there.

The ERCS did pay for the building of a church/house for the PRCM in Yangon. The church is on the main floor, and Rev. Titus' family lives upstairs. Everything is very plain and simple. In addition to the two children mentioned before, Titus and Cer Te have been blessed with two more daughters, Jeannette and Joanna. Besides the family, there are several others living in their home: Cer Te's elderly mother, a niece, and a cousin. Cer Te's sister's husband just recently deserted his family, so now Cer Te's sister, along with her three children, are living with them as well. They can accommodate all these people by simply putting down mats on the cement floor of the church.

We have been to Myanmar many times and each time is like a family reunion. There is a strong bond of love and friendship with those dear people. Here are the details of their family.

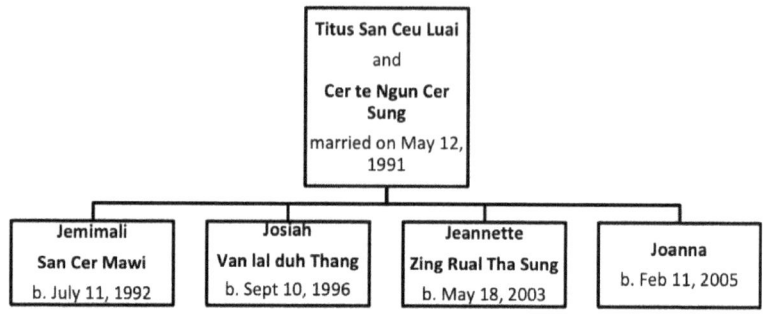

There have been many joys but also difficulties over the years. I recall one year when we were there; Titus came to Ruby Inn early one morning to see us. He said something had happened during the night that he had to share with us. His uncle was in trouble. His uncle had promised that he could secure jobs in Taiwan and Singapore for some men from the Chin State, and he had collected money from them in advance. It turned out that he wasn't able to get the jobs, so the men wanted their money back. That was fair enough, but Titus' uncle didn't have the money to return to them. These men threatened his uncle's life if he didn't pay them back. You have to understand that in this culture, that is a very real threat that they would certainly carry out—when they say something like that, they mean it.

During the night, two other uncles went to Titus' house to ask for help. They said that his uncle was very humble; he realized this was something very serious, and he desperately needed help. Titus told them that he had no money with which he could help his uncle, and it was only in the providence of God that the Korterings were in Myanmar. He would share the problem with them to see if they were able to help in this difficulty.

Rev. Titus felt that if at all possible, he should help his uncle; after all, this was his mother's brother, and his uncle's very life depended on it. He also felt this was the Christian thing to do; you don't return evil for evil, but you do good even to those who have treated you wrongly. It took quite some discussion, but in the end we gave Titus the money since we still had enough with us.

Titus brought the money to them right after he left us, and later in the evening, he went to visit his uncle along with two witnesses, his wife and his brother Timothy. His uncle had his wife and two brothers there as well. Titus explained that he did not have money; it was only because the Lord in his providence had brought the Korterings to Myanmar that he could share the need with them and get some help. He told his uncle, "The reason we are separated from each other is because of doctrinal differences and not because of any hate in my heart."

The uncle was extremely grateful (understandably) and thanked him for his help in this difficult time. He offered him the use of the school (FEFBC) for future seminars (with rent). (I don't believe they ever took up that offer—it works out well for them to rent rooms at School of the Blind.) We always had to smile that regardless of how much money we took along to Myanmar, we always came back empty-handed.

The URCM severed their connection with ERCS some time ago. Some of the pastors and congregations left the URCM and came to the PRCM at that time, along with some pastors from the EPCM, his uncle's denomination, and some Baptist men. Titus realized that many of these pastors and church members needed much instruction in the Reformed faith, and he worked diligently to teach them by conducting seminars in Yangon or elsewhere, sometimes lasting for up to one month.

Things were going fairly well until quite recently. When one of the PRCM students came back from studying at ARTS in Singapore, he influenced his family and relatives and took over the congregations in which they were members, organizing into the Evangelical Reformed Churches in Myanmar. This has greatly affected the membership of PRCM—some of the former congregations have split while other congregations have remained intact, but the PRCM is now considerably smaller. Only three pastors are left, besides Titus. This has taught Titus that the pastors and members must be Reformed before they are taken into the denomination.

"Now we are reorganizing our churches so that we cannot repeat the same fault. First, all over the country except Kyangin and Yangon we are going to regard as our home mission field, including Kale and Falam. So, when they join us, we will not regard them from day one as an instituted church. Rather, we will regard them as our mission field and teach them our distinctive and biblical regulations for quite a number of years. Then, if they show signs of maturity, then we will start to organize as an instituted church. While we are teaching them, we will not allow any foreigners to involve with our works as before. In that way, our people will think again the church is Christ's, not foreigners."

Titus is a hard and diligent worker. He is definitely a man of conviction and remains committed to the Reformed faith, trusting in God to keep this young denomination true to the Scriptures. This is what he shared with us. "I write down to you our distinctives, which are non-negotiable as well as no one is allowed to compromise if one calls himself PRCM. They are:

1. Among believers, there are no racism, no nationalism. All believers who trust Christ are one, they are equal, they all are members of one covenant family of God.
2. All our customs and cultures are born among us before we believe Christ, when we do not know Christ. So when we become Christian we must check all those customs, cultures, practices with the Word of God, and we must forsake what is against the Word of God and accept only what is according to the Word of God.
3. God is a triune God. He lives from eternity to eternity in perfect covenant friendship, love, fellowship, gloriously among the three persons, Father, Son, and Holy Spirit. The covenant that exists among them cannot be broken, can never be destroyed, therefore
    a. Husband and wife cannot divorce.
    b. If divorce happens for adultery, the innocent one cannot remarry.
    c. Only death can dissolve the marriage bond (Rom. 7:1–3, Matt. 19:9).

4. Believing parents and their children are included in the covenant of God, and only elect children of believers will be saved. (Rom. 9:11–13)
5. We live in this world according to our Reformed worldview (not common grace worldview), to glorify his name with our conduct. Our Reformed worldview has the standard and norm for all of everyday, earthly life. That is the law of God, which is in the holy Scriptures.
6. Our confessions are the three forms of unity and Church Order of Dordt (1618–19). We believe them with all our hearts, not only lip service, and we practice them strongly in our daily lives."

Just a little interesting side note. While we lived in Singapore, we were acquainted with Wayne and Julie King, who worked with the Summer Institute of Linguistics (SIL, Wycliffe Bible Translators) in East Malaysia. They were unable to get an employment pass, so every three months they would have to go out of the country and then re-enter in order to extend their stay. They would come to Singapore on these occasions, and if it were over a weekend, they would worship at CERC. We got to know them quite well as we had them over to our house many times. Wayne was in Singapore alone on one occasion and stayed at our house. Grandpa shared with him about Titus during that time, and his reply was, "That may very well be the most important reason you were called to work in Singapore all these many years."

It is just amazing to us, as we reflect on all these many events, how the Lord governs and directs all things according to his sovereign will. These are not things that we plan and try to work out, but God places these situations before us and gives us the strength to do the work in his service. Let's all learn to be patient and wait upon the Lord. No need for us to run ahead and try to rescue a situation, for God will guide all things according to his good pleasure and according to his timing.

Do remember Titus' family and the PRCM in your prayers, along with your prayers for the ERCS in these difficult times.

Written on September 23, 2005

Chapter 12

THE FIRST ARTS STUDENT

> Great is thy faithfulness, O God my Father,
> there is no shadow of turning with thee.
> Thou changest not, thy compassions, they fail not;
> as thou hast been, thou forever wilt be.
>
> Pardon for sin and a peace that endureth,
> thine own dear presence to cheer and to guide,
> strength for today and bright hope for tomorrow,
> blessings all mine, with ten thousand beside!
>
> Great is thy faithfulness!
> Great is thy faithfulness!
> Morning by morning new mercies I see;
> all I have needed thy hand hath provided.
> Great is thy faithfulness, Lord, unto me![*]

On March 27, 2006, while Grandpa and I were in India, we arranged to have a little time for an interview with our dear friends Paulraj and Kasthuri, with a view to sharing their story with you. I had my mini disc recorder running the whole time, but sad to say, when I tried to play it back, nothing was recorded. I really would prefer to have them tell their own story, so this was a major disappointment for me. I immediately sat down and made notes of what was said, and those notes, along with what we already knew of them from our longtime friendship, will be the content of this story.

---

[*] Thomas O. Chisholm (1923).

THE FIRST ARTS STUDENT

Paulraj grew up in the village of Periyakulam, Tamil Nadu, South India. He has one older sister and two younger sisters. His father had to work very hard to provide for the family. He had a yoke of oxen and a cart, and anyone could hire him to transport whatever had to be moved. Paul's parents were able to provide schooling for the older sister and him, but the two younger sisters were sent away for school; this practice is very common in India, as I'll explain later with Kasthuri's education.

Paul's older sister is married to John Ravichandran, a pastor in the Church of South India (CSI). The beginning of the CSI is interesting—there was a time in India when many missionaries from various denominations were working there, but then, as Paulraj tells it, "After church Reformation, Bartholomew Zeaganbalg was the first Reformed missionary to India, sent by Danish Reformed Mission, arriving on 19th July 1706, in a coastal village called Tharangam Paadi or Tranquber' in Tamil Nadu, India. In late nineteenth century, here took place a 'Sepoy Mutiny' ('sepoy' means local/Indian soldier), a local rivalry against the British rule in India, led way for killing of many 'Whites.' This killing did not spare Christian missionaries, irrespective of their good deeds for the benefit of the local people. Hence, the then British government forced all the foreign missionaries to leave for their own countries due to insecurity for their lives." Here you had all these small bands of Christians, Reformed, Methodist, Baptist, Lutheran, etc., without missionary leaders. The result was that all these Christians grouped together to form the Church of South India; consequently, this is not a spiritually strong denomination and there is a big difference among the pastors.

CSI is also the denomination in which Paulraj's family were members. The sister just under Paul is also married; they live in Chennai (Madras) and both she and her husband are employed there. The youngest of the family, Anbumani, is finishing up her higher education and hopes to one day teach the Reformed truths of the Bible to children in a training center/home for orphans, which they hope to organize through Ministry of Mercy (MOM). Arranged marriages are the norm in India, and since Anbumani is or soon will be of marriageable age, this will also be a concern for the family.

Paul is thirty-three years old at the present time. His schooling took place in the area where they lived, and after he completed his education, he worked for a Pastor Stephen in a children's home in a nearby village. Grandpa had met this Pastor Stephen on his first trip to India with Pastor Jai Mahtani in 1992, but that was prior to the time that Paul worked for him in the children's home. Grandpa met Pastor Stephen one more time at a seminar that was held in India, but since that time, their correspondence has died off, and they are no longer in contact with each other.

Grandpa evidently had given some materials to Pastor Stephen to study, and when Paul was working at the home, he saw and read a copy of *Ultimate Questions* by John Blanchard, and inside the book was the name of Pastor Jason Kortering. With Paul's very limited English at that time, he took a whole day to write a letter to Grandpa, introducing himself and seeking some instruction; this was the beginning of the communication between the two of them. Paul took a correspondence course with Grandpa, completing each lesson faithfully, sending it in to be graded, and then Grandpa returned the marked paper to him, along with a letter of comments and instruction and a new lesson. It is so amazing how the Lord directs and governs all things—"Weakest means fulfill his will." It is incredible to think of how God used the correspondence that Grandpa had with Pastor Stephen to be the means whereby Paulraj would be introduced to the Reformed faith, when he picked up that book while working for Pastor Stephen!

Paulraj later went to Heber College in Trichy, where his living accommodations were in a hostel. He was initially enrolled in a math course (not by choice), but then he switched to English as he was desirous of studying theology, and English would be a requirement for that. Paul became involved with a Rev. David George Kirupakaran during this time. (You will read more about Rev. Kirupakaran in Kasthuri's life story, and I'll be referring to him as Rev. K from now on; just don't confuse him with Pastor Kortering.) Paulraj was

THE FIRST ARTS STUDENT

able to work along with Rev. K on certain things, and later on, Rev. K wanted Paulraj to work with him full-time, both in his school and in assisting him with ministry. Paulraj expressed his willingness to take up theological training full-time, but he wanted to be trained in a Reformed Bible school. Rev. K, a godly man but with charismatic influence, could not help Paul in his expressed desire. Paul was already embracing the doctrines of grace by that time, so he had no interest in working along with Rev. K.

After Paul completed Heber College, he taught English in a polytechnic for two years and also completed his master's degree in English during that time. It was in 1999, while Paul was teaching at the polytechnic, that Grandpa and Bruce Klamer met up with him, and at that time, Paul expressed his long-term willingness to study theology from the Reformed perspective. He studied for one year at the Presbyterian Theological Seminary (PTS) in Dehra Dun, Northern India. Later, when the ARTS course in Singapore became available, Paul was able to take up those studies as well.

Now you have to hear about Kasthuri's background before I can go on telling about Paul and Kas' marriage. Kas' family was Hindu. Besides her parents and Kas, there is one older brother. Her father worked as a tailor and her mother helped with that. Her father had a drinking problem, which made it very hard on the family. Her parents were poor; the family lived in a thatched hut, and simply paying the school fees was beyond their means. They entertained the thought of having Kasthuri leave school and help in the tailoring business.

Kas was a good student and had good grades, so this is where Rev. K came into the picture in her life. Rev. K met with Kas' parents and agreed to be responsible for her school fees. He sponsored Kas almost from the beginning, but she lived at home with her parents through Standard 6, and after that went to live at Rev. K's house, where she was cared for and provided with her educational needs. Remember, we're talking here about a girl probably twelve years of age, so you can imagine how difficult it would be to leave parents and home at such a tender age.

Rev. K had some connections with supporters from Germany who provided a certain amount of money that Rev. K could use to support needy children, and Kas was one of these children. In the broad term, this could be referred to as an orphanage. Some children are orphans in the true sense of the word that both of the parents had died, some children are orphans because the parents cannot provide for them, and in some cases children are orphans because parents desert them. With the money Rev. K collected, Kas, one other girl, and one boy were sent away to a school about six hours from Salem for their further studies. She would return to Rev. K's house during the school holidays, and she would help Mrs. K in many ways during those times.

While in their home, Kas had time to learn the basics of the Christian faith, and that brought a great change in her life. Kas' family was Hindu, but through Rev. K's family, Kas was beginning to learn something about Christianity. The Ks would allow her to visit her parents for a day or two during the holidays, and while at home with her parents, Kas would be expected to follow all the Hindu customs. During her visits home, she was careful not to let on to the family that she was learning about the Bible and was forsaking Hinduism. Kas repeatedly mentioned to us how she thanks God for his leading in her life.

It's always interesting to observe different cultures and then try to imagine how we would function under such circumstances. As a young girl, Kasthuri had quite an unusual experience. When she completed 10th Standard (sixteen years old), she had to leave school for a year in order to accompany a sixty-five-year-old missionary to another mission field in India. Her task was to assist him in his household activities and also go with him in his ministry visits as his interpreter. She was able to interpret his English sermons into Tamil. She said the Christianity that she learned at that time was very simple and had no doctrine.

Kasthuri eventually was able to enroll in and complete the nursing course at the Christian Medical College (CMC) Hospital in Vellore. (I'll tell you more about that a little later on in the story.)

THE FIRST ARTS STUDENT

Both Paul's and Kas' families were thinking about the marriage of their children about this time, but their approaches were from opposite directions. Paul's father spoke to him about marriage and was looking out for suitable girls for Paul to consider. Paul asked his father if he could have something to say in this regard, and the father happily agreed to this as he knew Paul would seek a Christian wife.

When Paul was working by Rev. K, Kas was studying in Trichy, so Paul only saw Kas when she was by Rev. K's house during the school holiday. Paul later studied in Trichy, but by that time, Kas was finished with her schooling there. She must have made a terrific impression on Paul because Paul remembered her and thought that she was the girl he desired to marry. He didn't have a clue how to contact Kas, so he wrote to a former school friend to ask if he knew how he would be able to contact this girl. Paul also wrote to Rev. K to inform him that he was interested in marrying Kas. Once Paul received her address, he wrote a letter to Kas stating his purpose in contacting her. Kas' mother was also seeking out someone for Kas to marry, and she sent a Hindu boy for Kas to consider. Kas, by this time having embraced Christianity, chose Paul, who was a Christian.

Up until this time, Kas had not told her family that she was a Christian and that her desire was to marry a Christian man, but now the time had come that she would have to take a stand. She first spoke with her brother about Paul, and he made clear to her what the consequences would certainly be—she would definitely be excommunicated from the family and from the village. Kas' mother was very angry and beat Kas when she found out that Kas was a Christian.

Rev. K had to intervene for Paul and Kas. All the key relatives were asked to come together, and in front of them all, Rev. K asked Kasthuri if she had become a Christian and if she had chosen to marry Paul, who is a Christian man. Kasthuri's answer was yes, that was what she desired for her life. This answer meant that she was officially cast out from the family, and her parents signaled this with a push of their hands, then walked away from her. This is just so hard for us to imagine, but Scripture tells us, "He that loveth father or mother more than me is not worthy of me…And he that taketh not his cross, and followeth after me, is not worthy of me. He that findeth his life shall lose it: and he that loseth his life for my sake shall find it" (Matt. 10:37–39). The only way we can explain such strength is "marvelous grace of our loving Lord."

Plans were made for the wedding of Paul and Kas. Kas had her nursing degree by this time, and she was bonded to work in the hospital in Vellore to pay for her schooling. She received some wages, but all that she earned had to be given to Rev. K to pay for the schooling he had provided for her, and he in turn gave pocket money to Kas. In preparation for the marriage, Rev. K began to allow Kas to save her wages to cover the expenses of the wedding.

It was surprising to us that Rev. K had so much to say regarding the wedding, and he could tell Paul and Kas what they had to do and what they had to pay. It is true, though, that he was the father figure in her life throughout all these years, and in their culture it would be very improper for them to approach Rev. K with their ideas of what they would like and where they would like to cut down on expenses. It is hard for us to understand, but we admired Paul and Kas for their humility and for their desire not to cause any trouble.

Paul and Kas were married on May 30, 2001. Kas entered the marriage with some Pentecostal beliefs although she had never spoken in tongues, etc. Paul felt that Kas would learn the Reformed faith as they went along once they were married. Had we known this, we certainly would have cautioned them about marriage, but we only found this out during the interview. Kas said her friends had warned her; they said that Paul was a heretic. Paul and Kas had many arguments over religion at the beginning of their marriage. Paul patiently taught her about the five points of Calvinism, but she found the doctrine of limited atonement very hard to accept.

Arrangements were being made for Paul to come to Singapore to study at Asian Reformed Theological School (ARTS), and since the young couple was just married and Kasthuri was new to the Reformed faith, it was decided that it would certainly be beneficial

THE FIRST ARTS STUDENT

for Kas to sit in on the teaching sessions and learn right along with Paul. If Paul was to become a pastor, she as his wife would also be involved, so a good understanding of the truth was essential for her as well. Kas said the changing point in her life came when she studied at ARTS in Singapore. She saw how all of Scripture harmonized, and the Lord worked in her heart that she embraced the Reformed faith. Both of them were good students and worked diligently.

Upon their return to India, Kasthuri had to go back to work at the hospital to complete her bond. She was pregnant at the time, so this wasn't easy for her to do. Their son Jason was born on December 7, 2002, so when it came time for Paul to return to Singapore for his second session at ARTS, he had to come alone. Paul's parents came from Periyakulam and stayed with Kas and Jason during that time.

Paul and Kas and their two children (Joan was born February 26, 2005) live in Vellore, Tamil Nadu, South India. Paul's parents and Kas' parents are also living with them at the present time. In the Indian culture, sons carry the responsibility of their family for their whole life, while girls marry out of their own family and share with their husband in his responsibilities toward his family. Paul is the only son in his family and therefore is responsible for his parents, and Kas as his wife shares in that responsibility. Kas' brother, according to culture, should be the one caring for Kas' parents, but her brother has a drinking problem and does not assume that responsibility. Thankfully, Paul and Kas are able to overlook culture and follow the biblical principle of providing for all the parents out of love.

Although Paul and Kas gladly care for both sets of parents, it does hit them financially. They would find it difficult to approach Paul's sisters and ask them to help with the support of Paul's parents as this would cast a bad reflection on Kasthuri, since according to culture, this would be interpreted to mean that Kasthuri is not willing to accept the responsibility of her husband's parents. We considered with Paul and Kas the instruction God gives in 1 Timothy 5:8. With Paul's family all being confessing Christians, we felt this text could be explained to the family members with love and understanding so that all the children could contribute something to the support of their parents rather than leaving it all to Paul and Kas.

It has been a great blessing to have Kas' parents living with the family as they are now hearing the gospel also. Kas' father was converted some time ago; he later had a stroke and is unable to speak but he is doing alright physically. Her mother, who at one time beat Kas for being a Christian, now enjoys the environment of a Christian home, listens daily to Scripture reading, teaching, and prayer, and also attends the worship services each Sabbath day. They give thanks that she is beginning to grow in her understanding of the Word of God.

Paul and Kas are such dear people; we just wish all of you could meet them. They are so committed to the Reformed faith and are willing to give everything they have in order to share this precious truth with others. Grandpa and I believe that our parents, in their day, would often deny themselves in order to have something to give to others, but this is hardly true in America anymore, probably for 99 percent of us; our giving is out of our abundance. It's refreshing to see a young family eagerly and joyfully serving the Lord whatever the cost. The Lord is certainly blessing their work, which gives them much joy, encouragement, and determination to press on.

After Paul completed the second session of ARTS, he returned to India to take up the work there. It wasn't clear to him, at that point, if the Lord was calling him to be a pastor. Both Paul and Kas definitely felt that they no longer could be a part of the Church of South India. The Lord had led them to the Reformed faith, and that is what they desired to share with others. We can appreciate how difficult it is to begin a new work in India where the Reformed faith is hardly known. Paul's pleasing personality and willingness to speak with everyone is a great asset.

Paul began by publishing a small pamphlet in which he translated a few articles and also wrote some of his own; this was well received but it was also costly. The ERCS was supporting the work of Paul's ministry at that time, but they are no longer doing this. Paul had a deep desire to share with others what he had studied in Singapore, so

THE FIRST ARTS STUDENT

in early 2005, he was able to rent a room for a few months to conduct classes in Sola Deo Gratia Academy, unofficially, but still with structure. With all their enthusiasm, Paul and Kas prepared a leaflet to advertise this course and personally distributed the leaflets. The course was held three evenings each week, with the sessions lasting one and a half hours, and Paul would teach, using the material he had studied at ARTS. Their funds ran out after a few months, so they had to vacate the place and continue the program at an apartment, where they paid a minimal rent.

The Lord blessed this work, and the fruit of it is seen now in the Protestant Reformed Fellowship. The course served as the means whereby seven men came to embrace the Reformed faith and grow in their desire to learn more. These men now form the core group of the fellowship, and there are some thirty-five to fifty people attending the three or four Bible studies that are held each week, as well as the Sunday morning house/church worship service that developed out of the Sunday evening Bible study. We were able to witness all this, and what a joy it was for us! What we heard over and over again is how thrilled they are to hear the messages Paulraj brings to them because they can see it is what the Bible teaches. They want to know the Bible and have the comfort and assurance that God's Word gives them.

We don't know what the Lord has in store for them. They truly desire that eventually they may be organized into a church. And we pray for them that the Lord will bring that to pass. There is a great need for financial support. There are eight people living in Paul and Kas' house, and their home is also open to people of the fellowship. Some of them are singles who live in heathen homes, so Paul and Kas' house becomes a refuge for them, a place where they can have spiritual fellowship and pray.

In order to help meet expenses, Paulraj tried to take up some employment, but the company he worked for had a hard time making ends meet and could not pay their employees for some time. Even for those who do have jobs in Vellore, the wages are very minimal and can barely provide a living for them. For the poor in their midst, they are mainly concerned that they have rice and assistance with medical needs, if necessary.

When we consider the trust that has been built up over the thirteen plus years we have known Paulraj, and we see his sincerity and love for the truth, we feel that the Lord has not only placed before us a mission field, ripe unto harvest. He has also supplied a local man to work in this field, one who is among his own people, speaks their language, knows their culture, understands them better than an outsider ever could, and is willing to give his life for the work.

Paulraj feels he needs more instruction at this point, as he strives to lead this group into the truth. Hopefully this need can be met by arranging to have some pastors go to India to conduct a seminar for two or three weeks at a time. Such visits would also give an opportunity to evaluate the work and encourage the saints there. If we were to assist this group financially, it would cost only a fraction of what it would cost to have one of our own missionaries there.

Should a church eventually be organized, they would have the goal of getting the Ministry of Mercy (MOM) up and running. There are many children in India (even some children from the fellowship, two orphaned boys being brought to church by an aunt and two very young children of a widow in her twenties who must work to eke out a living) who need shelter, food, good instruction, etc., but that is all in the future, the Lord willing. The Lord has done great things, and we give him all the thanks and praise.

Part Three

Mission Trips

> The ends of all the earth shall hear
> And turn unto the Lord in fear;
> All kindreds of the earth shall own
> And worship Him as God alone.
>
> For His the kingdom, His of right,
> He rules the nations by His might;
> All earth to Him her homage brings,
> The Lord of lords, the King of kings.*

---

* No. 48, 5-6, in *The Psalter*.

Myanmar — January 5-19, 1996

After experiencing two most wonderful weeks in Myanmar, I hope I will be able to convey in this report how it has truly enriched our lives. We really count it a great privilege to be used by the Lord for the preaching of the Reformed faith.

Before I begin, I must introduce you to a few people.

Moses: his vision for Myanmar was to reach out to the people in the villages with the good news of the gospel. He had the advantage of knowing many people because of his previous work as a veterinarian, relatives in different areas, and the clan to which he belongs. He began as a church planter and organized churches here and there. At the time the ERCS came into the picture, he was hoping to begin a school for training church leaders.

Kip Vel: wife of Moses and the mother of their six children. She is a very gifted person and came to Singapore for theological training at Far Eastern Bible College (FEBC) in order to prepare to be an instructor in the Bible school they would begin in Myanmar.

Fung Dun: brother of Moses, who also came to Singapore for training in FEBC so that he would be qualified to teach in the Bible school as well.

While in Singapore, Kip Vel and Fung Dun attended First Evangelical Reformed Church (FERC) and acquainted them with the situation in Myanmar. Although financial assistance would be helpful, their main concern was to develop in their understanding of the Reformed faith, and they asked the ERCS to provide teaching sessions in Myanmar for the church leaders there.

Some time later, about twelve people from the ERCS made a trip to Yangon, Myanmar, for the purpose of evaluating the field for possible mission work, etc. This visit was followed up with Pastor Lau making a trip to Myanmar, with a smaller group of people, and conducting a teaching seminar on the five points of Calvinism. Grandpa was asked to take the next teaching session, which is the reason for this trip.

Friday, January 5. We left Changi Airport on Silk Air along with two ladies from FERC (Fiona Tye and See Leh Wah) and Fung Dun. Fung Dun had completed his studies in Singapore and was returning to Myanmar for good. The flight went well, very short compared with our travels to the U.S.—only three hours. Myanmar is one and a half hours behind Singapore, so we were closer to you, time wise. Our very first impression upon seeing the Yangon Airport was that it was much better than we expected.

The people who were going to attend the seminar had to leave their homes several days earlier. It is not easy to travel within Myanmar, especially if it means traveling as cheaply as possible. Sometimes it requires riding in the back of a truck on top of a load of grain, standing up in a bus for a long distance, or it could be walking for a whole day in order to make the next connection; simply stated, it takes a lot of effort and determination. The first few seminars that the ERCS held in Myanmar were also attended by some women who came along with their husbands, and by some older young people, all very eager to hear and learn more of the Reformed truth.

There were about fifty people at the airport to welcome us when we came. These people included the leadership of the church in Yangon and some of the travel-weary visitors for the seminar. Only about twelve came into the airport itself; the rest waited outside the gate, since it cost five kyats (pronounce it chets) to enter the building. Five kyats is less than U.S. 5 cents, but in a poor country, people are very mindful of how they use their money.

Myanmar money, incidentally, is all paper. Years ago they also had coins, but the coins aren't worth much anymore. One kyat is equal to approximately one U.S. cent. On the official market you would only get six kyats for one U.S. dollar, but on the black market you get anywhere from 110 to 120 kyats for one U.S. dollar. Any foreigner arriving in Myanmar has to exchange U.S. $300.00 for 30 FECs (Foreign Exchange Currency), which you can then exchange for kyats as you need them. The unused FECs are non-refundable.

MISSION TRIPS: MYANMAR—JANUARY 5-19, 1996

You can imagine how much paper you get when you exchange your money. The kyats come in denominations of 1, 2, 5, 10, 20, 45, 50, 100, 200, and 500. The funny part is that they are gone so quickly because, even though things are not expensive, you have to fork out quite a few for everything.

By law, all foreigners must stay in registered hotels while in Myanmar. I believe this is one way they help the economy in their country. It is also good for us because I think it would be difficult for us to live in with the locals on their level. The cost of the hotel room is in U.S. dollars, and they accept the FECs without converting them to kyats, so it works out well.

Our initial shock was seeing the "taxi bus" in which the people came to the airport. The taxi bus is a covered pickup truck with open sides and just a simple seat along each side. You would be totally amazed at how many people can fit in the back of these trucks. It's almost unbelievable! One contributing factor is that the Burmese people are very small, short, and thin. There will be at least eight people sitting on each side, and more standing up in the center, hanging onto a bar across the top. In addition to that, there are others hanging onto the back. There is a little step at the back for getting in, and one time I actually counted ten people hanging onto the back. As long as they can get one foot on the step, and then get a hand on somewhere, they are all set. It looks terribly dangerous, but I guess they are used to it.

The hotel van was at the airport to pick us up. We first greeted all the people and took some pictures, and then the people all returned to the village where the seminar was to be held, and we went to the hotel. The hotel was very nice—not fancy, but certainly very adequate for our needs. It was a small hotel, only eleven rooms, so we became very well acquainted with the staff. They treated us like celebrities, always opening the door for us and bowing. When we came home, they would dash out to the truck to open that door too. When we came to the dining room, they would place the napkin on our lap. It got to be a bit much.

I think they gave Grandpa and me the most convenient room because we were staying two weeks. We had hot showers, electricity, even air-conditioning. Breakfast was provided along with the cost of the room. We had to pay U.S. $30 per night for our room. They really treated us super, and it was almost sad leaving there. When later on we saw how the people live in the villages, it was almost embarrassing how good we had it.

We could also take our dinner at the hotel if necessary, at a reasonable cost. Friday night we ate at the hotel with Fiona and Leh Wah. All of us who came from Singapore and were staying at the hotel would spend some time together each night, talking over the events of the day, sharing insights, making plans, reading the Bible, and praying.

Saturday, January 6. Shortly after 7:00, we heard quite a bit of noise outside, like children having recitations, so we thought there must be a school nearby. After breakfast, Fiona, Leh Wah, and I went for a walk, and we came across this school. We went on the campus to look around, and a man came up and asked if he could help us. We told him we were staying at the hotel and that we had heard all the recitations and were a bit curious. He was the English teacher, and he took some time to show us around. The Saturday classes are for remedial teaching, and regular school sessions are held from Monday to Friday.

You might picture in your mind the schools and facilities you are used to, but this is so completely different. Everything is very old. The school was gloomy and poorly lit. The walls were bare wood and the desks were ancient. We couldn't believe the library. The books were stacked in piles without the spines showing, so it didn't appear very useful. He said the school was in need of books and they would appreciate our sending them some books, if we could. The school grounds are dirt and rough. The canteen is just a bunch of old rickety tables.

This proved to be an interesting contact though, because the teacher later introduced us to his cousin's wife, who is a Christian. The teacher is about fifty years old, unmarried, and a Buddhist. He told us that a teacher's beginning salary is 950 kyats per month, and the maximum is around 1,350. (We're talking here of about U.S.

MISSION TRIPS: MYANMAR—JANUARY 5-19, 1996

$9.50 to $13.50.)

Elder Siew Chee Seng from FERC arrived on Saturday morning. In the afternoon we all went to the village for the registration of the delegates. It was quite a procedure, mostly because of the language barrier. We had made registration forms in Singapore and also took name tags along. A few people who knew both English and Burmese or Chin were able to help us. Elder Siew was the photographer. We first numbered the name tags so that the number would show on their picture, and then we numbered the registration forms, so that we would know which person went with which form. Just as all the Chinese looked alike to us when we first came to Singapore, all the Burmese looked alike when we came to Myanmar. Besides that, all the names are strange.

If we are going to get to know these people, we need their pictures and names together, along with the other details we asked for. It was fun and a challenge, to say the least. Anyway, we felt we were prepared, so that we didn't have to take precious time on Monday morning for registration.

Tracy was the person who worked along with me on Saturday afternoon. Her own personal story is interesting too. Tracy is the niece of Pastor Moses and is living with their family at present. She works full-time for the church, doing some translating and secretarial work, for which she receives a little pocket money. When she was ten years old, her aunt and uncle took her along to the U.S. and promised her mother that they would return her to Myanmar at age eighteen. (Tracy's father died when she was three years old.) She lived in Atlanta, Georgia, where her uncle was a Baptist minister. By the time Tracy came back to Myanmar, she had completed school through grade 10. She stayed in Myanmar for a year and then went to India for six years and taught English.

Now she has been back in Myanmar for a year, but she desires to go for more training to a Bible school or Christian college in Singapore or the U.S., to acquire a degree so she would be able to teach in a Bible school in Myanmar, work in translations, teach other women, and witness in the villages. Her heart is really set on helping people in her own country. It's hard to slow such enthusiastic people down a bit and tell them they must be patient and wait for the Lord's leading in all of this. She is a very sweet girl and it's a joy to know her.

After registration we took a short walk to see the property that the ERCS had previously purchased for Grace Church. There is a house and a shack on the property. The house is actually what they are using for the church now, and the pastor, who is a bachelor, lives in a tiny room in the back of the church.

While we were in Yangon and there were more people around for the seminar and church services, the meetings were held at Moses' house. Moses, as you will remember, is the husband of Kip Vel (the lady who studied in Singapore), and he is one of the leaders in the URCM. He has a two-story house, rather well-built. The main floor is one large room (comparable to a nice-sized living room) with a small kitchen behind (the kitchen consists of a hot plate and a few open shelves for dishes and pans). The whole family, and anyone else who needs a place to stay, lives upstairs. The rooms upstairs are made by hanging pieces of fabric on clotheslines.

Sunday, January 7. In the morning we went to Galilee Church, which is in another small village, and to get there we had to travel over many bumpy roads. Friends of Fung Dun were able to loan their vehicles for our use during our stay in Myanmar. One car was driven by Stephen, a member of a Baptist church, and the truck we used was owned by a friend and driven by the son of another friend. Talk about having connections! Sunday we used both vehicles. When we reached the village, the ladies of Galilee offered some food to us, but we had just had our breakfast at the hotel so we could easily wait until after the service. The church is only a small room made of wooden boards. It has a bare wooden floor. Nothing is painted. And it has a thatch roof. Everyone sat on the floor, except us; they provided some chairs for us to sit on.

There must have been about thirty people who came from the

MISSION TRIPS: MYANMAR—JANUARY 5-19, 1996

Grace Church area in one very crowded taxi bus. Galilee Church has quite a few young children, so the first number was the Sunday school children singing a couple of songs. Next, a little boy sang a solo very nicely. After that, a Sunday school teacher sang while playing her guitar. Their only accompaniment is guitar, and the people just sing so joyfully. It was really a thrill to be there. Then the church service began, and Grandpa preached that morning from Nehemiah: building the walls of Jerusalem. His sermon was interpreted by Fung Dun in the Chin language, and then by another man into the Burmese language.

I had a bag of candy along, and after church, when we were standing outside, I started handing out candy to the children. It was so cute. Besides the children of the church, other children came running from all directions to get a piece of candy. Even some mothers carrying children walked over. The adults were just as eager as the children to get a piece of candy. There were many times when we thought a video would be fun, but in the eyes of the people, simply having a camera was quite a thing already.

We walked over to the pastor's house for our noon meal. They had it set up outside with a canvas over the top for shade. I'm sure they were giving us their very best, and probably even extending themselves because we were there, but this being our first time in Myanmar, we wondered if we would get sick from the food. The rice was cooked outside over a fire and they even prepared some chicken for us. We're thankful that the Lord kept us all healthy during the entire time. Some of the young girls stood in back of us during the meal and were fanning to keep the flies away.

After that we went to Grace Church for a service at 3:30. They asked Elder Siew to give the message, and this was interpreted by Fung Dun. Fiona, Leh Wah, Elder Siew, and Grandpa and I had dinner at the hotel and then enjoyed some nice fellowship in the evening.

Monday, January 8. The seminar began at 8:00. We used the truck for our transportation for the seminar. I sat in the back a couple of times, but more often I rated the front seat along with the driver,

Lian Te. Some advantage to being the oldest person around! Lian Te knows very little English but he is definitely trying to learn. When I tried to talk to him, he would usually just shrug his shoulders, but he had the friendliest smile. The ride took approximately twenty-five minutes, more or less, depending on whether we had to wait to cross the one-lane bridge.

We had taken fifty cheap ballpoint pens and a ream of paper along. It was so amusing to us how everything we offered was snatched up so quickly. This is something we would so easily take for granted, but it was special for them.

Pastor Lau was the instructor at the last conference on the five points of Calvinism. Grandpa thought he would start out with a little review. It took longer than he had planned, pretty much the whole morning session, because he had to do a bit of re-explaining for them.

Grandpa's original plan was to teach three courses during the seminar. Then he decided it would be better to treat one course first, rather than three different courses each day. The one on the covenant was top priority, so he began with that. It went rather slowly because it all had to have two translations, and he wanted to explain it thoroughly and give time for questions. So it wasn't long and he changed his goal to two courses. The way it turned out, he covered one course, and in addition to that gave a brief introduction to the Heidelberg Catechism.

Because these people are poor, they eat only two meals a day. The meals consist of rice, sometimes with a little meat or vegetable, and sometimes plain. Each morning, before the conference, they would have a cup of coffee along with a dough fritter. By the time the morning session was over at 11:00, they were hungry for their rice.

It was surprising to us that they were able to use two houses, near to Moses' house, for the conference. One house was where the wives and daughters of the men stayed, and the other house was for the men and the dining hall. The men's house is still under construction, so no one had to vacate that property. I don't know how it happened that the other house was available.

MISSION TRIPS: MYANMAR—JANUARY 5-19, 1996

None of these village houses had furniture. The dining hall was set up in three rows. The seats were formed by setting down bricks, only one high, and laying a plank across them. The tables were made the same way by putting two or three bricks on top of each other and then three planks for the table effect. These people sat right next to each other with their knees up against their bodies. Now go ahead, see if you can do that and manage to eat.

They had a little temporary kitchen set up between Moses' house and the next house. There was one working table and two or three fire pits on which they could cook large kettles of rice and pots of veggies. After eating, the young girls would do the cleanup. They would get down on their haunches to wash the dishes in a pan that was setting on the ground. It was cute that while these girls were cutting vegetables, washing dishes, or whatever, we could hear them singing their hearts out, even trying to harmonize.

They wouldn't think of having us eat with them or eating what they eat. On Monday, Fung Dun, Moses, Tracy, Lian Te, Fiona, Leh Wah, Elder Siew, Grandpa, and I went to a Burmese restaurant for lunch. The restaurant seemed clean enough to us, but we sure wondered about a few of the things that were served. Afterward we stopped at a fruit stand and bought large apples and tangerines (one hundred in all) for all the people at the conference.

In the afternoon Grandpa started teaching on the covenant. Fung Dun first translated it into Burmese, then into Chin. He did a good job and stuck right with it all week. He also had to listen to the questions and give them back to Grandpa in English. We could tell from the questions that Grandpa's teaching was getting translated properly. We had our dinner that night at the hotel. Grandpa went to our room to prepare for the next day, and the rest of our group chatted about our impressions and experiences and then had a time of prayer together.

Tuesday, January 9. Grandpa got started right away on Tuesday morning with more instruction on the covenant. I told Tracy that I would really like to meet with the women during the noon break, after lunch was finished. The afternoon session would start at 2:00. She rounded up all the ladies and we met together in the ladies' house. They all sat on the floor, but they brought in some chairs for Fiona, Leh Wah, and me. I made some opening remarks, expressing our thanks that the Lord had brought us there safely and that we had the opportunity of meeting all of them, and our desire to get to know them better.

I was surprised at how quickly they responded and opened up. They had questions about how we conduct a Ladies' Fellowship in Singapore, so I explained that to them, and told them about some of the difficulties the women in Singapore encounter, being first-generation Christians. They are very concerned for the women and their families in the villages and have a great desire to witness to them, to share the gospel with them, and to help in whatever way they can.

One question they asked was, when they have their fellowship, the women preach; is this right or wrong? This goes so painstakingly slow with interpretation, but you have to ask more questions to get a complete picture of what is going on. They encountered some objection to "women preaching" by some of the people. What it boils down to is defining their terms. The women were not preaching. There was no call to worship. They were simply meeting together, and one was sharing or explaining a portion of Scripture and what it meant to her.

Other things they brought up were family problems. For example, a mother has a sixteen-year-old son who is rebellious against religion. The method of discipline they used when he was young was to have him sit on the table; he could not look to the right or to the left, but could only look at the Bible in his lap and memorize the verse they assigned to him. The women said they don't spank their children very much. More often they bend the index finger and strike the child on the head with the knuckle, or they will talk with them. A young girl asked about a teenaged brother who gives in to peer pressure and listens more to his friends than to his parents.

One mother is a widow and has four children. Because it is so difficult to earn money in Myanmar, she sometimes has to go into

MISSION TRIPS: MYANMAR—JANUARY 5-19, 1996

India to buy and sell in order to provide for the family. We asked, "How frequently and for how long must she do this?" The answer was about four times a year and anywhere from two weeks to a month at a time. During those times, she leaves her four children alone at home; the oldest is seventeen and the youngest is eight. Our time was up already because we were having a picture-taking session, but we promised to get back with them the next day.

In addition to the many group pictures that were taken, everyone had to have their picture taken with Grandpa on one side and me on the other—it was their little keepsake. I don't know what our smiles looked like toward the end. I'm sure there were over fifty pictures taken that noon.

Fiona, Leh Wah, and I left then and went shopping at Bogyoke Aung San Market. The two girls would be leaving on Thursday so they had to do a bit of sightseeing too. The marketplace is all small shops, has a lot of character, and is a good place for souvenir shopping. We had a fun afternoon and later met Grandpa and Elder Siew at the hotel for dinner. That night we chose to have the one Western set meal (includes the salad, entree, dessert, and beverage) the hotel offered, but it wasn't all that great. We decided they were better at preparing their own cuisine.

Wednesday, January 10. Everyone was on time to begin another day of the conference. About mid-morning when Grandpa was lecturing, he paused for Fung Dun's interpretation, but when nothing was said, Grandpa looked over at Fung Dun. Fung Dun had a frustrated, worried look on his face, and motioned for his brother Moses to go outside. The front door was open and there was a government truck outside with some officials looking in the direction of the church. For a moment he was scared, but he felt everything would be all right because prior to the conference, they had gotten the okay from the local councilmen. After we had the picture-taking session in the middle of the road on Tuesday, it might have been reported that something strange was going on; there were some Caucasians in the village for several days. Everything turned out all right. Moses explained the situation, and the government officials were satisfied, I guess, because they drove off and we didn't hear a thing from them.

We were invited to the house of Moses' neighbor for our noon meal. His eighteen-year-old son passed away in November 1994, when the group from Singapore was in Myanmar, and they asked Elder Siew, who was also along at that time, to give the funeral message. The wife is a Christian. Their oldest daughter, also a Christian, is very intelligent and is studying in the U.S. to be a doctor. She is there on a U.S. scholarship. They attend the Baptist church.

He opened with prayer before the meal, but he said that he and his youngest daughter were not "born again" and he asked that we pray for them. They were very hospitable. He even came to the airport to see us off when it was time to go back to Singapore. He's a good friend of Moses and will do anything to help. They are trying to fix up their house a little, making rooms with doors instead of using fabric to separate the rooms, and they will also attach the outhouse to the house and run a pipe to a drain field or something like that. There was no furniture in the house, just a couple small tables, and they borrowed some chairs from the church for our visit.

We continued meeting with the ladies after lunch. Fung Dun had to be the interpreter this time because Tracy was busy with someone else. They explained how they try to provide for others. Rice is their only meal. They allow a small cup measure of rice for each person. So if six people are eating, they will measure out six of those portions. Then they will reach in with their hand and take a handful out and put it in a container. "That," they say, "is for the Lord." They accumulate that rice, and then all the ladies put their rice together and give it to the "poor."

Before coming to the Reformed church, they were members of larger churches, so there was more rice to give away. Now they belong to a small church, and they feel bad that they don't have as much to give. I used the illustration of the widow's mite, and that in God's sight they were giving generously of what they had. I tried my best to encourage them, and they expressed appreciation for my meeting with them.

MISSION TRIPS: MYANMAR—JANUARY 5-19, 1996

In the afternoon, Fiona, Leh Wah, and I met up with the English teacher whom we had met on Saturday. He took us to visit his cousin's wife. His cousin is an orthopedic doctor, and their two sons are also doctors. One is in the U.S. specializing in internal medicine, and the younger one is putting in his year of government-required medical service before he goes on to specialize. The whole family is Christian.

The cousin's wife was a school teacher for over twenty years and is now retired. She speaks excellent English, so we thought she must have studied abroad, but she was never out of Myanmar. She is busy now with translating English works into Burmese. Burmese is written with all little circles and curlicues. She is working on a Bible story book at present, starting with the New Testament, and having it printed in sections. When she completes it, she hopes it can be printed in one volume. She gave each of us one of the sections that is finished. She said, "The Lord has been so good to me all my life, I just want to give the rest of my life in serving him." She offered that if we have anything that we need translated into Burmese, she would be very happy to do it for us free of charge. She goes into the villages every Saturday and Sunday to witness to the poor people. She goes empty-handed because she doesn't want them to listen to her because she brings something for them. When it was time to leave, she got her youngest son, who is single and lives at home, to drive us around, show us Chinatown, and take us back to the hotel. It was so nice to get in the car and have a tape of familiar Christian hymns playing.

Thursday, January 11. We said goodbye to Fiona and Leh Wah before leaving for the conference. Now that the girls were gone, I stayed at the conference all day. Elder Siew was away most of the day. He wanted to do some shopping and he also had to take care of the finances of the conference. Fung Dun, Tracy, Grandpa, and I walked out to the main road to a little restaurant for lunch.

Fiona, Leh Wah, Elder Siew, and Grandpa and I contributed some extra money and gave it to the ladies so they could prepare a special evening meal for all the people there. We didn't see what the people ate, but I hope it was the same food they cooked for us. It was absolutely delicious and was prepared very nicely. The chief cook for the conference was Hla Hla, and she's an expert! After the dinner we went back to the hotel. The people at the conference had some kind of service each evening, but since it was all in Burmese or Chin, without interpretation, it wasn't necessary for us to stay, nor did they expect us to.

Friday, January 12. We said goodbye to Elder Siew before leaving for the conference. Each day at the conference was so very special. Grandpa was enjoying every minute of it, both in the teaching and in the interaction with those who attended.

At noon I met with the widow lady alone and then with the orphanage lady (and my interpreter, of course). I must tell you about the orphanage lady yet. This is a couple up in the Falam province. They have four children of their own and have taken in ten orphans. We don't hear of orphans very often, but in Myanmar it is very common, due in part to the fact that they cannot afford medical attention when they are sick, so many people die very young. The church really feels a burden for these children, because sometimes there are Christian orphans, and if there is not a place for them, they will be provided for in the Buddhist orphanage and indoctrinated in Buddhism. This mother told me how she instructs her children that God has blessed them with parents, and now they have a calling to be kind to these orphans and help them. Their children gladly receive these orphans in their home and treat them as brothers and sisters. They all live in one small rented house, or I could better call it a room.

It's really something to see the poverty of these people. You can't remain untouched. They do not have running water. They have no washing machines, no refrigerators, and no telephones. They sleep right on the floor without any mattress or rug. They must use an outhouse, which is a little shack on stilts with an eastern toilet (flat on the floor) with a pipe that goes down into the ground. They have a bucket of water with a dipping pan in the outhouse, which one can use for flushing. In each neighborhood there is a well, and one can go there to buy water by the bucketful. Baths are taken outside

MISSION TRIPS: MYANMAR—JANUARY 5-19, 1996

by pouring water over oneself with a pan. All the laundry is done by hand and hung over a line to dry. (I asked at the hotel if they had a washing machine for their laundry and she told me, "No, we don't. We do it all by hand." Can you imagine washing sheets and towels every day by hand?)

I haven't figured out how the people get along during the rainy season. The road is higher up than where the houses are, so I guess that is tolerable. The houses are all built on stilts. We were told that during the rainy season there is a lake with fish swimming in it, all around the house. Natural question is, how do they get about during the rainy season with so much water around? Everyone wears flip-flops, and they simply take them off and let the mud ooze through their toes and they slip and slide through it.

These people are poor physically, but they are spiritually rich. We have such an abundance, and it just seems as if our lives have so much clutter (materialism, entertainment, etc.) that draws us away from things spiritual. Their life centers in the church. Their thoughts are not on what they can get but on what they have: salvation in Jesus Christ. I don't think we could even exist on their level, but I'm sure we could get along with a whole lot less than we have.

After Fiona, Leh Wah, and Elder Siew left, we were told that the noon meal would be prepared for us. Grandpa and I were glad. We wanted to have the opportunity to eat as they eat. But...no way. We didn't get to eat with them, and they continued to fuss for us, preparing very nice special dishes and bringing them over to where the conference was, so that we could sit on chairs by the desk. We didn't have to eat alone. Fung Dun, Moses, and Tracy always ate with us, and once the executive board of the URCM had lunch with us.

Saturday, January 13. Grandpa finished up his instruction on the covenant by "stretch time" and coffee at 10:15. They had some chairs and benches set up along the walls for us and for some of the men during the entire conference, and the rest of the people sat on straw mats on the floor. The mats were about five feet square, and I wouldn't dare guess how many people could sit on one mat. It surprised us that some of the people did not even get up during the break time, but just remained sitting on the floor, waiting until we got started again. (That means sitting on the floor for three to three and a half hours with legs crossed some way or other!)

With about forty-five minutes left for the morning session, Grandpa took the time to tell them about himself: the family he was born into, how his parents desired for him to be a minister, and how the Lord led him in his youth. He told them about our marriage and family, the churches we were in, about our working now in Singapore, and the great blessing it is to bring the gospel to others. He also shared several Scripture verses that have always meant a lot to him. After that, there was opportunity to ask a few questions.

Another beautiful noon meal was served, and then in the afternoon Grandpa had the introduction to the Heidelberg Catechism. Grandpa and I went back to the hotel again, and just had a simple meal of fried rice since we had such a big dinner at noon.

Sunday, January 14. Sunday again and Grandpa preached at Grace Church. All through the conference, and again on Sunday, we were just struck by how heartily the people sang. No question about it, that really means a lot to them, and they have great joy in singing. They do have a little book made up in English as well. In it they have hymns that they also have in their language, so we are able to sing together: "Jesus Is a Rock in a Weary Land," "Bringing In the Sheaves," "How Great Thou Art," etc. In the afternoon, Tracy and I worked on translating some of the testimonies that the people had written. It went faster for her if she just translated, so I did all the writing.

Hla Hla and her helpers prepared a special dinner for Sunday night. I had watched them for a while, so I knew what we were getting and what to avoid. One dish was liver and fish eggs. Grandpa took about three bites of that dish before deciding he couldn't handle any more of it. He fed the rest to the cat who was frequently around. They also prepared some beef with mushrooms, which was delicious! Another thing that they prepare so nicely is their mixed vegetables. They serve it on a platter, and it's so colorful and pretty.

MISSION TRIPS: MYANMAR—JANUARY 5-19, 1996

Grandpa and I were so tired in the evening after a busy day, and since all the others had gone back to Singapore, we were able to go to bed earlier at night, but that also meant waking up earlier in the morning. Our minds would start working a mile a minute, thinking about the people and all our experiences. Grandpa wrote quite a few reports in his mind during that time.

Monday, January 15. Grandpa's sixtieth birthday, and how special it was to spend it in Myanmar! We had an outing that day with about thirty people, some people from around Yangon and others who hadn't started on their return home yet. We visited the zoo. Grandpa and I felt we would have fit in better had we been in a cage along with the animals, judging from the way people were looking at us. We were told that many people in Myanmar have never seen a Westerner before.

We saw the Shwedagon Pagoda, which is the largest in the world and has been covered many times with gold. Enshrined in the pagoda are eight hairs of Buddha. (What a lot of idolatry! It gives such a sick feeling to see all these people bowing down and praying to their gods.) After that we walked around by the seaport and then rode through the downtown area of Yangon. Our guides pointed out various buildings, like the American embassy, etc.

After all that activity, we went back to Grace Church for a birthday party. Moses' son also had a birthday that day, his seventeenth, so it was a double birthday party. Moses gave a few remarks in Burmese, and then they asked Grandpa to make some remarks. He shared some parting thoughts, testimony, and words of appreciation, and he assured them of our prayers. We sang "Happy Birthday" and had birthday cake.

Then there was one request: "Can Pastor and Mrs. Kortering sing a song for us? We hear Mrs. Kortering singing alto and it sounds so nice." So we sang "How Great Thou Art," and Paul, son of Moses, accompanied us on the guitar. While singing the chorus after the last verse, we had our first electrical blackout. All the lights went out, but we continued on, "How great thou art, How great thou art."

Then it was time to say goodbye to all those who were at the conference. By that time a real bond of friendship had been established, so the hugs and handshakes were quite meaningful. This was done by candlelight, and by the time we were getting in the car to go to the hotel, the lights came on again. We reached the hotel around eight. The only thing we'd had to eat since breakfast was the birthday cake, but we really didn't feel all that hungry either. A plate of fried rice was just right for our dinner. The people there are used to two meals a day, so they didn't take any food along for the day. They were very happy to see that I had a bag of candy to share with them.

Tuesday, January 16. It was our first quiet day, and we spent the whole day at the hotel. The hotel has a nice green area complete with tables with sun umbrellas and chairs, so it was very pleasant sitting outdoors. We both did a lot of writing that day, which is helping me greatly in writing this account of our stay there. Grandpa made notes for his report.

Tracy called on the phone and asked if she, Hla Hla, and Moses could come to the hotel to visit us for just a little while. Much to our surprise, Tracy gave me a shawl that was handmade by her mother. Up in the Chin state, they have special shawls that are made for certain occasions, and this was one of those shawls. The background is black with a very colorful design woven on it. By the way, Tracy was calling me "Mother" soon after we got there. She wanted to know all about our family and feels as if she has gained five sisters.

Hla Hla gave me a little package also and wanted me to open it (the usual custom is like Singapore: don't open gifts till later). In the package were jade stones laid out in size for a necklace, bracelet, and earrings. Her son-in-law, who lives in Kale Province, is a stone cutter, and these stones were cut by him. It all looks very pretty, but I suppose it could be quite costly to have them made up because it would require a setting for each stone. We'll have to take them to a jeweler and have them evaluated before deciding what to do with them.

Grace Church wishes to do an outreach by providing a home for elderly people, and Hla Hla will be the one to manage it.

MISSION TRIPS: MYANMAR—JANUARY 5-19, 1996

Arrangements are already in place for a house that will be provided by a widow lady, who will be one of the residents. They have to do a little renovating before they can move in. They would like to have some non-Christian residents so they can witness to them. She says, "It may be that the Lord will save them, so they do not have to fear when they die." This home will accommodate ten people.

Wednesday, January 17. Grandpa had agreed to speak for the chapel services at the Far Eastern Fundamental Bible College. We had to be there at 8:30 and we arrived just on time. He had made a speech on the subject of demons while in Singapore and thought he could use it at FEFBC's chapel service. It worked out very well. All the classes at Far Eastern are taught in English. They do this because they want all their students to learn English, as there are more books available in English for their Bible study.

Remember my talking about Rev. Titus, who is studying in Singapore in order to be a professor in this school? He is so Reformed and gets all excited about learning from Grandpa. Just can't get it fast enough. It is Titus' uncle who is at the head of FEFBC. Titus attends Far Eastern Bible College in Singapore and is basically repeating all the instruction he has had before, in order to get his degree. He is grateful to have learned Hebrew and Greek. We also met Titus' wife, Cer Te (who does not speak English), their little daughter Jemima, and Cer Te's mother. While Titus is in Singapore, his wife is staying at the hostel at FEFBC. Titus has a year and a half left to study in Singapore. When he went back to Myanmar over Christmas, he talked with the professors about covenant theology. He said they were quite open to listen, which was encouraging to him.

After that we went to the kindergarten at Galilee. The kindergarten is an outreach of the church for the children in the neighborhood. It is run by two women of the church. All the children, forty-eight of them, are from homes within walking distance of the church. There was one who was two and a half, and the rest are between three and five. If anything melts your heart, it's that!

The fee for kindergarten is one kyat per day. That's one U.S. cent.

They told us that some of the parents cannot afford it and their children are allowed to come free. While Fung Dun was in Singapore, he got some discontinued school uniforms from a kindergarten, so most of the children wore the same little green outfit. The kindergarten is held in the same building as the Galilee Church, which I described at the beginning. You have to cross a little board bridge from the road to the steps. The building is small, made of bare wood, with a bare wooden floor. Because it's built on stilts, you can see light come up between the floorboards.

We got there just at lunchtime. The room is so small that it's like a human carpet when the children are in it. The kids take their own lunch, rice and perhaps something with it. They share the water, using only a few cups for all of them. Some of the kids ate using their fingers, and others had spoons. The teachers had to go around helping the kids a little bit. After lunch they could go outside for a short while. During that time, one of the teachers swept the rice from the floor, pushing it to an opening in the floorboards, and down it went to the ground.

We asked if the children could sing a couple of songs for us when they came in. They sang two choruses in English. I caught some of the words; one must have been about the Trinity because I heard "three in one, three in one," and the other was "Jesus Loves You and Me." Then it was nap time. One of the teachers opened a wooden box in the corner and started handing out pillows, and all the kids lay down on the floor. They were all so sweet and precious. What really struck me was that they were so well-behaved and orderly.

There was absolutely nothing in the kindergarten room—no chairs and no tables for the children. I don't know if they ever get to write and color. We brought some supplies along and I hope they will be able to use them. On the chalkboard they had the ABCs and numbers, so I guess they are trying to teach them that, but the teachers really don't speak English either. We communicated with the teachers through Fung Dun.

We went outside with the teachers to take a picture, and other

MISSION TRIPS: MYANMAR—JANUARY 5-19, 1996

neighbor children started gathering around. They probably recognized me as the lady with the candy, but by that time I didn't have another piece left. I felt bad about that. I gave the teachers what I had left of granola bars, etc., to share with the school children.

Steven was driving us around that day, and Fung Dun and Moses were with us. After that, Steven took us to the university that he attends and introduced these Western people to his teachers. He was skipping school that day to show us around, but when a friend told him they were having an English test at 3:00, he promptly drove us back to the hotel so he could still go for the test.

Thursday, January 18. This was our last day in Myanmar, so we took it slow in the morning and were ready to leave the hotel around 11:00 to do a little souvenir shopping and looking around. We bought some tangerines for our lunch. (One has to learn how to find decent restaurants in Yangon. We saw plenty we didn't care to go into.) We went back to the hotel and packed things up. We had roasted chicken for dinner—definitely not our best meal.

Friday, January 19. The send-off group at the airport was Moses, Fung Dun, Moses' neighbor, Rev. Bawi (pronounced Boy), Rev. James, Tracy, and the truck driver, Lian Te. Saying goodbye was not easy. They hope and pray we will be able to come again sometime, and so do we. We really came to love them as dear saints in the Lord. The flight home was good, and Pastor Lau was at Changi Airport to pick us up and take us home.

Now just a few more interesting tidbits to share.

We found the people to be very warmhearted and friendly. Even though the people we met are so very poor, they do not complain. They are genuinely happy people who show true happiness does not come in material possessions. They express a real joy in the Lord. They're very eager to learn and understand. They sing so enthusiastically. And they show such love and concern for each other! It was just a real joy to be with them for those couple weeks.

One of the ladies told me, through an interpreter, that she felt so bad that she could not speak English. Believe me, I felt bad that

I could not speak Burmese or Chin. Right now a person could not enter Myanmar as a missionary, but we realize how important it would be, if a person were to work there, to know the language.

These people are content to have their very basic needs supplied. They don't ask for money to improve their living conditions. The ERCS will have to work through this and decide how much they can help. The cost of the conference was paid by the ERCS: travel for the delegates, food, and Grandpa's travel. We paid for my trip. The others who went from Singapore paid for their own trip as well.

The money that each church needs is just enough for their pastor's family to live on, and the rest would be for outreach. Many of their families are large: one pastor has eleven children, others have four, six, and seven. There is an Indian family in Grace Church. The mother gave birth on Saturday night to their tenth child. Many Indian children are pretty, and those little kids are very lovable. The father was in church with the family on Sunday morning, and they sang a song together, with the father playing the guitar.

We noticed that the church people have plenty of time (some are unemployed; someone told us unemployment is 150 percent, meaning extremely high, of course) so they do a lot of thinking and planning for outreach, but they don't have the money to carry it out. In Singapore the people have plenty of money, but they are so busy working that they don't have time. In the northern part of Myanmar (Kale and Falam) there are some farmers, so things are a bit easier up there and there is more possibility of their being self-supporting in a few years' time.

Yangon is a large city, bigger than Singapore, with a population of around three million. The city itself is quite nice, although it would be quite a culture shock for one coming from the U.S. At one time Yangon was considered to be the most beautiful city in Southeast Asia, but since the military has taken over the government, that is no longer true. We were surprised to see digital countdowns beneath their traffic lights. We had never seen that before, so here in this undeveloped country it seemed like something quite modern.

MISSION TRIPS: MYANMAR—JANUARY 5-19, 1996

When the traffic light changes from green or red, the digital timer counts down from thirty seconds, so it's possible to tell just how long it will be before the light changes again. Driving in Myanmar is on the right side of the road, same as we do in the U.S., but the funny thing is that they get a lot of their used vehicles from countries that drive on the left side, so the steering wheels on those vehicles are on the right side of the car. If they are going to pass on the left, they have to pull out quite far before they can see if another vehicle is coming.

The main roads are paved and quite wide. There might be a center dividing line but no lane marks. Lines really wouldn't mean anything anyway. People pass on the right and on the left and simply blow their horns all the time to signal they are passing. In the villages, the people walk down the roads, so drivers also blow their horns to get them to move over.

There are some modern buildings in the city. It is common to see shops set up just about anywhere. In town we saw suit jackets folded and set in piles on the sidewalk, and the fabric shops were simply heaps of fabric laying there. There are many little coffee shops. Stools are tiny (about eight to ten inches high) and the tables a little higher. It looks like children's toy furniture.

A very familiar sight in Myanmar is all the Buddhist monks walking around. They have shaved heads and they wear saffron-colored—I can't really call them robes—I think they are just long pieces of fabric wrapped a certain way around their bodies, with one shoulder exposed. Most Buddhist boys will spend one or two of their school years in a monastery, so you see young children dressed this way too, with their heads shaved. Some may decide, at that age, to stay in the monastery for their life's work, but many of the boys will return to their homes. Aside from that, one doesn't see a lot of Buddhist religious activity, like there is in Singapore with the burning of joss sticks and hell money, etc.

The weather was absolutely beautiful, like the best of California. No rain, sunny, and clear blue sky. Cool at night, and even though it was hot during the day it wasn't humid like Singapore. Wow! Did we ever notice the humidity when we came back home! People in Myanmar wear jackets, sweaters, and scarves in the morning when it is a bit cooler, but to us it was very refreshing and we didn't put our sweaters on at all. Mosquitoes are abundant in the evening—another reason why it was good we could get back to our hotel early.

One time when Kip Vel was studying in Singapore, she gave me a mint-green crocheted shawl when she returned from Myanmar. With Singapore heat, I knew I would never be wearing it in Singapore, so I had it on the coffee table for a while. Now I learned what I am supposed to do with it. The women fold up these pretty shawls and set them on top of their heads, or wind them around their heads with some of the fringes hanging down, to keep the sun from their heads.

We met the friend of Fung Dun who so generously loaned us the truck all week. In visiting with him (English-speaking, by the way), we learned that he earns 1,250 kyats per month. He has a family of four children and, because they have quite a few guests at their home, they need two large bags of rice each month. One bag (probably fifty to seventy-five pounds) costs 1,250 kyats. There is no way that people can survive in Myanmar without making deals or working the black market. He told us that the prime minister has a salary of 3,000 kyats per month. It's only the government officials and their families that are rich because of all the kickbacks.

Officially you can buy only two gallons of petrol per week, reasonably priced, so you are forced to buy what you need on the black market at a higher price—190 kyats per gallon. You have to know how to look for the places that sell petrol. When you see the little petrol sign on a building, you park along the road, and they bring the petrol to the car in a large metal pitcher and pour it in using a funnel. This is illegal and you could be fined, but then you simply settle for a bribe, and you're on your way. There are "under the table" deals all the time. The question arises whether this is alright to do, and we wrestled with it as well. The biggest thing is exchanging money on the black market. In addition to that, there are many other issues like buying petrol, etc.

MISSION TRIPS: MYANMAR—JANUARY 5-19, 1996

In 1988, there was an election in Myanmar and Aung San Suu Kyi was elected. The military refused to let her take office and put her under house arrest. There was a major bloodbath and the military killed thousands of people. They have been in control since that time and life for the Myanmar citizens has only become more and more difficult. The people only become poorer and poorer while the military enjoys luxuries. There is no way the people can survive without their trying to eke out a living in whatever way they can.

For clothing, men and women wear longyis (pronounced lon chee). The longyis are made with two yards of fabric sewn together with one seam to make a circle. Women's longyis may have several darts sewn in back to make them lay smooth, and a band sewn on top, especially if made from a silky fabric. Women step inside, pull the extra fabric to the left, hold it tight against their body, and then pull the extra fabric to the right and tuck it in. Men stand in the center of their longyis and pull the extra fabric from both sides to the center, forming a pleat, and they have some special way of flipping it over and making a knot. You see people all over, anywhere and everywhere, adjusting their longyis. They pull them apart and redo them.

Some fabrics are a bit dressier than others and they are worn with shirts, blouses, T-shirts, and sweaters. Everyone looks very decently dressed. The ERCS has already had a clothing drive for Myanmar. I saw shorts on an adult only one time. Children are seen with dresses and different kinds of clothing. Men dress sometime with trousers, and the women might have some other clothing too, but it's mostly longyis.

Much work is done manually in Myanmar: construction, road work, unloading ships, etc. The government can require a person to work for a month without pay on a road project or whatever. This could mean working under the hot sun and smashing large pieces of rock with a hammer—life is not easy! We saw streams of people carrying baskets of cement to a construction site, and we saw the same thing at the seaport with loading and unloading.

I guess that brings me to the end of my story. It was a wonderful experience for us, and we're glad we were able to share it together.

I took notes during all the lectures because that kept me busy during the translating parts. Grandpa did very well and he enjoyed it immensely. This was real mission work! We did so much talking about everything while we were there, and there's so much to discuss now as to method, money, etc. It's all very interesting and a real blessing to be involved in this work.

❦

Myanmar — November, 1997

The Evangelical Reformed Churches in Singapore (ERCS) asked Professor Herman Hanko to be the guest speaker at the Reformation Day lectures in 1997. These lectures are always a highlight on the church calendar in Singapore, and Prof. Hanko agreed to come for this special event. Mr. and Mrs. Rich Bos accompanied Prof. and Mrs. Hanko on this trip. By the way, Prof. Hanko and Mrs. Bos are brother and sister, and Mrs. Bos (Elaine) is a friend of mine from way back when we were teenagers. At the same time our nephew Steve Faber was visiting in Singapore and staying by our house. They all stayed with us, and we had a great time of fellowship together. Included in the plans was a trip to Myanmar, where Prof. Hanko would have an opportunity to give a seminar in a third-world country and have the new experience of working with interpretation.

The six of us went to Myanmar (Prof. and Mrs. Hanko, Mr. and Mrs. Rich Bos, Steve Faber, and myself), along with Dr. Daniel Kwek and Elder Siew Chee Seng from FERC, and Pastor Moses (a Myanmar pastor studying in Singapore). We were told that many of the Myanmar nationals fly on Myanmar Air and that it's more desirable to go on Silk Air (Singapore Air). When I inquired about cost, I found out that Silk Air was SGD840 compared with SGD590 on Myanmar Air. Naturally, we chose Myanmar Air, and we weren't one bit disappointed. Service was excellent, meals were good, and I

MISSION TRIPS: MYANMAR—NOVEMBER, 1997

certainly wouldn't hesitate to use that airline again. The SGD590 was a group price; individually it would have been SGD780.

We stayed at Ruby Inn. It's a family operated hotel: father, mother, and their daughter Ruby. This is the same place where Pastor Lau and Grandpa stayed when they went in June 1997. They have twelve rooms and it's kind of nice staying in a small place like that—the owners are so very helpful and you get to know them on a rather friendly basis. They served a full breakfast each morning, they did our laundry (marked our things with different colored threads so they could return the laundry to the right room), they were our money-changers, they answered all our many questions, etc. Nice, pleasant people.

We had taken along a hot pot, mugs, coffee, and tea, for in the evening, but only used it the first night. The following night we asked if they could furnish the coffee, and if we could use the dining room for an hour or so; it would be nice to sit around the table while having some fellowship and devotions together. They were happy to accommodate us and just added it to our bill at the end of our stay. My room was only US $15 per night (the room was a bit smaller but very adequate), and when I was going to settle my bill, Ruby put her hand up by her mouth and whispered, "Don't tell them, but I'm not going to charge you for the evening coffees." We all got a kick out of that—the others were charged about one U.S. dollar each.

Friday was the anniversary celebration at Galilee Church so right off we had to travel to the village. Being the second time for me and the Singaporeans, we knew what to expect, but for the rest, it was quite a shock. It is so hard to describe the road conditions—potholes in Michigan are nothing compared to over there. Titus' younger brother, Timothy, drives a taxi truck so he was available for us the entire time. They were saying that a set of tires only lasts about six months—I hope those are used retreads and not new ones!

Before the program we walked over to the chicken farm, which is quite near to the church. Dr. Daniel Kwek and Lee Meng Hsien (men from FERC) invested in a chicken farm, which provides work and wages for four families. It was really neat to see this and we were quite impressed. They were clean, well-maintained, and not terribly smelly. There were several buildings and the chickens were divided according to age: youngest chicks, the middle batch, and the older ones.

Prof. Hanko spoke for the anniversary program and they had several special numbers. After the program, they served a noon meal that was prepared outside the church. This never fails to amaze me: they prepare such a beautiful and delicious meal without any of the conveniences that we are so used to.

While waiting around, we decided to take a walk in the village—a definite no-no. No one told us that ahead of time, but it's something I probably should have known and thought of. Anyway, we strolled down the road, snapping pictures of cute little kids and anything else we saw interesting. It would be neat for you to see Steve's video sometime. He has pictures that no one else has; surprising that some of his film was not confiscated. Finally Pastor Moses came along and said to us, "Get back to the church." We immediately turned around and went back. It was quite a while before he returned and was able to tell us that he got it all straightened out, everything was okay. Does that mean he had to pay a bribe?! We don't know. We did ask if it would cause any trouble for them later, and he said it wouldn't.

We had our dinner at a restaurant that evening. I don't know what happened to my left knee about that time, but I noticed in the restaurant that it was really hurting. (There's a little arthritis in that knee but this was hurting a whole lot more than that.) After dinner we went to Rev. Michael Zahou, who is a Reformed Baptist, and Prof. Hanko spoke for quite a large gathering there that evening. It's such a common occurrence that the lights go out, but they are all prepared with their candles. Kip Vel told us that very rarely do they have electricity the whole evening.

Rev. Zahou has a Bible school and most of those who attended the meeting were students. We could see the dormitories from the main building where we were; basically they are only shacks with not much in them. Another thing that always strikes me is that people come out of these places looking as clean and neat as can be. They

MISSION TRIPS: MYANMAR—NOVEMBER, 1997

adapt to living in poverty! The Lord has given us so much—may we always be a thankful people and never complain.

Saturday was going to be our outing, and I had pretty much made up my mind to stay behind because of my knee. They were going to the Pagoda, and I had already seen that so I wouldn't be missing much. But it didn't take much of their talking to convince me to go along anyway. On the way we stopped to pick up some Tiger Balm and an elastic bandage for my knee, and I hobbled around for the day. When we stopped at the store in town and got out of the truck, someone said, "Mom, hi!" I turned around and there stood Tracy, the girl who interpreted for me on the first trip. We were so happy to see each other once again. She has a job now in Yangon, working for the Yellow Pages Directory. We went to see the Pagoda. It gave me the same sick feeling I had the first time when seeing all these people bowing down and worshiping the idols. In the afternoon we went to a gem factory and the Bogyoke market (the place where I bought most of the Myanmar souvenirs in '96).

Our dinner that evening was at Titus' house. His wife prepared such a beautiful meal for us. You just know they stretch themselves for these special occasions—it's definitely not the way they usually eat. We do give them some extra money when we go there; otherwise you'd feel terribly guilty having a delicious spread like that.

Titus has such a nice family; it was a joy to see him in his own environment among his people. His wife is very sweet and smiles, but she doesn't understand English so several times Titus would tell us what she said and would tell her what we said. She and the other women who were there did not sit at the table with us. His little five-year-old daughter Jemima is a cutie. You ask her, "How are you?" and she answers, "Fine, thank you." Josiah is about thirteen or fourteen months old now and is doing well once again after having had dengue fever just before Grandpa went to Myanmar in June.

Titus' father came down for the conference. He's a very well-mannered gentleman, speaks English, and we had interesting conversation with him. He was seriously wounded in a land mine accident and was flat on his back in the hospital for seven months. He is on a pension now of 1000 kyats per month; divide that by 250 (the current exchange rate on the black market) and you get 4 U.S. dollars per month. He and his wife are in their sixties and are caring for several orphans. Titus' mother wasn't there. He has an older brother, Joshua, who is pastoring the church that Titus had before, and a sister, Priscilla, who works in an office in Yangon, and she comes down and spends the weekend with Titus' family. All of them are very pleasant people, warm-hearted, smiley, and easy to talk with.

Titus' house is nice by Myanmar standards. Very simple. The bedroom, where the whole family sleeps, and the study are one room. The bed has a mosquito net over it. There's a pile of books there and he treasures every one of them. The best time for him to work on the computer is during the night because that's when the electricity is the most stable. He gave us a copy of the first Standard Bearer written in Burmese and also his translation of the Heidelberg Catechism into Burmese. The SB includes some translated articles and some that were written by him. He is such an industrious and likeable person. Everyone who meets him is instantly impressed with his enthusiasm for the Reformed faith.

Sunday morning we worshiped at Grace Church and had lunch with them and then went on to Titus' house for an evening service at 4:00. It gets dark there early—by 5:00 it's very dark already. Titus asked Prof. Hanko to preach the same message he had Friday morning at the anniversary service of Galilee Church, and Titus did the interpretation. We stayed and visited with all the people for a while after the service.

Monday, Tuesday, and Wednesday was the conference. Titus interpreted into Burmese and Pastor Moses interpreted into Chin. The conference was on "The Covenant of Grace." Prof. Hanko really did a good job—both in content and making it very plain, using very practical illustrations, and he worked well with the interpreters. I pretty much wrote down everything he said; by the time the interpreters were finished, I was ready for the next sentences.

On Tuesday, Mrs. Hanko, Mrs. Bos, and I just stayed for the morning session and then we went to the Bogyoke market for shopping. Steve went along with Dr. Kwek to meet up with an acquaintance of his who studied in Singapore and worked at a hospital in Yangon. After their visit, they also went to the market. We saw them there, so all of us could go back to the hotel together. We had all our evening meals in a restaurant.

The fellowship at the end of each day was very enjoyable also. We would sit around the table with our coffee and some goodies we had taken along from Singapore, and chat about the activities of the day, impressions, observations, etc., and then have devotions together. The whole group got along well together. I believe Steve thoroughly enjoyed every minute of his Singapore/Myanmar experience, and the people here enjoyed him as well. The last night in Myanmar, Steve said something to the effect that he never knew he could have such a good time with all older people, and...wiser. (The "wiser" coming as an afterthought.) Elder Siew mentioned to me that he was impressed with Steve; it was encouraging to see a young man with good values and interest in mission work.

On Thursday, November 6, it was back to Singapore for the Hankos, Mr. and Mrs. Bos, and me. Elder Siew, Dr. Kwek, and Steve went on to the Chin state along with Pastor Moses. They weren't able to travel as far as they had planned, but they did have a successful trip and some meaningful visits as well. They returned to Singapore the following Monday, and after a few more days packed with activities, Steve left for the U.S. on Friday morning.

Myanmar, 1999

We are grateful for the privilege of returning to Myanmar once again so Grandpa can teach a seminar in Yangon, Myanmar, on the subject of church government. This time we have a laptop computer with us, so instead of making notes and writing about it when we get back to Singapore, I hope to write about it as we go along.

Everything went well with the trip, for which we are thankful. We carried along a new Digitec notebook computer for Titus. Titus does have a desktop computer, but the electricity is very unstable in Myanmar, making it quite difficult for him when he is doing translation work. The battery of the notebook computer is good for about three hours. Needless to say, Titus is delighted!

We settled in at Ruby Inn. I had a splitting headache and after a bit of unpacking, I thought I better lie down and sleep it off. I got myself to thinking that I missed my coffee Saturday morning and it was probably the lack of caffeine that gave me the headache. Certainly I don't like to think that I'm so dependent on having my coffee, but after drinking some and then having dinner that evening, I was feeling as good as ever.

We had a nice Sunday. Grandpa preached at Grace Church in North Dagon where Pastor Moses is the minister. The church was full, since many of the men who would be attending the conference were there. After the morning worship service, they have a Women's Fellowship Meeting and Grandpa was asked to speak for that too. We had Sunday dinner by Moses and Kip Vel's house and then took a taxi back to Ruby Inn.

About two years ago, Kip Vel's brother passed away, and then in January 1999 her sister-in-law died. This couple had four children between the ages of twelve and nineteen who will now be cared for by Moses and Kip Vel. Moses and Kip Vel's idea is to rent the house next door to their own house for 6000 kyats per month. (The exchange rate on this trip is 350 kyats to one U.S. dollar, so we're talking here of around U.S. $17. To do this they would need help from the ERCS.) If they are able to do this, they would like to take in more orphans and children of very poor families and hire a Christian woman to be in charge. Because all the children receive public education, they are very concerned for their spiritual education at home.

We were picked up from the hotel at 4:00 by Tial Thanga and

went to his home for dinner, fellowship, and a Bible study. Dave Postma from Hudsonville, Michigan (some of you may know him), is in contact with Tial Thanga. Sunday night was the only night we could visit with them because he was leaving on Monday for a month. It was a very interesting visit.

Tial Thanga is in charge of the Reformed Theological Seminary here in Yangon. The students in the seminary have different church affiliations but they are taught the Reformed truth. They are planning to have an intense English course at the seminary during the three-month summer holiday. Tial Thanga's English professor from Jackson, Mississippi, will teach this course. He indicated that men from the URCM would certainly be welcomed to take the course as well. Sounds like a good possibility, if it all materializes.

Tial Thanga's family lives on the seventh floor of a building and you have to walk up! There's a narrow stairway with steps of various heights and very dark. With him taking the lead, it wasn't too bad. He carried a flashlight and just walked slow and steady. We were surprised when we saw their apartment; it was quite large, light, and cheery. Just think of moving into such an apartment and carrying the furniture up there. And how about the weekly groceries? I guess that would be a family project and each one could carry a few bags. Shortly after we were in the house, there was quite a storm with strong winds.

The Thangas have four children. The oldest girl is sixteen, a foster child. She is from a Buddhist home. For some reason a home was needed for this girl. Thanga asked the father if the girl could come and live with them. The father's reply was, "Why not?" So they took the girl in; she is one of the family now and has become a Christian. They also have an eleven-year-old girl and two boys, four and five years old. That evening, they invited a group of ten people to their home. They are also doing some translation work; we must put him in touch with Titus so they don't go through all the work of translating something that is already done.

Monday, April 19. Ruby Inn is quite near to the airport, making it very convenient for many church workers and missionaries who come to Myanmar. Right now there are three men staying at the hotel who are charismatic. They may get wound up in their services, but they can be pretty noisy in the hotel as well.

Rooms at the Christian School of the Blind have been rented for the seminar. The school carries on as well while we are there, but they still are able to accommodate our group of men. There are about forty-five men attending from four denominations (United Reformed, Protestant Reformed, Christian Reformed, and Evangelical Reformed).

The dormitory building is along the front of the property. There is a large water reserve tank just outside the dormitory that is used for bathing. We meet in a large upstairs room in another building, and there are benches and ceiling fans. Don't imagine anything fancy, but it's certainly a 100 percent improvement over what we had before. At least the men aren't sitting on the floor all day. There's some construction going on so it can get a bit noisy at times. It's also close to the airport so at times they have to quit talking while a plane is overhead. We can also hear some of the blind students trying to play the piano ("Silent Night" most of the time) but all in all, it still goes well.

The dining room is downstairs. First the blind students eat and then the meal is served to our group. The food has been good: rice with a few veggies, and some soup. There are square tables with stools so four people sit together to eat. The men have all three meals at the dining hall and we just take our lunch there. Titus told Grandpa that he'll notice the men improving as time goes on—the reason being that they are fed better than at home so they have more energy and are more alert. Breakfast for us is served right at Ruby Inn and we go out to a restaurant for our dinner.

I just wish I could convey to you the poverty of these people. They are encouraging the men to contribute something for the conference to have a sense of value for it and also so they have the desire to make a sacrifice to attend. If someone is poor, they would not forbid him to come, but if they are able, they contribute 200 kyats (U.S. 60 cents) for three weeks. We are so filthy rich, aren't we? Grandpa and I spend more than that four times a day just on a taxi. Money

MISSION TRIPS: MYANMAR, 1999

and missions is such a difficult subject, but it certainly would not be right not to show mercy and compassion to these dear people. (In the end, nothing was collected from the men and ERCS took care of all the expenses of the seminar in addition to the deacons dispensing a large amount of benevolence for the various needs, a great deal of which was medical.)

The School of the Blind is quite near to Ruby Inn. One of the hotel workers will go up to the main road to hail a taxi for us and we can reach School of the Blind in about seven minutes' time. We usually come back for a short rest after lunch, and then go back for the afternoon session. Taxi one way costs 250 kyats (U.S. 73 cents). (This is funny: Titus was getting a cab for us this afternoon and the driver wanted 300 kyats. He let it go because it was too much. What it amounts to is U.S. 15 cents more.)

It strikes us that things have improved somewhat in the town of Yangon. For one thing there are more car taxis available so we aren't riding in the back of a truck all the time. Roads are in better condition. Even the road in front of Moses' house is paved—that's really newsworthy!

Wednesday, April 21. The charismatic preacher was at the breakfast table with us this morning. He asked if they had bothered us last night. Evidently Ruby went to their room thinking that a real fight was going on. He said they were just having a beautiful time, the Holy Spirit was just filling their room, and they were engaged in holy laughter. I'm glad we didn't hear any of it. And yes, we did have some discussion with them.

It's Wednesday already and the third day of teaching is finished. Grandpa is a good teacher and is having the time of his life and enjoying every minute of it. (He said to me today he wishes he could do this full-time: go to all these countries and teach the Reformed faith.) I feel really blessed that I can be along and enjoy the classes. The material is all familiar but it's good to have a review. The last hour in the afternoon is for questions and Grandpa really likes that too. They can ask questions about the lessons or any other questions they might have. They don't hesitate to ask, so it has been quite lively. This afternoon we had, "Behold, I stand at the door and knock," and some other questions on man's responsibility.

On the way to the meetings we pass through a little village, and this morning I just thought of our family and how your hearts would melt to see all these little children living in such poor housing. We saw two young boys, who were only around five or six, with the Buddhist saffron monk robes on–sad, huh?

Pastor Poh from the Reformed Baptist Church in Kuala Lumpur, Malaysia, and Pastor Peter Kek from Johor Bahru, Malaysia, are here now for a week. These are men we know because of the ministers' fraternals and the conference held each year in September that Grandpa attends.

Saturday, April 24. It's Saturday morning and Grandpa is going over messages for tomorrow, so I can do a bit of catching up. We are getting picked up at 8:00 on Sunday and will have about a forty-five-minute ride to the Evangelical Reformed Church (there are three or four of their men attending the seminar) where Grandpa will preach at 9:00. From there we go to Titus' church for a service at 11:30. Grandpa will preach and Titus will have the baptism service for their first convert. A niece and a cousin live with Titus' family; the niece is a student, and the cousin works. The niece witnessed to a friend at school and brought her to church. Titus instructed her for about a year and now she is going to be baptized. I can just imagine their joy, can't you? Titus' new house/church will be dedicated on May 9, the last Sunday we are here, and Grandpa will preach for that service too.

We just met with the retired Christian school teacher whom we first met in 1996 (Wednesday, January 10). There is a nice shaded sitting area outside by Ruby Inn where we could visit with her. We are investigating possibilities for teaching English to the pastors in Myanmar. It was a good contact; they have three three-month sessions a year and the cost is only 1000 kyats per session (U.S. $3). This same group instructed some students to prepare for study in the polytechnic in Singapore and they did very well. I mentioned the

MISSION TRIPS: MYANMAR, 1999

other English course being taught at the Reformed Theological Seminary by a professor from America. You wonder whether this would be an advantage or disadvantage as he would not know the Burmese word to relate it to.

After the seminar class on Friday, we went to Galilee Church. Anyone who had gone there before would be surprised how everything has changed, well not quite everything, but we traveled there on all paved roads! and that's a great improvement. There has been a lot of construction. We saw a huge development of apartment houses and the sad part is that they are standing empty because people cannot afford to buy them. The villages are the same with their tiny huts and many people milling around.

We were asked to look at some land with a view to growing mushrooms. The idea is to have mushroom farming where the chicken farm was. The buildings of the chicken farm are in bad shape, but what can you expect with that kind of construction and a thin thatch roof? The land was covered with water, and I guess you'd have to build it up so it wouldn't be flooded in order to grow anything there. (Now it looks like there will be four plots for mushrooms in the area of Grace rather than Galilee.)

The seminar is going well. Grandpa isn't able to cover as much material as he prepared, but there has been good feedback and the men are happy to be learning. When Grandpa was explaining about equality in the ministry (pastors are equal and all contribute, and not some more important or have more to say), I really liked how he showed this from Acts 15. When you read that, you can just about picture the apostles having their meeting. They have a problem, they discuss it, they all contribute: Peter, Paul, James, etc. When they are finished, they come to a conclusion "for it seemed good to the Holy Ghost, and to us" (v. 28). Read it and think about a classis or synod meeting—it's interesting and you understand how we have our Reformed church government.

Grandpa borrowed and read a book from Pastor Poh entitled *Thinking about Christianity and the Chins in Myanmar* edited by

Cung Lian Hup (published in commemoration of the Chin Evangel Centenary, 1899–1999). It is Baptist but it gives a good insight into the history of missions in that area where the URCM has churches today. Grandpa came across a poem that I thought would be nice to include in my story. We quote the poem's introduction as well.

"The call for social concern and responsibility is urgent. The poor and the needy, the unfortunate and the underprivileged are many. To illustrate my point I would like to quote a poetry written by a homeless widow who had gone to her pastors to tell her plight so many times. The pastor was sympathetic and promised to pray for her. The following poetry was submitted to the pastor.

> *I was hungry,*
> *And you formed a humanities group to discuss my hunger.*
> *I was imprisoned,*
> *And you crept off quietly to your chapel and prayed for my release.*
> *I was naked,*
> *And in your mind you debated the morality of my appearance.*
> *I was sick,*
> *And you knelt and thanked God for your health.*
> *I was homeless,*
> *And you preached to me of the spiritual shelter of the love of God.*
> *I was lonely,*
> *And you left me alone to pray for me.*
> *You seem so holy, so close to God.*
> *But I am still very hungry—and lonely—and cold."*

Sunday, April 25. It is now Sunday evening, and we are back at the hotel after a busy, extremely hot, but nevertheless a wonderful Sunday and good fellowship with God's people here in Myanmar. Pastor Titus is a friend of Pastor Bwee of the Evangelical Reformed Church in Myanmar. Pastor Bwee has a training center where he holds a three-month training course once a year: December, January, and February, after the harvest is in and before the next planting, as many pastors are farmers in addition to the work of the ministry. Titus also helps out as

MISSION TRIPS: MYANMAR, 1999

an instructor during that time. A few men from ERCM are attending the seminar and Pastor Bwee asked Grandpa to preach in his church today. Pastor Bwee had his theological training in Korea.

The ERCM does not receive any foreign help aside from some occasional love gifts. Since the ERCM members are generally very poor, the pastors cannot expect the congregation to be able to support them. The training center/church is in a new town and the ERCM is the first Christian witness there. Pastor Bwee can only take five students at a time because he has to pay all the expenses for the training sessions. He is an industrious person—he bought a piece of land with some trees and has to cut down one tree every year in order to get enough money to have the training course. They also use the land to grow vegetables. He's not rich, but evidently has very good management. He has done a lot of translating and has a lot of material available for the pastors. Pastor Bwee is really enjoying the classes Grandpa is teaching at the seminar, and he told me this morning that he would like to write a summary of the church government class.

The next place was Titus' church/house. We sang several Psalter numbers with the tunes we have and that he translated into Burmese! Can you believe it? We sang three: numbers 2, 3, and 116. This was the first time they used them in their worship service, but he said they had been practicing for a while. He has an uncle who is very good at music and knows notes and timing. Titus translated the words, and this uncle (three years younger than Titus) put the translation in verse rhyme so it could be set to the same music. This uncle is a brother to the uncle who excommunicated Titus from the church. When I asked Titus about it, he said this uncle said they do not get good preaching in the other church.

And you know what else—the Canons of Dordt are now available in the Burmese language! It is so exciting to see the enthusiasm of the people for the Reformed faith! The Lord is truly blessing the spread of the gospel in this country.

But at the same time, the charismatics are hard at work, and next week they are holding a crusade in Yangon in their grandiose way in a large hotel. (P.S. After several nights of meetings, the government shut it down—too threatening probably, with so many people attending, or was it the raucous noise?)

Next weekend Titus' family will be moving into their new house. This is a church/house that was provided by the ERCS. We saw it today; it's just a couple blocks from where they live now. The main floor is the church sanctuary, a bathroom and shower, and a simple kitchen. The family lives upstairs where there are bedrooms, a small study, a front room, bathroom, and another simple kitchen. They have a well with a pump, but it didn't have enough power to bring the water up to the second floor so they had to build a holding tank and then with another pump, they will be able to have water upstairs. The house is a big improvement for them and the church is much more suitable, where others will feel free to come, rather than coming into someone's house.

I have had a sore throat and may be coming down with a cold. Not too bad yet and I just hope I don't lose my voice. The hotel owner just stopped by our room with a longyi for Grandpa. I think if he wore it to a meeting, he'd be afraid it would drop. We must find out how they should be tied. I can't quite picture Grandpa adjusting a longyi in public.

Tuesday, April 27. Tuesday evening so I better do some catching up. The seminar is going great. Grandpa is encouraged that the men are really hanging in there. We are about halfway now and they are sticking right with it—taking their notes and asking lots of questions. The last hour of every day is for questions, and there is no sign yet of running out of questions. The interpreters are working hard too. Titus translates from English to Burmese and another pastor translates from the Burmese into Chin.

The weather here is extremely hot and the men don't get any relief at night. Grandpa and I have this air-conditioned room and sometimes have to pull a blanket over, and the men don't have a fan or a bed; they sleep on whatever pads they brought along with them. Probably it is as good as they have at home, but it is a far cry from the comforts we know.

MISSION TRIPS: MYANMAR, 1999

My day was really special. I met with about twelve women at Grace Church. I didn't want to spend the whole time talking about things that might not relate to them, so after sharing some thoughts and explanation on Proverbs 22:6, we opened it up for questions. The women were quite responsive and open. Kip Vel had to serve as interpreter. We met from nine to noon, without taking a break, and then we had lunch by Hla Hla, the lady who runs the old people's home next to the church. After the meeting was finished, we had a time of personal sharing about our life, etc. It's nice to get to know these women a little more intimately with their struggles and difficulties. After they spoke, I would just try to give them some encouragement. There are still other areas of life that they would like to discuss, so we are meeting again next Tuesday.

About a half hour before the end, a young man walked in and sat in the back bench. He was nice-looking, clean and neat. The people knew who he was, but I didn't until a bit later when they told me he was the husband of one of the women. She is a Christian, he is a Buddhist, and they have a daughter about three years old. He asked if he could ask a question. He said, "I am a Buddhist and my wife is a Christian. I am searching to know God. I don't want to become a Christian because of man's persuasion. If I become a Christian, I want to be a true Christian. At this point my mind is open."

This was completely unexpected, but you must use opportunities that the Lord gives when he gives them. I didn't have a nervous feeling but really felt that the Lord was giving me the words to speak. The advantage to having an interpreter is that it gives you just a bit of time to organize what you are going to say next. It was a good experience for me to talk with him and also to encourage the wife.

I showed them the family pictures. Three people have already remarked that Aunt Lori looks like Princess Diana (they say Dinah) and one lady said Cory looked like Prince Andrew (Charles' brother). They think all the children look so cute (of course I agree) and they like to hear little family details.

You hear about some sad family situations from their pre-Christian days and how that has changed since they became Christians. But there still are problems. One lady shared that she left her husband four years ago after she just couldn't take his abuse any longer. The mother and four children live with her sister, who professes to be a Christian but doesn't live like one. The sister is a businesswoman, provides the home for this family, and supports them, but this church member is very concerned about the spiritual influence her sister will have on her children. She even has to read her Bible when the sister is not around.

I have to tell you about this little story too. Our meeting was held in the church, which is just a small room. There are no fans so the door is wide open. There are a couple rows of benches in the back of the room where the women sat, and then they set up a small table in front of them where Kip Vel and I sat. From where I was, I could look right out the door. Across the road from the church is a lake (looks quite brown and dirty). A couple boys, probably six or seven years old, came to the lake, dropped their shorts, and went skinny dipping. A little later they came out of the water, ran around and played until they were dry, and on went the shorts again. A little later some more kids came and together they did it over again. It was cute and they were having lots of fun, unaware that an old lady was observing them.

Wednesday, April 28. Today turned out to be quite different at the seminar. For one thing, it was much cooler. There was a hard rain shower last night and again today. To the locals, it was really cool; it didn't take long for them to turn off the fans. In the subject of church government, Grandpa was up to the subject of deacons, and that led to a big discussion on the Singapore help.

It was important to get it all out, so Grandpa patiently took the time for it. They need much help in the medical area. They told of a father of three children who needed surgery for a gastric problem. No way could the family afford medical help and assistance didn't come from Singapore for it, and the man died about three months ago. Communication must be improved for one thing. It makes your heart sad to hear stories like that. The whole discussion boiled down to a couple questions that everyone must think about and then it will be discussed again on Friday.

Friday, April 30. It is Friday afternoon and I decided not to go for this session so Grandpa is gone now. We can hardly believe that two weeks of teaching are over already. Grandpa was teaching about how to handle differences in the church—matters of principle and matters of preference, procedure for protest and appeal, etc. All this is completely new to them. What the churches here know is one-man rule. It will take a long time for them to understand and implement it but hopefully the church leaders can understand and instruct the people. Pastor Titus is familiar with it from Grandpa's instruction while he was in Singapore and is thoroughly committed to everything Reformed—he is one very enthusiastic student! I sat in the back and observed this morning that the men were really paying attention. There could be some interesting questions this afternoon.

It is really neat for me to sit in on all this instruction. I have heard most of it before but it is just like taking a refresher course, and I really enjoy having the time to do this. Not many women have this opportunity and privilege. Some things are new or have been forgotten. Grandpa explained the congregational meeting as a council or consistory meeting to which the congregation (male members) is invited to meet with them and help make some decisions. What an easy and understandable way to explain why women do not vote in the church based on 1 Timothy 2:12.

A young Baptist girl sat in on a few of the meetings, and she was there again yesterday afternoon when articles 3 and 4 of the Canons, Head 2 were being taught: the infinite worth of the atonement. She usually comes and sits next to me, so afterward I asked her if this explanation was new to her. She said she had never heard it before but "Uncle explains it so well, he is a good teacher."

Tomorrow (Saturday) two deacons from ERCS will be coming to Myanmar. They will only be staying a few days, going back to Singapore on Tuesday. They have to take care of some diaconate matters with the churches here, and also consideration is being given to starting four small plots for mushroom farming. If it goes well, they could possibly set up some more. Evidently it's fairly easy to do as the company supplies everything except the land and buys the harvest. The people only have to tend to it.

We haven't gotten to town yet. If it gets to the point where it looks like there won't be time to do it, I might skip an afternoon meeting again next week and go off on my own. The old shopping mall is fun even if you don't buy.

Sunday, May 2. Well, I'm sure this is the first time I write a few lines before breakfast on Sunday morning. The two deacons from ERCS came in yesterday afternoon so we'll meet for breakfast in Ruby's dining room around 8:15. Grandpa and I will be picked up at 10:00 for a church service at Galilee at 11:00. The deacons are going to Grace Church. One of them will give the message and the other one will have the Ladies Fellowship (with the men most likely joining in too).

Grandpa and I both have colds. We're inclined to think it's from mold in the air-conditioning in this room. It hasn't slowed us down or kept us from any of the activities and we're thankful that Grandpa's voice is holding out for all the teaching and preaching. You all know me with my cough, cough, cough. Not too bad during the day but at night I sure can get those terrible coughing fits. I took a cup of hot water around 12:30 last night and that helped to quiet things down. I believe this is my first cold since the one I had two years ago in Michigan so certainly nothing to complain about.

I was so busy just before coming to Myanmar that I pretty much forgot about extra medicine. Grandpa and I seldom take anything aside from our prescriptions, so it just wasn't on my mind. Now I plan to get it all together and just have it ready for traveling. One of the deacons, Mohan, works for a pharmaceutical company in Singapore, and whenever their employees travel, they pack up an assortment of medicine for them. So he came to our rescue with some medicine for cough (me) and sore throat (Grandpa).

Tuesday, May 4. When the deacons were here, they thought of the idea to take a survey, so we took about twenty minutes for that

MISSION TRIPS: MYANMAR, 1999

on Monday. We encouraged the men to be very honest in their evaluations and also asked for additional comments, which could be helpful when arranging future seminars.

The money here is really strange. I remember when Grandpa and I went to Myanmar in 1996; the exchange rate was something like 120 kyats to the U.S. dollar. This time when we came, it was 342 kyats and just this past weekend it was 350. A family man from Titus' church works in construction. He earns 250 kyats per day, hardly enough for his family's "daily bread." He also works on Sunday because otherwise the family cannot eat. This past Sunday evening Titus went to the construction site and had a service with about fifteen people who were working there. A teacher earns about 1500 kyats per month (U.S. $4.50).

Last night the deacons were all finished with their work and being their last night, they were interested in doing something different. The four of us took a cab and went to Chinatown for a couple hours. We ate our dinner at a roadside restaurant and walked around the shops. What a mass of people; it sure was interesting and we had a good time.

The cab driver on the way home drove like Jehu—furiously! We didn't dare say anything for fear we would provoke him and make it worse. Speed limit is 65 km and Mohan, who was sitting in the front seat, saw it reach 110! He was passing everyone, weaving in and out like crazy, even coming down the little lane to the hotel; he couldn't wait a second but had to pass. Believe you me, we all breathed a sigh of relief to get back here safe and sound. All our other taxi drivers have been very reasonable and aside from last night, we find it much calmer than India.

Thursday, May 6. It's already Thursday afternoon and things are winding down for us over here. The men are having their outing this afternoon but we had something else to do. The pastor from Kale asked if it was possible to get a used portable typewriter. (Sounds kind of ancient, doesn't it?) We sure wanted to help him if we could, so this afternoon Titus took us to a place downtown where they sold used ones. He had one without a case but we preferred a case with it. The man said, "Take a seat and give me a few minutes." He left the shop and came back with a nice typewriter in a case. Of course we were curious where he was able to get it and his answer was, "At an embassy nearby that has an auction of things they don't need." Okay, fine with us: 20,000 kyats (U.S. $57). There will be another very happy man tomorrow morning when he sees this.

Now Grandpa, Titus, and his brother Joshua are visiting on the veranda. We will all go for dinner pretty soon and then they will take a cab back. We have lots of stuff (books, vitamins, used clothing for the children, tea, etc.) for them but were waiting until they moved to their new house so now they can take it along.

Yesterday (Wednesday instead of on Tuesday) we had the ladies fellowship at Grace Church. I took a cab out to North Dagon, got to the church, and everything was closed. Hla Hla lives right next door so I went over there. She said it was supposed to be the next day. Kip Vel, the one who did the arranging, and myself were the only ones planning on Wednesday. The lifestyle there is so different that Hla Hla walked through the village a bit and informed the women and soon there were twelve at the meeting. We started a little later but time isn't that important, and we still had a good meeting until 12:30.

As I grow older, it seems all the pieces of the puzzle of life are coming together and the picture becomes bigger and clearer and I'm amazed at how the events of my life, even back to childhood days, are so meaningful and helpful for what I experience now. It's a great blessing to see how God in wisdom directs all things, and now to be able to share this and encourage others way on the other side of the world.

Problems are similar all over the world, but they come with different circumstances and with people at varying stages of spiritual growth. The oldest lady at the meeting yesterday is seventy-seven. She has asthma and is as thin as a toothpick—I'd be surprised if she weighs sixty pounds. (I wonder what that picture will look like with her sitting next to me!) She is one of the women who Hla Hla takes care of. She's a widow, and the mother of five sons who were all killed as

MISSION TRIPS: MYANMAR, 1999

soldiers in the army. She has no family to care for her. The other lady at Hla Hla (the Old People's Home, but there are only two women living there now) is seventy-two. They take her to church and she was at the meeting too, but she has not been converted yet from Buddhism.

There were two young girls there, sisters aged thirteen and twenty-one. (It is school holidays now until June, which explains the younger girl being there.) They are from a family of six children: three older brothers, the twenty-one-year-old, and two younger sisters. Both the parents and the brothers work to support the family. One of the questions raised the week before was about teenagers and their activities so I thought it would be a good question to inquire how this young girl spends her time. I found out that she had to leave school after finishing 2nd Standard (ten years of age) and care for the family while the parents worked. She does everything, cooking, cleaning, and laundry (and without the conveniences we know).

I guess most of the time was discussing poverty and how to deal with it. I knew that was one of the questions ahead of time so could do a bit of homework, and it wasn't difficult to find Bible texts and songs to comfort and encourage them. You can hardly begin to imagine their struggles but it's so very important how they handle it: not questioning the Lord's wisdom but constantly relying on God and trusting in him. Sometimes we can be blind to the blessings of affliction, but what a tremendous witness if they do not become bitter. Godliness with contentment is great gain.

"Thou, O God, hast prepared of thy goodness for the poor." Psalm 68:10

Friday, May 7. This morning was the last session of the seminar and this afternoon Grandpa is at a ministers' fraternal. We gave the typewriter away this morning to the men from the Kale district. Grandpa brought it out at break time and showed them how to use the different features. All the men gathered around to see the big attraction. I just had to snap a picture; it was too cute for words. You would think they were looking at the very latest model of computers or the latest model car, they were so excited and happy. The men from that district had to have their picture taken with us and their "new" office machine.

Then after the teaching session was over, we had a little closing ceremony. Grandpa shared a few thoughts on Philippians 4 (ten minutes) and then the certificates were handed out. It's so cute, Titus is the inside man and he gives us all the feedback of the comments the men make. He said the men were really excited about getting a certificate for attendance; they would talk about being sure to be on time for roll call. Then when we had them laminated, that was really special; otherwise they would get messy in their bags on the way home.

Grandpa has started working on his report already and will spend some more time with it tomorrow. It sure will be nice to have it all finished by the time he is home. Sunday Grandpa will preach in Titus' church. It will be the first service in their new place.

Saturday, May 8. Grandpa put in a full morning of work so his report is shaping up. This afternoon we went to a new mall near to the hotel. We went past it several times on our trips to the School of the Blind so we thought we better check it out. It is not fully occupied yet, and they are still working on some of the stores. In addition to the supermarket there are fewer than ten stores, so it didn't take very long. We were most interested in seeing the supermarket just to know what things are available here. The mall is basically Singapore stores. It's only on the ground level and the upper floors are condos. The grocery store was fantastic for Myanmar, a real *super*market! We should have stopped there much sooner.

The maximum time a person can stay in Myanmar at present is one month, and all tourists are required to stay in a licensed hotel—their way of bringing business into the country. We're always thinking if someone were able to live here and work with the people, would they be able to manage with what's available? I think they could alright and from that point of view, it was nice seeing the store.

We were planning to go home on Tuesday but now are trying to move it up a day. The work is finished and to tell the truth, we're out of money over here so no use going to the Bogyoke Market. It's really

MISSION TRIPS: MYANMAR, 1999

fun to shop there with oodles of stuff to look at. We aren't sorry, of course, that we're out of money—we've really enjoyed being able to give for all the many needs here. We thought we took plenty along of our own and from the reserve funds, and I guess we did alright, haven't been short at all, and it's only for ourselves (and you) that we don't have any left. Funny, isn't it, because we are taking back a large suitcase that is completely empty.

Every foreigner who comes into the country has to change US $300 into kyats. It's not refundable so everyone spends at least that much—not difficult to do, as it can be used for paying the hotel bill too. There's a man at Ruby Inn now who wasn't aware of this requirement, and he arrived here with Canadian traveler's checks—even those are impossible to cash. He was stuck at the airport, and I don't understand exactly how they finally finagled it but it took quite some doing. There's another long-term Canadian staying here, so he has helped him out by taking some of the traveler's checks and will deposit them when he goes home in June.

I have to tell you this: I didn't take along enough hair spray so I had to try to buy some at a little shop in the neighborhood. There were four cans on the shelf, and they were behind lock and key like jewelry in the stores back home. I couldn't help thinking of the aisles of hair spray at Meijer! The price wasn't bad but the smell is horrible; I'll be glad to throw it out when we get home.

The first day we arrived in Myanmar, a filling in one of my teeth fell out. It didn't really bother me because it wasn't sharp and it is way in the back. A few days later one of Grandpa's teeth chipped. Like I wrote before, I got a cough, and then Grandpa did too. I wondered why he had to get everything I do—shucks, I can't expect any sympathy when he has the same thing I have. Now we are on our last day here and I had another piece of tooth fall off. Dear me, what's happening to this old lady? This time it's on the upper right side but on the outside of the tooth; I might smile less in public until it's fixed.

Sunday, May 9. Today we were by Titus' church for the first service in their new building. He invited all the construction workers' families. In order to come to the seminar each day, Titus borrowed a motorcycle from a mechanic friend, so this friend was invited too. He told Grandpa ahead of time that many unbelievers would be at the service. Grandpa preached on Jesus healing the blind man: once I was blind, but now I see. Titus even had the village uppity-up (I forget what they call them around here) at the service. There were around seventy in attendance that Sunday morning so the church was full. After the service they served a lunch for everyone.

Grandpa and I have an idea. We usually like to take a little break in January, and we thought it would be nice to come to Myanmar just for the purpose of spending some time with the people and helping them. Pastor Moses has such an old computer; it is one that someone just wanted to get rid of, it's broken and parts are not available for it anymore. We would like to get him set up with a good used one. We'd also like to go up to Titus' home village and help his brother Joshua, who is the pastor there, get a used computer too. We would try to buy the computers in Yangon and then hire a taxi to go to their village.

I have to tell you about our evening with Tracy. Remember Tracy? She was the young girl who interpreted for me on our first trip to Myanmar. We received a short letter from her at Christmastime, and she wrote that she was married and had a baby. I tried calling her repeatedly but couldn't get through. Finally I got through to her and she said their telephone had been out of order for one month (that is how long it takes for Myanmar to get at repairs).

Her husband is a Korean Australian working in Myanmar. We didn't ask his age, but he looks much older and Grandpa and I calculated he must be close to fifty (he moved to Australia at the age of twenty around 1970). Tracy is thirty.

We had an interesting evening with them. They picked us up in an air-conditioned station wagon (fairly new) and we went to their house. Tracy works part-time for the Yellow Pages International Directory so my natural question was, who cares for the baby when she is working? She said her mother did. Her family was from the

MISSION TRIPS: MYANMAR, 1999

north in the Chin state, but now her mother and two brothers and a niece are living with them. The house they live in is large, well-constructed, and very different from the homes of the other people we know in Myanmar. There's a large refrigerator in the kitchen, so definitely wealthier. After meeting the family, they took us out for dinner (just the four of us) to the fanciest place we ever went to in Myanmar.

Her husband's nickname is Foo-sy (guessing at the spelling here) and he supervises the servicing of shipping vessel engines. His company also harvests prawns in the Myanmar bay. He was friendly, very gracious to entertain people whom he never met before, but we didn't have much in common. Grandpa asked him if he was a Christian, and his answer was that he attended a mission school. The dinner was shark fin soup (only eaten on special occasions in Singapore because it is so expensive, and here they came out with a large bowl of it and kept filling the individual bowls as soon as they were getting empty), mutton roast that was so very tender and tasted just like beef roast, a large beautiful fish, some mixed vegetables, and steamed rice.

We had told them to just take us someplace simple, but you could tell they had in mind to make it a special treat. After dinner Tracy asked if I wanted to go to the "ladies," and that's when we had just a couple private minutes together. She told me that her husband's father was a Roman Catholic and his mother was a Buddhist. She is very thankful to God for her husband and believes if she works slowly with him and prays, he will become a better Christian. He is so good to her and really has provided for her and her whole family. The house they live in, telephone (which is very expensive in Myanmar), and the car are all provided by the company he works for. If and when she is able to obtain a passport, she, her husband, and their daughter will move to Australia.

Tracy's family is very poor, so I asked what would happen to the family when they could no longer live with them. Her husband has already bought a proper home with a much larger paddy field in Kale for her mother so she would not have any financial problems. Tracy's brothers are twenty-eight and eighteen. He has arranged for one of the brothers to be trained in welding, and the other brother as an auto mechanic.

We asked what church they are going to now and she said that she and her family have joined a Chin-speaking church but her husband doesn't understand Chin. The English-speaking church is quite far away. We wanted to take a taxi home and save them the time of bringing us all the way back, but he said, "No, no, please come." He was a neat, clean, decent person, kind and caring. We pray that the Lord will bless and keep this family in his gracious care.

Down the road from Ruby Inn is a Buddhist monastery. I'm glad we had air-conditioning in the room to block out some of the noise of their chanting. While we were there it was the full-moon festival. These monks were chanting around the clock—taking turns by the hour, and it was really amplified so that all the village around could hear it. What a racket! Finally that week was over, but their chanting is also done daily from around 5:30 to 7:00 a.m. Usually on our way to the school at 8:45 we would see around twelve monks (all ages from eight to fifty) walking down the lane to the monastery carrying their beggar bowls (I really don't know if that's what you call them but I guess they are for people to put their offerings in).

Monday, May 10. We are thankful to be home in Singapore once again. It is nice to be home a day early to get some things done around here, especially since we plan to be off to the Philippines next week Thursday, the Lord willing.

Myanmar, 2001

As I have done for other trips in the past, I have again written a brief summary of our activities in Myanmar. Rich and Elaine Bos accompanied us on this trip and while we were there, the Lord spoke to us through the hand of death by calling Rich to his eternal

MISSION TRIPS: MYANMAR, 2001

home. We're thankful that Rich and Elaine desired to go with us, and although it was not like we thought it would be, we confess that the Lord is good and his way is the best way. Rich joyfully served the Lord with his involvement in this mission activity, and now he is at home with the Lord. What follows is an account of the activities we enjoyed up till the night of his death.

This is one story I begin by backing up so you know what took place in the planning stages. It was just a year ago that our application for a visa to go to Myanmar was rejected. After patiently waiting one whole year, we were so very thankful that a visa was immediately granted right in Singapore without one bit of difficulty.

Our dear friends Rich and Elaine Bos were keen to join us on this trip, so they came to Singapore the week before on April 11. They were due to arrive in Singapore on Tuesday night, the 10th, but their flight was late in leaving Grand Rapids, so consequently they missed their flight from Chicago to Narita (Tokyo, Japan). If they were delayed a whole day, we would have had a problem getting their visas on time since the Myanmar Embassy in Singapore was going to be closed for a few days for the Water Festival. (The Water Festival in Myanmar is a fun time and you mustn't be afraid to get wet. Anyone is free to throw buckets of water or spray someone with a hose.) Rich and Elaine were able to transfer to Singapore Air and arrived by us on Wednesday morning. Wednesday afternoon they had passport pictures taken, and on Thursday we went down for their visas and picked up our tickets.

We spent much of our spare time that weekend packing up supplies for Myanmar. Besides all the many things that were collected at the PRC seventy-fifth anniversary celebration held in Grand Rapids, Michigan, in the summer of 2000, we had lots of vitamins that the Boses brought along from International Aid and shirts that we received from members of the ERCS. We thought it would be nice to bring shirts along for all the men at the seminar. There was no shortage; we may even have enough to give two to each person.

We packed three suitcases and three boxes. I called Myanmar Air and explained that we were taking supplies to give to the people there and wondered if we could have an extra allowance for luggage. They agreed to 30 kilograms per person instead of 20. (One kilogram is equal to 2.2 pounds, so 30 kilograms is 66 pounds.) We were really running over, so we were prepared to pay for some extra baggage if we had to. We prayed about this: if God wanted all these things to reach Myanmar, he could certainly bring it to pass. So we weren't anxious about it but simply left it in his hands.

Our flight was on Monday, April 16, at 1:30 p.m. We checked in and the total weight was 145kg (25kg above our allowance). We told them that we had received permission for extra weight and most of it would be given away. After a little consultation between the men behind the counter, they let it all go through and said, "We like charity." We breathed a sigh of relief; the first hurdle was over. We were never on such an empty flight—there were only about thirty passengers on board a 737! Another strange thing was that we took off ten minutes early. It must be that all the passengers had boarded so no need to wait longer. The flight went well.

We had sixteen pieces of luggage in all: six heavy ones of stuff, a small suitcase for each couple, each person with a carry-on, and each person with a "purse." Elaine and I decided that the word "purse" took on new meaning for this trip—actually they were pretty good-sized bags that could hold quite a bit. We got to customs, and they wanted to check one suitcase and one box. We told them it was all donated items that would be given away. They scrummaged through it a bit and asked what was in the other suitcases and boxes, and we just told them it was more of the same kind of stuff. They helped us close it up and sent us on our way. When we packed, we set some things aside to give to them in case they asked for it, but we didn't have to give up anything! Wow! We were so thankful that the Lord provided so graciously; thanks be to him!

Ruby Inn: it feels like coming home once again. We are in room 9, and Boses are in room 8 for a couple nights and then will transfer to room 10. Their room is hot so we sat around in our room for a while, and after the weather cooled down a little, we went outside. Monday was the last day of the Water Festival so many business places and restaurants were closed. It reminded us of Chinese New Year in Singapore, the few days when most everything is shut down and business comes to a virtual standstill. We were told if we waited until after 8:00, they wouldn't be throwing water anymore.

Mr. Aung from Ruby Inn took us to a Thai restaurant down the road and we walked back to the hotel afterward. At the restaurant, they first seated us in an air-conditioned room and we placed our order. Then I guess a larger group was going to come and they were trying desperately to figure out how to arrange the remaining tables. Finally Grandpa asked if they would like us to move, which they gladly accepted. They brought us to a smaller room where we were by ourselves.

Rich, Elaine, and I ordered fried rice with chicken and Grandpa ordered the same only with noodles instead of rice. Grandpa's dish really looked good and he thought we'd all be jealous. He had just taken a couple bites and the waitress walked in and whipped the dish away and set down his noodle dish. She was out of the room in a flash. We laughed so hard—I'm sure the dish went directly to the person who ordered it. I said to Grandpa, "I wonder how many bites the other person took of your dinner before they realized they had the wrong dish." We paid 4000 kyats for our dinner, which converts to less than U.S. $8 for the four of us.

We met in the dining room of Ruby Inn for breakfast at 8:00. You can't eat a breakfast like that every morning: juice, papaya, homemade custard pudding by Ruby's mom (delicious), two slices of toast, scrambled egg, and coffee.

All the meetings for this seminar were held at the School of the Blind, and we would hire a taxi for both ways. The four of us could go in the same cab for about an eight-minute ride for 300 kyats. This time in Myanmar, the exchange rate is 550 kyats to U.S. $1 so each trip cost approximately 55 cents.

Grandpa began the day with a devotional on 2 Timothy 3:15–16.

Then he outlined briefly what he intends to cover in this course on ecclesiology. Elaine and I didn't go back for the afternoon session. We stayed at Ruby Inn and started sorting out all the stuff we had taken along. I was having a headache and when it didn't go away with Excedrin, I took some other medicine. It wasn't long after that and I was throwing up. Elaine quickly packed up the stuff we had on the bed and went to their room. I laid down but didn't sleep. After about an hour or so, the headache was gone and I felt well enough to go with them for dinner. Traveling and a headache—I sure wonder if they go together. We had our dinner that night at a little restaurant within walking distance of the hotel.

We heard some disappointing news. Titus' brother Joshua has decided not to study for the ministry. This was quite a shock to Titus as well, and it means that the PRC in the home village is without a minister, and also that Joshua will not be coming to Singapore in September to study. But we did meet another young man by the name of Roland who is now considering joining the PRCM. He is with the CRCM (not connected with the CRC in the U.S.). He seems to be a very gifted young man and will have to be examined to see if he believes and agrees with all the points of doctrine as taught in the PRCM.

On Wednesday morning we all went to class again. Elaine and I stayed home in the afternoon and arranged all the things we brought along. It was quite a job as we had to make up about forty bags, but we work well together. We gave toothbrushes for each member of the family of all those in attendance, several tubes of toothpaste, a couple bars of soap, Band-Aids, diarrhea medicine, pain reliever, antiseptic cream, and child and adult vitamins. We had plenty of vitamins so we could give a good supply to everyone.

The shirts, which were donated in Singapore, were taken along to the conference for distribution. We were short about ten shirts from each receiving two. They were so happy with them! It was a delight to see their great joy, enthusiasm, and appreciation. The next day we brought along some towels for the men who did not get two shirts. They were not disappointed. One man held his towel happily to his chest and said, "So nice, I've never had one before." The other supplies will be handed out at the end of the seminar.

Grandpa just told me that the man who received the portable manual typewriter the last time we were in Myanmar came to him again to thank him and tell him that they are still using it and appreciate so much having it.

Thursday afternoon Elaine and I went to Bogyoke market. That is such a unique and fun place to go shopping for gift items, but I have to keep reminding myself that there's only a certain amount of room to take stuff back. Ruby wanted to go along shopping, and she also took a friend with her. We figured it was more for the free ride (we looked at many things they were interested in that we weren't). Grandpa managed to get his next day's preparation done before dinner since we were out, so we were able to have a relaxing time and more visiting over dinner that evening. It was enjoyable for all of us.

There's a new law in Yangon—no more motorcycles in the city! What a change that has brought to Yangon! Because of this, Titus had to sell his motorcycle, and he was able to buy an old (very old), small pickup for the same amount of money. It would be hard to imagine Singapore without motorcycles.

Friday night was free so we asked Ruby for some suggestion of what to do. She suggested Karaweik, which is a huge restaurant built in the shape of a Chinese boat. It was a big buffet with a great assortment of main dishes, drinks, and desserts. It cost 2,000 kyats per person (under U.S. $4). During the dinner they have a cultural show that was quite interesting.

Saturday morning we wanted to visit the mushroom farm by Galilee Church. We didn't have directions or an address so we weren't successful in finding it, but we had a fantastic time anyway. We went through several villages and were struck again with the poor living conditions of the people. One place looked like a market and small shops so we decided to stop and investigate. It was fun, the people are all so friendly, and we met a young man there who spoke English and was willing to show us around and explain things to us. Grandpa took some good pictures. We bought a long-sleeve white shirt, which we'll give to someone, for 1,000 kyats ($2) and a couple towels.

Grandpa had studying to do in the afternoon so the rest of us relaxed and read. Around 6:00 we went to the "mall." I can't think of which mall I'd compare it to: small and only a few stores, but what a contrast to what we saw in the morning, the poor and the rich of Myanmar. There is a big supermarket where most everything is available but at a price the majority of people can't afford. After that we walked across the street to a Chinese restaurant for dinner.

Sunday, April 22. We went to the morning worship service at Grace Church. When we arrived at 10:40, Pastor Bawi was teaching a Sunday school lesson (I'm unable to tell you what it was about because we couldn't understand a word). The church service began at 11:00 and Grandpa preached from Ezekiel 37:11. There was a large group because many men from the seminar were there. They sang hymns that morning instead of their Burmese songs so we could sing along in English: "Great Is Thy Faithfulness," "Jesus Is a Rock in a Weary Land," "Bringing in the Sheaves."

We stopped in at the old people's home next door to the church. Two women died since the last time we were there, but three more came so now there are four women. You might be interested in their ages: eighty-one, seventy-five, seventy-two, and sixty-six—that last one is younger than your grandmother!

We were back to Ruby Inn by 1:30. There were leftovers from Saturday night's dinner, which we had for lunch. We have to get used to ordering food here; the servings are very large, so we must order less. At 3:00 Titus and his brother Timothy came to get us since Grandpa was preaching for the PRCM in the afternoon and we weren't sure of the way. The PRCM has eighteen songs translated from the Psalter, which they sing very well, and it is a special thrill for all of us to hear God's people in this distant land sing the same songs we do but in a different language. The afternoon sermon was on the first commandment, Q&A 94 and 95 of the Heidelberg Catechism.

MISSION TRIPS: MYANMAR, 2001

We stayed around for fellowship after the service and that's when you just wish you could speak Burmese. It can be quite frustrating trying to communicate.

Monday, April 23. We were up bright and early so we could leave on our little trip at 5:30. Rich, Elaine, and I planned to go away for a few days and see some Myanmar scenery. Grandpa didn't go with us, of course, because he's teaching at the seminar this week. He has plenty to keep him busy in addition to teaching, so he'll be just fine. We hired a driver with an air-conditioned car for five days. April happens to be the hottest month in Myanmar and even though the car is not exactly cool, I'm sure it's tons better than having hot air blow in your face all day. The driver is good and drives carefully.

It was quite a day and we saw so many interesting sights. We were all struck once again with the extreme poverty in this country. We saw many oxen-pulled carts, people carrying their water, washing clothes in the river and laying them out to dry, crushing rock for paving roads, melting tar by the roadside, and the list could go on and on. Most of the homes are shacks and many are not even good shacks. The wood is not painted. There's no grass, just sand and dirt everywhere. There are many pagodas, some in the middle of nowhere.

It's a sobering thought: there's nothing in us that we deserve anything more than these people who have to work hard for next to nothing. The Lord has given us so much, spiritually and physically. May we always be thankful but also willing to share what the Lord has given us.

One thing about having a private driver, they know where to stop so you can eat in decent restaurants and not along the road. Breakfast and lunch were in hotel dining rooms; do not imagine anything grandiose, but it was very acceptable. Breakfast was in the town of Bago, lunch in Toungoo, and tonight we are staying at Meiktila. Nothing fancy here but I guess we can survive the night. (There are four geckos playing around on the walls right now as I write this. Well, as long as they stay there, not too bad. I just don't want them on my bed.) This hotel is close to being a disaster, nice owners but very dirty. Ruby Inn suddenly looks quite attractive in comparison.

Tuesday, April 24. After having breakfast at the hotel, we were on our way again by 7:00. The destination for today was Pyin-Oo-Lwin, a trip of five or six hours. It was a delightful day from beginning to end. The scenery along the way was similar to what we saw yesterday. We did go over a mountain pass with many switchbacks. It just felt like autumn in the air and near the top there were some trees with colored leaves. After not seeing colored leaves for ten years, I really enjoyed it, even though it was just a little bit. There were numerous fruit stands along the road. We stopped and picked up some fresh mangos, four for 200 kyats (U.S. 9 cents each).

We're staying tonight at the Mya Nan Dar Hotel: large rooms, everything neat and clean, just the way we like it. The food in the restaurant is good too and so very cheap, you wonder how they can make any profit on it. Tonight we had steamed rice with veggies and cashew nuts. We also ordered sweet and sour pork and Chinese cabbage. With only one serving of each dish, we had enough to divide between the three of us and still didn't finish it all. It came to 1800 kyats or U.S. $3.21, $1.07 for each of us. Unbelievable, isn't it; I can't even afford to cook at that price. But many people earn so little, they can't even afford that.

This afternoon our driver, Paul, took us to see some waterfalls. We spent about forty-five minutes there walking around and snapping pictures. The falls were not spectacular but still nice to see. They had a big section where they were selling fresh vegetables and local products. All the writing was in Burmese so we couldn't tell what anything was. Just before we were going to leave, we noticed another falls so we walked over there too. It was quite a sight to behold! There were many people in the water; you could almost call it a community bathing spot. There were people standing under the falls in their longyis and kids having the greatest time just jumping around in the water.

Next stop was to visit a pagoda and Chinese temple, and it was obvious our driver didn't know where to take us. He drove right past

MISSION TRIPS: MYANMAR, 2001

a large pagoda high up on a hill, and when he did that, I thought there must be something bigger yet that he was going to show us. He took us to a temple with some gardens around it, but really it was nothing worth stopping for and we were back to the car in a flash. The pagodas and temples aren't a big attraction for us anyway and I think we'll see more of that tomorrow.

Then we went to a huge market and that was great fun. It was streets and streets of shops with all kinds of stuff. It would be fun to spend a day—kind of like Shipshewana but with different kinds of stuff and very cheap. We bought more bath towels, soap, toothbrushes, and toothpaste because more men came to the seminar after we had divided up the stuff. By the time we spent an hour and a half there, our hands were full and it was 5:00 so time to get back to our hotel anyway. There are no buses in this town and transportation is by horse-drawn carriage. Up to four people can go in a carriage. I didn't time how long it took but my guess is about twenty minutes and it cost about U.S. $1. Attached to the carriage is a canvas sling that catches the horses' droppings; quite clever.

Wednesday, April 25. We left Mya Nan Dar Hotel at 7:00 and our destination for today is Bagan (emphasis on last syllable). The morning and afternoon rides were complete opposites. In the morning we saw so many neat sights and the roads were excellent by Myanmar standards. This afternoon it was more like a one-lane road for two-way traffic and also in poor condition. The area was desolate and forsaken and the land was barren and dry. Very hot today: when we reached our hotel, they told us it was 45 degrees Celsius—*over 100 degrees Fahrenheit!* We were thankful for an air-conditioned car, which really wasn't all that cool (we were still sweating), but it would have been much worse without it.

This morning was fantastic; we were just seeing one thing after another and were snapping pictures left and right. Mandalay is a large city with good buildings and looks like a prosperous place, no shacks like in the villages. We stopped to take pictures of the old city wall and had a cup of tea by a little stand along the road. We saw many places where they were crushing rock and stopped by one of them for picture taking. There were many, many workers there and our driver told us that the workers were prisoners. I asked what kind of crimes they would be in prison for, and he answered "political."

There was a pile of large pieces of rock and kids were filling baskets with these pieces. Two ladies worked together to lift the basket on top of one person's head, and she would carry it to the machine and dump it in. The machine had two chutes; out of one came very small pieces of rock and out of the other came very fine crushed rock. A basket was under each chute, and again two ladies would be working together lifting it up on one of their heads and then carrying it to the right pile. No one was just standing around; by the time one group had their basket, there was another group to take the next one. We tried lifting one up. I don't know how much it weighed but it was *heavy*!

An interesting sight was large wagons with huge loads of straw drawn by a yoke of oxen with a farmer perched high on the top. First there was one wagon, then we saw two together, and the winner was when we saw seven of them in a row. It reminded us of Joseph in Egypt, and his brothers returning home with their wagon loads of grain.

We saw a lady busy hand-scrubbing clothing. These people are so delightful, they smile easily and laugh and simply love to have their picture taken. You take one and more people come around instantly to have their picture taken too. When I took the picture of the washwoman, another lady took me by the arm and said, more, more. She had a group of six or eight together in no time flat. It's so cute; they can just giggle and giggle when you take pictures.

Then I spotted a machine that presses the juice out of sugar cane. We have them in Singapore too, but I wanted the Boses to see it. In order to get them to run the machine, we ordered two glasses of sugar cane juice for 100 kyats. When they finished making it, we gave it to the children who had gathered around to drink. We really didn't dare to drink it because they had put ice with it. The children gladly drank it and that gave us still another cute picture.

I happened to notice a barber in a small open shop, cutting a

MISSION TRIPS: MYANMAR, 2001

little boy's hair with a razor. I took a picture from the back, but they motioned to come in front to get the boy's face on the picture. He must have been a proud Grandpady.

Tonight we are in Bagan. What a place! You can't believe it. The whole area is literally dotted with pagodas of all sizes. Our driver is a Baptist and explained he didn't have interest in all the pagodas and he's not familiar with this area so suggested we have a tour guide in Bagan. A tour guide from the hotel went with us for a couple hours after we arrived here.

We saw the largest, the highest, the grandest, and about two thousand more. The reason why there are so many, just in this area, is because the kings lived here. The pagodas were all built and paid for by wealthy people. They are also very old, the oldest ones being over a millennium and the latest one built around 1250. What thoughts go through your mind! How God's wrath must be upon all those who trust in other gods. I think of the parable of the rich man and Lazarus, if Buddha could come from the dead and warn all his followers that their religion is false.

We're glad we saw what we did but we've had enough. The only thing that would interest us in the morning would be the market, but we're passing that up and will start heading back. Thursday will be about a ten-hour day of travel, and we hope to be back in Yangon sometime Friday afternoon.

Thursday, April 26. Breakfast was at the hotel, as usual. Breakfast is pretty much the same every day: toast and jelly, choice of egg (fried, scrambled, or omelet, generally undercooked so I must ask right away that they cook it longer; this morning was the first time they had it right), juice, piece of fruit, and coffee. We were on our way by 7:00.

Paul, the driver, had been telling us about this certain palm tree with toddy fruit. This morning we were able to stop and see it and have a demonstration. Why we actually stopped was to inquire why people had chimneys by their huts. You can't believe how friendly these people are, they were just so happy and willing to show and explain everything to us. Good thing we have a local with us for interpretation.

There are two kinds of toddy fruit, male and female. The female fruit grows in clusters like long narrow bananas. About six or eight of these pieces are tied together, and each morning the man climbs up the tree, cuts a slice from the fruit, attaches a small round jug to the cluster, and then the juice from the fruit collects in the jug. They have a light-weight ladder made of bamboo attached to the tree. He first shimmied partway up the tree to reach the ladder and then to the fruit.

Then they showed us to their house and inside was a stove of sorts, about three bricks high and four feet long, which led to the chimney. That's where they cooked the juice. The stove was heated with the stalks from sugar cane plants. There were three large wok-shaped pans on the stove with different stages of the cooking process going on. You'd have to see the environment to appreciate the process. The home is one room with a dirt floor and not a piece of furniture. Still they had this whole process running as slick as could be. Some of the juice is made into candy, some is fermented for alcohol, and some is used as juice. We gave them some kyats in appreciation for their explaining everything to us, and they gave us some of the candy in little baskets that the wife had woven.

Their ingenuity is nothing short of amazing. The baskets are so neat and not a thread, pin, or anything else is used, just pieces of sugar cane stalks that haven't much other use. We think of you often and how you would enjoy seeing the extremely simple life but still being productive.

The male toddy fruit grows the size of a closed fist and in a cluster. The only way they use it is to cut it in pieces and feed it to animals.

The next interesting thing we saw was an ox-driven grinding wheel. They were extracting the juice from peanuts. These people raise peanuts and also sesame seeds. There again it was all so primitive but as neat as could be. The couple has three children, and our driver thought the children would be uneducated as there's no school in the area. They had us sample some of the peanuts and sesame

MISSION TRIPS: MYANMAR, 2001

seeds. We wanted to buy some but as they bagged it up, they said it was a present. We gave them some kyats anyway and then she also gave some baskets, smaller ones but done so neatly and evenly, and made in such a way that they could be opened and closed. Another thing they gave was an eight inch long, hand-rolled thing that they smoke, their version of a cigar, I guess.

People don't have running water and have to either fetch it from the river or go to a well. We saw people drawing water from a well so we had to investigate. They have a cart on which is mounted a large barrel (probably thirty gallons). They have a plastic bucket, probably a gallon or so, with a long rope that they let down into the well. This well happened to be very deep, and they had to pull it a long way up. They empty it into the big barrel and when the barrel is full, they're on their way. It took two of them to push the cart up to the road. Three people were busy drawing water when we came and another three came while we were there so there is lots of activity at the well.

We're thankful for a careful driver. The road was narrow and many times he had to give way to let lorries or buses pass. It wouldn't be so bad if there was a decent shoulder to drive on, but many times he had to slow down way ahead since there was a drop-off to the shoulder and it was quite rough.

We have a nice hotel tonight, clean and comfortable. It's Hotel Amazing Kaytu in Taungoo, Myanmar. Paul, the driver, treated us for dinner tonight. We really wanted to treat him but we'll give him a tip instead when we get back. He shared some of his life history with us; it seemed he just wanted to have some people to talk with. He married at eighteen years of age and his wife left him and the children (two girls) when they were very young. The one is studying medicine in London and the other is taking accounting in Yangon. I sure don't understand his source of money: he's been to London three times, he has a car, lives in an apartment, but doesn't have a job. He was in the air force for nine and a half years and withdrew just a half year before being eligible for benefits. He said he didn't want anything from the military. I didn't dare to ask him anything about the government.

He belongs to the Baptist church but doesn't attend. The reason he gave is that the pastor is his father-in-law and he doesn't live according to what he preaches and that causes offense. He said he prays but only reads his Bible occasionally. He even lived in Singapore for eight years. During that time, the mother-in-law cared for the girls and he came back once a year to visit them. I'm not clear on what happened but he got into some trouble at Changi Airport when someone handed him a package to take along. It would be interesting to know more about that but we better leave well enough alone.

Friday, April 27. We started out around 7:30 and drove straight through to Yangon. Talk about a bad road, you just can't believe how bad they can be. One good thing is that it's not quite as hectic as India, but I really felt for our driver; all the slowing down, yielding to vehicles bigger than his own, getting off on the shoulder, weaving around whatever is going down the road, doesn't make for easy driving. We arrived back at Ruby Inn by 12:30 and Grandpa was there on his lunch break.

Grandpa had a good week while we were away, kind of lonely, but he survived alright. There were also very few guests by Ruby so it was pretty quiet. He is so enthused about the seminar. The general topic this time is the church. What he has been doing each day is beginning with a devotional for about an hour. They first sing a few songs (there are some good singers at the seminar), and then Grandpa takes a text on some aspect of the church and explains it. At the same time it shows them how to open up a text.

The men are just drinking it all in, taking notes all the time, and are coming up with excellent questions. The meeting room is air-conditioned, real luxury, and we can certainly tell the difference it makes with the men. They stay alert the whole time. Grandpa is quite impressed with the spiritual growth of the men and their desire to learn and understand more of the Reformed faith.

Saturday, April 28. In the morning we stayed by the hotel. Grandpa had plenty of things to go over and the rest of us could write or read. We left for lunch at 11:30, and after that Elaine and I

MISSION TRIPS: MYANMAR, 2001

went to Bogyoke market while Rich and Grandpa went to Rev. Titus to help him with setting up the new computer. The market is always a fun place to go; everything is a bargain but it sounds so funny when we ask the price and they say 25,000 (that's only U.S. $5).

We all got home about the same time. We're getting our pictures developed over here so we went to collect them, but they were having problems with their machine so only had two rolls finished. The Million Coin Restaurant had just opened up again after some renovations so that's where we had our dinner. Wow! What a treat to have some Western food again.

Sunday, April 29. We had a delightful and blessed Sunday. We went to Rev. Titus' church in the morning and Grandpa preached from Daniel 1. A sixteen-year-old boy was going to be baptized at this service but his parents whisked him away to prevent his baptism. We know that God overrules all of this but what persecution this young person must endure for his faith. It's nice to hear this group of people singing the Psalter again in their language. We learned later in the week that the parents of the young boy want him to spend at least two weeks in a Buddhist monastery before making a decision about baptism in a Christian church.

We went to Grace Church for the evening worship service. I have to tell you about the taxi we had on the way out there; it was definitely on its last leg. There was no covering on the inside of the doors, no handles for the windows, wires hanging loose in the front, the seats weren't any better—springs were shot. We actually wondered if we were going to make it. He just kept chugging along but two times the thing just couldn't go anymore and he had to pull over to the side of the road, lift the bonnet, and jiggle something. It was funny beyond words and we had a time controlling our laughter.

Remember Tracy? We met her already on our first trip here and she interpreted for me when I spoke with the women. She knew we were here and called yesterday morning. They moved and don't have a phone yet. Since we were here the last time, she has had another child (a boy). We might have opportunity to see them on Saturday.

They hope to move to Australia but getting the legal part taken care of takes time. Her husband is a Korean Australian so they are working on immigration for her.

Monday, April 30. It was good to join them in class once again after our little outing last week. We brought along a candy treat for break time today and we'll try to pick up some fruit for tomorrow. There were still more people today so they ran out of food. Elaine and I graciously bowed out at lunchtime because we weren't coming for the afternoon session. To evaluate the food at the seminar, let's just say it's not delicious to our palate but it certainly is edible and the locals are all enjoying it.

Last week the exchange rate was 630 kyats to U.S. $1. This made a big difference when I had to convert money to pay for the seminar. Actually it will be costing less than the estimated budget. Two men are sick so there are a couple medical bills to settle as well.

We have our pictures developed already of last week's trip. The camera I used is a cheapy, no zoom lens, but certainly better than having nothing. Yesterday afternoon they took group pictures and now we have a copy for each of the men.

We took all the supplies along this afternoon and distributed them after the meeting. The people are all so very grateful for everything and it is a joy to be able to give them this little bit of assistance. We made up a bag for all the attendees of the seminar, forty-seven in all.

Yesterday Rich and Grandpa had a glass of iced tea and today Rich was feeling pretty sick and Grandpa wasn't feeling great but he still continued on with the teaching. Elaine was sick the first week too and so was Rich. Mostly diarrhea, but today Rich was running a fever and Ruby arranged for their doctor to come and check him. The doctor gave two injections and some medicine and thought he would be feeling better the next day.

They plan to finish up with the seminar by tomorrow noon. We will have a little closing ceremony for the men to receive certificates and pictures. Tomorrow afternoon Pastor Cheah comes in and

MISSION TRIPS: MYANMAR, 2001

they will have meetings for the next couple days with men from the URCM and PRCM. That gives the rest of us some time to browse around in the very interesting downtown area.

We do have permission to go to Rev. Titus' home village, so the Lord willing, if everyone feels well, we will make that trip next week. We plan to hire a vehicle and drive the first day to Pye, where we can stay in a hotel. It is about a two-hour drive the next day to the village and then the pastor/missionary there would like us to see his work too. Titus is planning to go along with us.

The seminar finished up today. The subject they worked with was the church and worship. This afternoon Pastor Cheah arrived and he took along another box of supplies. The whole group was together again tonight for a "banquet": they ordered food packets of chicken biryani and a bottle of pop, and at the same time we distributed the extra box of goods.

This concludes what I had written before Wednesday evening.

May 2, 2001. The day started out with Rich feeling a little better but as the day went on, he was feeling more sick, mostly gastric pains but also some difficulty in breathing. Elaine stayed home with him while we went for the dinner. When we returned, we went to their room to check how he was doing. He seemed to be getting worse, so they had called for a doctor. A different doctor came that second evening and administered two shots but quite quickly Rich slipped into a coma while the doctor was still with him. The neighbors of Ruby Inn provided transportation to the hospital but before we reached there, Rich had passed away.

God's all-sufficient grace was truly evident in Elaine, and he lovingly sustained her during this difficult time. Being in Myanmar at such a time had its own difficulties, but the Lord graciously provided all the way. The Lord's ways are higher than our ways, and in his infinite love and mercy he took Rich to his eternal home from Myanmar while he was busily involved in what he loved to do: attending the seminar and meeting and fellowshiping with the people in this foreign land.

Calls were made to the family to inform them that their father had passed away, but at that point there was very little information available. We didn't know immediately the cause of death nor what arrangements could be made.

The next hours and days were busy with making all the necessary arrangements. Here again we felt the Lord's guidance and direction. We felt so completely helpless in this third-world country and so many decisions had to be made. An autopsy was required by law and the doctor at the mortuary was a very kind and understanding man. Mr. John Haynes at the American embassy worked nonstop to cut through all the red tape and make the necessary arrangements for the body to be returned to Michigan. When the ERCS heard about this, they immediately worked on changing Elaine's flight back and making a reservation for me so I could accompany her home.

And so again the Lord has spoken to many through the death of this godly man. There was a great outpouring of love, first among the saints in Myanmar, then in Singapore, and finally in the United States. It struck us that God's people in different lands were upholding the bereaved family in their prayers.

We arrived in Singapore on Saturday around 1:00 p.m. and at 5:00 p.m. there was a memorial service at FERC. Then there was the long flight from Singapore to Grand Rapids, Michigan, where Elaine was once again united with her children and grandchildren. The funeral was held on Tuesday, May 8, at the Faith Protestant Reformed Church. Prof. H. Hanko, brother of Elaine, preached a very comforting message from 1 John 3:1–2. We pray that God may graciously enfold the family in his arms of love and comfort their hearts.

> *Behold, what manner of love the Father hath bestowed upon us, that we should be called the sons of God: therefore the world knoweth us not, because it knew him not. Beloved, now are we the sons of God, and it doth not yet appear what we shall be: but we know that, when he shall appear, we shall be like him; for we shall see him as he is.*

MISSION TRIPS: MYANMAR—JANUARY 16-23, 2006

Myanmar—January 16-23, 2006

This trip to Myanmar was a very special blessing for both of us. We thought the last time we went, in 2003, could very well be our last trip there. After the death of Pastor Cheah and our return to Singapore for seven months, the Lord opened up the opportunity for us to go yet another time. This trip was entirely on our own, no teaching seminar; we just went mainly to visit with Rev. Titus and others whom we had come to know in that country.

We stayed as usual at Ruby Inn, which has become our "home" in Myanmar after so many visits, and they treat us like family. The week we were at Ruby Inn was a week of transition for them. They have leased out the place for five years with the option to buy, and the new management is taking over on January 25, 2006. Saturday was moving day for them although they kept things running quite smoothly. The family moved to a rental home (fancy, fancy at U.S. $600 a month—they had to show it to us) while they are having a new home built on Bawga Lane (same street the inn is on) but nearer to the main road. He told us that some rich Burmese general is putting up the money for the hotel but a Japanese will run it. I don't think things will be quite the same at Ruby Inn in the future.

When we arrived at the airport in Myanmar, we thought something must be wrong: no Titus. Titus would always start waving as soon as he spotted us, and this time no one was there waving. Mr. Aung from Ruby Inn had come to get us, and we figured Titus would eventually show up, we were just concerned that something had happened. It turned out that Grandpa gave him the time we were scheduled to leave Myanmar rather than the time we would arrive. Titus did go down to the airport with his whole family (the children missed a day of school), and when we didn't show up, he called Ruby Inn and found out we had arrived an hour before. The airport is only a five or ten minute ride from where we stay so it didn't take long for him to get to Ruby Inn.

It was about noon so we took them all to Country View for lunch. Country View is nearby, just to the end of the lane and then a short block. The food is good there and by our standards very cheap, roughly U.S. $1 to $1.25 per person. (We found out the next day that while they were visiting with us on Monday, their dog gave birth to six puppies. When they came home, they found them all lying right in front of the bathroom door.)

We spent some time with the family, but you just can't imagine how difficult it is with the language barrier. You can't expect Titus to be interpreting every single thing they say and we say, and it feels awkward to speak only with Titus and leave them out of the conversation. They seem to be used to it because they just chatter among themselves. One thing is the same: we all smile alike. Nevertheless, you feel a certain closeness to them. Titus always writes that he interprets our letters to them and how happy they are to hear from us. They stayed until about 2:30 and then were on their way.

It was great to see them all again. The children have grown up. Jeannette is two years and eight months, and the new baby, Joanna, whom we hadn't seen before, will be a year in February. She started walking at eight months. They are such sweet children.

You might think this is strange, but we did absolutely no sightseeing the whole week. We had been to Yangon many times before and really had no interest in going to the same places again. Each morning Titus came to Ruby Inn at 9:30, we had a neat little place to meet under a big tree, and we visited with him till lunchtime, took him out for lunch, and he would go home again around 2:00. The week was given mainly to mentoring him, learning more of the situation in Myanmar, and giving encouragement. So what follows are interesting things we talked about.

One big item of concern is the church split that has taken place in the Protestant Reformed Churches in Myanmar (PRCM). The PRCM grew quite rapidly since organization, and Titus realized at that time the great importance of instructing the pastors in the Reformed distinctives. Daniel, a member of the PRCM, was sent to Singapore for training in the Asian Reformed Theological School (ARTS) program. Titus saw in him a man who had leadership abilities and could be a coworker with him, but that was not to happen. When Daniel returned, he led the PRCM to a split. Of course, we were concerned as to what had taken place.

The first thing Titus told us was the "broad reason": clans. Titus and many church members are from the Zahou clan, and Daniel and many of his relatives are from the Haka clan. He explained about loyalty to the clan you are from. Even the uncle who deposed Titus back in the mid-1990s is from the Zahou clan, so he believes Titus is right in this case. Be that as it may, we asked, "Is that all? It was nothing doctrinal?"

The plan for Daniel was that he would work as a missionary in Mandalay after completing his studies in Singapore. They requested Daniel to come down to Yangon to meet with the classis but he refused for some reason, which the classis thought was reasonable, so they assigned some delegates to go up to Mandalay to meet with him. He was to sign his agreement with the church order. He hesitated at first and expressed that he wanted to be under the Kale church (Haka clan) rather than the Yangon church. The elders explained that would have to be done in the proper way, according to Reformed church government, with his submitting the request and grounds to the classis, etc. I believe it was article 53 (commit to the three forms of unity and the church order) that he objected to, but in the end, he did sign it.

Then, unknown to the church elders, he made a trip to Falam (mainly Haka clan) and split the church, separating himself and the Haka clan from the PRCM. He was deposed from the PRCM for insubordination. The new church that he started is called Evangelical Reformed Church in Myanmar (ERCM). He took the name of the ERCS but that did not mean that Singapore was going along with him rather than Titus. So sad, isn't it, all these churches splitting up.

Elders from the PRCM went to Falam to explain what took place, and the result in one of the congregations was that nine families

(Haka) came back to the PRCM. Daniel has two uncles who are pastors in the PRCM, and when visited, they said they must remain faithful to their nephew. What remains for the PRCM is a church in Falam Town and three other churches in villages nearby, two churches in Irawaddi (Titus' hometown), and one in Yangon. There are two faithful pastors in Falam. The Falam churches were organized before the split, so the PRCM churches there do have elders and deacons. However, they are treated now as "special missions" until they become more mature in the Reformed faith.

Before we left for Myanmar, Grandpa received a letter from Rev. Titus explaining that a man from one of the village congregations in Falam was beaten up by a group of young boys and was taken to the hospital. He asked if we could help with the medical costs of around U.S. $300. Now for the background. In the Falam village of Old Hnah Thiel, the original PRCM there had twenty families. After the split they were left with three families, and nine Haka families came back (referred to above) so they have a church of twelve families now.

The fifty-year-old man who was beaten up is from the Haka clan and one of those who returned to the church. One night, near the end of 2005, while he was with his wife, five young boys attacked him quite severely, causing some internal bleeding (blood in urine and stool). The wife cried out for help so people from the village came to the rescue. He was unconscious for one and a half days. One of the boys involved is a cousin of Daniel and from the ERCM. Generally clan members are loyal to their own clan but here some hatred was obvious.

This man had to be taken to the hospital in Falam Town, which is thirty miles from the village. Four men from the PRCM had to carry him on foot for fifteen miles and then take him on the bus for another fifteen miles. His injuries are not life-threatening, but he does have to stay in Falam Town until he recovers enough to make the trip back. Three men (farmers) have returned to the village and one man has stayed back to accompany him home. He has been discharged from the hospital, because he would be more susceptible to germs if he stayed there, and is recovering now at an elder's home in Falam Town. (This family is caring for the injured man and also the elder who is waiting to go home with him.) They have to take him to the hospital periodically for check-ups. At the time we left Myanmar, he was still in Falam Town.

After the attack, the boys who beat him fled to India to avoid being charged with the crime. Daniel's uncle, the father of one of the boys, came to the family to ask their forgiveness for what his son had done. This uncle is in charge of the village government so you can just imagine what a scandal this became. The police did become involved when this happened, but the family has withdrawn charges against them.

It's really neat how Titus is instructing the church members to give. They do receive some benevolent assistance, but before dipping into that, they try to raise as much as they can among their own membership. Titus was telling us about a church member in Yangon who was in the hospital. They took a special collection for him in the Sunday worship service and came up with 7000 kyats (about U.S. $6.50). When this was told to the man, tears came to his eyes. He was so touched that the church could come up with that much for him.

For a time, Titus taught some subjects in the theological school of the Evangelical Reformed Church. One of the students was from the village of Rakhain on the border of Bangladesh. Titus came to know him quite well. His mother died when he was young, and his father remarried and two daughters were born to that second marriage. When he was studying in Yangon, his father passed away. He had in mind to become a missionary in Mandalay, but his stepmother threatened to hang herself if he did not return home, because it simply wasn't safe for three women to be living alone in that particular village. Consequently, he did return home to the village and the Lord is using him there in spreading the Reformed faith. Now there is a beginning of a church there and they would like for Titus to come and teach sometime this year or next. To get there from Yangon, travel is three days and nights by bus, one day on a ship, and then the rest of the way by canoe. Nothing comes easy.

Titus has to be careful because his health has not been good. He realizes how necessary it is for him to know his limitations; he would like to go, go, go, but his body cannot take it. He was going to the doctor but didn't get much help from the medications that were prescribed. Finally he asked the children's doctor if she could help him. He was experiencing some numbness in his feet and the problem was with his heart, not enough circulation. She was able to prescribe some other medications that have proven helpful, so Titus is doing much better now. He does look well and so does the rest of the family.

On Sunday we went to Rev. Titus' house. I should tell you a little about the family and all the others who live in that household. First of all there is Titus and his wife Cer Te with their four children: Jemima, Josiah, Jeannette, and Joanna, and Cer Te's mother, then there is a niece and a cousin who have been living with them for several years already, next is Cer Te's sister with her three children (her sister married a widower and he wanted to spend some time with the children from the first marriage; this caused some friction between them because it meant leaving the family, traveling some distance, staying several months, and not earning a living for the family in Yangon during that time. In the end, he did leave the family, but Titus is working with them with view to reconciliation), and then there is one more, a church member from Irawaddi who is studying in Yangon, making a total of fourteen people!

They live in a church/house, church on the main floor, living quarters upstairs. The girls sleep on pads on the cement floor of the church. When pastors and elders come to Yangon from the other churches, they put up at Titus' house too. Titus said even though they are so very poor, they still do like their life and like to live, but when they had their Old Year's service he said they all were so happy and said, "We're one year closer to the coming of the Lord."

Grandpa preached on Sunday with Rev. Titus interpreting. The sermon was from Romans 8:35–39. I was struck how Grandpa could apply the message to these people, enter into their situation, and encourage them. We sometimes joke that they have a Protestant

MISSION TRIPS: MYANMAR—JANUARY 16-23, 2006

Reformed dog in Myanmar. Grandpa was just starting the sermon; the male dog walked in and laid down right in front as he always does. Moments later the female dog came but she didn't stay long. At the close of the service they sing Amen, Amen, A...men. When they started singing that, the dog got up and walked out. It was a bit comical, just like he could tell it was time to leave.

They have had a chicken farm for several years already, and this gives some work for all the people living there. Previously, this chicken setup was right next to the church. You could practically reach your hand out the church window and touch the chicken coop. Things have changed some. Titus has a friend from Korea, whom he met while they were attending the Far Eastern Bible College in Singapore. We know him too; he was by our house for dinner with Titus. I don't know the correct spelling of his name but when he introduced himself he said Liki Lee, like a leaky faucet. Titus still has contact with him and occasionally Liki comes to Myanmar. He said when he has extra money he is willing to share it with Titus. He bought the first chicken coop lot for U.S. $800, and then later he bought the two lots behind the chicken coop and behind the church for U.S. $1,300 each. He thought it would be better for Titus not to have the neighbors so close, in case they would get sick of it and cause trouble.

In addition to that, Titus had to change the chicken farm. It was required that there be a cement foundation in order to maintain cleanliness. So the old chicken coops are cleared out and the new chicken coop was set up on the lot behind where the old one was. We are impressed with Titus' management; the girls can pretty much handle the feeding, collecting of eggs, and cleaning, and Titus picks up the feed as needed. Right now they are collecting about 400 to 450 eggs per day (500 chickens). He sells them just a bit cheaper than the market so all the neighbors are happy and come to buy his eggs. He budgets the income, a certain percent to cover expenses, a certain percent for when they have to buy more chickens, etc. With what they are able to save from the business, he is planning to erect another chicken coop and buy more chickens. This will give them chickens at various stages of growth and they will always have eggs, instead of having to have several months without eggs.

On the lot behind the church, he has planted a very nice vegetable garden, which is a huge help for the family so they can have more vegetables in their diet. Titus maintains the garden by himself; it is his exercise, his relaxation and revitalization. The church members and neighbors also benefit from the garden from time to time.

A recent self-help project that the ERCS contributed was a rice mill in Kale at the cost of U.S. $5,500. This was done before the church split, and now after the church split there is no longer a PRCM in Kale. Naturally you would think that the continuing church there, ERCM, would run the mill, as they were also part of the group. But the mill is not in operation. Why? He told us that even though the PRCM is not there anymore, everyone knows about the church split and wouldn't go to that mill. I don't know, that's hard for me to understand. There are other rice mills working in that part of the country. If they do good work and have a good price, why wouldn't people go there?

Another thing we discussed is what it would take for the church there to be self-supporting. At the present time there are several of us who are contributing to the monthly support of Rev. Titus' family. We don't have to think for a minute that he keeps it for himself. He gave many examples of how they try to eke out some for others and help in whatever way they can. It seems the way to go is buying a rice paddy farm. This would give work and provide for two families of the church, and the profits would go to the church. If the Lord prospers the work, he believes the church could be self-supporting in about a year's time.

He has talked about this before when the cost would have been approximately U.S. $8,000. At the present time, the economy is poor because the government has shifted from Yangon to another place. Consequently, land is much cheaper now and a twenty-acre farm could be purchased for U.S. $4,000. There is land available and the owners are willing to sell because they are tired of all the work.

MISSION TRIPS: MYANMAR—JANUARY 16-23, 2006

The church, on the other hand, would love to farm some land in the hopes that they would not have to be dependent on foreign money. We were concerned about jealousy on the part of the other congregations, but he explained that would not happen because in Irawaddi there are cement factories where the people work, and in Falam the people are really oppressed by the military government and it would not be possible for them to have such projects. The Yangon church contributes to meeting the needs of the Falam congregation.

I should tell you a little bit about the government in Myanmar. The military government lost in the election in 1988, but they promptly put under house arrest Aung San Suu Kyi, the lady who won, and they have taken over the government by force ever since. It is very oppressive to say the least. Falam, Myanmar, is near the India border and the military is very powerful and brutal there. If there is something you have that they want, they will simply take it from you; Titus mentioned a vehicle, a pig, a piece of equipment, whatever. This makes the people afraid to have certain things because it could so easily be taken from them.

Not only that, they also have forced labor. They don't hire someone to do work, they simply come to a home and demand that the father or an older son work for a certain number of days. This is toil; I think of the children of Israel in Egypt. For example, road repair: they will dump a huge pile of large pieces of rock on the road, and with a hammer the workers have to smash it up so they can fix the road.

They are keeping the people under their control, keeping them poor and in subjection. And if the people dare to oppose them, the punishment only becomes more severe. Your heart really goes out to these people who are held under such bondage. The only rich people in the land are government officials, generals, and such like. They live in the rich homes and drive the new cars and eat in the upper-class restaurants. One wonders if there is ever going to be relief for the poor. It's bad in Yangon too, but not as bad as Falam; the border is always more patrolled so the military is exceptionally strong in Falam.

That was a little side story. Now back to the farm. Before Titus studied he worked as a farmer, so he is quite knowledgeable about the whole process. He explained that they are able to have two crops each year. One is the rice crop from July to October, and the other crop is beans from November to February, for export to China. Another possibility is having a chicken setup there as well for additional work.

We are giving the idea of the paddy farm some serious thought. Over the years the PRCA churches have taken collections for projects in Myanmar so it would seem this would fall in that category. But... that is not for us to say, and how long it would take for something like that to be approved is hard to tell. If we can swing it, we'd just like to do it personally. We know it is quite an investment and we don't know how successful it will be; that is only known to the Lord and it is in his hands. Those who are contributing monthly now are all getting older and we don't know how long we'll be able to keep it up, so if the church in Myanmar can be helped to provide for themselves, that would be a great blessing. Another consideration is that now we are still able to transfer money into that country. Hard telling how long it will be that way, so you like them to be independent, if at all possible.

You might wonder what we did each afternoon after Titus went home. We would get ourselves a cup of coffee, sit by a table that they have nestled among the various fruit trees and flowers, and discuss further what we had talked over with him. Talk, talk, talk, throwing out ideas and thoughts.

The situation with the ERCS and the PRCM is very uncertain at present. The PRCM wants nothing of divorce and remarriage; they hold strictly to the no remarriage position. It remains to be seen whether CERC will be able to take on the PRCM by themselves after the whole situation is settled here. Another concern is the translation work. Titus likes to put out a Standard Bearer four to six times a year. Each issue costs about U.S. $200. The Standard Bearer is well received in the PRCM but also in the broader church world; people have commented how much they have learned from it. Then there is other translation work that Titus would like to do but here again he has to learn when he must stop. It's a delight to see someone so enthused about the work of the Lord.

He also has the desire to instruct the pastors and elders, and to do this costs approximately U.S. $1,000. He has three groups of men: one group of six, another of four, and then a group of two. This means that Titus has to go through the teaching three times. The men travel down to Yangon and stay in the house by Titus for two weeks, eating at their table and having their laundry taken care of. (Titus laughingly told us the family is happy when it is all finished because they have to adjust the sleeping arrangements and share the bathroom when there are guests. Don't think their bathroom is like yours; they have a squat toilet, and shower with a bucket and pan.)

They have thirteen Psalter numbers that have been translated and fit to the tunes we know, and the people sing them heartily. I even noticed Josiah singing without looking at the book, so they are also committing them to memory. Another three songs are completed, which they are learning, and another three are in the pipeline. The musician in the group (he teaches music in some of the Bible schools in Myanmar) would like to give more time to the project of arranging the Psalter numbers so they could sing more of the songs, but that will only be possible if he receives a little remuneration (like U.S. $25 a month) so he can let up on some of his other work. Somehow there seems to be no end to the help that they need.

There was also some time, briefly, to discuss some theological issues. Titus wanted to understand more of Logos, Christ the Word, so that was one thing. Then Grandpa shared with him the lectures he gave on covenant—going through four lectures in one morning is about as brief as you can make it.

We talked with Titus about the importance of training another man for giving some leadership in the church. He does have someone in mind. This young man is twenty-nine years old, married with two young daughters. He has middle school education and is not English speaking, but Titus does see in him sincerity, love for the Word, eagerness to learn, and good judgment.

I didn't say anything yet about the weather. It was simply fantastic, absolutely beautiful. It wasn't hot; there were nice breezes and low humidity. Wow! What a contrast from hot and humid Singapore. While it was a relief to us, the locals were chilly—many of them wore sweaters or jackets. Our bed in Singapore is more comfortable than the beds we had in Myanmar but the shower at Ruby Inn is excellent. One thing that certainly is to our advantage is that foreigners must stay in a registered hotel while visiting in Myanmar. It would really be tough if we were expected to stay in with the locals.

On Friday night we brought Titus' whole troop and his brother Timothy's family out for dinner. We've taken them there before and it's a highlight for the family. The dinner is buffet so they can eat as much as they like and choose their own food. It's great to see them all enjoy it so much. In addition to the food is a cultural program, which is an added attraction.

On Saturday we visited with Pastor Moses and Kip Vel from the URCM. In the beginning of the ERCS' work in Myanmar they worked with this group, so we know them quite well. They have broken the relationship with ERCS, although they still do attend the seminars ERCS holds in Myanmar. Moses has set up his own school now and has about ten students. He has a four-year program and conducts it for eight months out of a year.

About a year ago their property was destroyed by a fire. This included their church and the building next door that they used for the school. Providentially, the wind was blowing in the right direction so all the neighboring houses were not destroyed. This could have been a major disaster if the fire had spread: houses are near to each other, and some even have thatched roofs. Here again we saw how the government operates. When there's a fire in Myanmar, it has to be that someone is guilty, so in this case two of the students were charged with negligence and a fine had to be paid. Actually the fire was caused by wind, which made the electricity to arc.

Now they are holding their worship services in Pastor Moses' house. They had to remove one of the walls to make the room larger.

MISSION TRIPS: MYANMAR—JANUARY 16-23, 2006

They are renting the house next door for the school, and a house across the street for the men to stay in. They hope and pray that they will be able to rebuild, but they have to do some serious fundraising before that will happen.

There is something interesting about their family. Some years back Kip Vel shared with me how she would like to see her children move away from Myanmar. I cautioned her at the time: the Lord gave you these children, this is their home, this is their country, and if they leave, you will not be able to see them. Are you sure this is what the Lord would want you to do? Her answer was, "I want the best for my children. It's very difficult for them here."

All the children except the youngest, Joseph, are living in Atlanta, Georgia. Their daughter Maria is married to an American and has a two-year-old child. Moses and Kip Vel were not able to go to the wedding and have never met the son-in-law or the grandchild. Priscilla is engaged to a minister's son and will be married in July 2006. The man is ten years her senior and is from the Chin tribe but living in America. The minister translated the Bible into the Falam language. He recently made a trip to Myanmar and visited with Moses and Kip Vel and on his son's behalf asked for their permission for the wedding. Their son Paul doesn't have a girlfriend, and Titus has a Burmese girlfriend, who also lives in Atlanta.

The children are working and contribute a lot for their parents' work in Myanmar. Together they paid U.S. $4,000 to have a phone hooked up in the home. In a phone call to his parents Titus said, "Mommy, I don't have any money to buy meat" (after they bought the phone). The mother's answer was, "The Lord will bless you." When they had to rent the house for the school, they asked their children to please cover the cost of it. The owners of this house live in the United States, so the children can send a monthly check to them. When one need is taken care of, there's another need that must be met; that is Myanmar.

It was on these little trips—out for dinner, to Moses' house, and to Titus on Sunday—when we took a taxi that we got to see the real

Myanmar once again. The taxis are quite beat up, the roads are as bumpy as bumpy can be, men are still making the gravel by hand for road repairs. People are still living in flimsy bamboo houses. All along the way are tiny shops where they hope to sell a little to make a meager living. The buses are crowded to overflowing, literally that is, because men are hanging onto the back with just one foot on a step. We talked about family and friends in America, wondering what your thoughts would be if you saw the living conditions of these people. It's quite an experience and one that really gets to your heart.

We were told that in May 2005, bombs went off in three malls in Yangon on the same day. I believe they said around forty people were killed. Now when you go into the mall, everyone is scanned. Although they don't know for certain, the common folk believe it was an inside job because the military men were warned ahead of time not to be in the malls. Titus said their people are too poor to shop in the malls; they seldom, if ever, go in there. We went there because we wanted to buy a game for the children. We settled for Chinese checkers simply because there wasn't much selection. We gave them our set of Uno; we played it once with Titus so he could teach the family and they were all pretty excited with it.

I guess that week doesn't exactly sound like vacation, but it was definitely a week we thoroughly enjoyed, and we feel greatly blessed to be used by the Lord in this way. We only pray for good judgment and wisdom to make the right decisions. We recalled how the people loved to sing (in their language) "Oh, Jesus is a rock in a weary land." How true, Myanmar is certainly a weary land but the Christians we know are joyful in the Lord. The short while they live on this earth is nothing compared to the hope that they have in Christ.

For us, we go there for a little while and then we return to our own place with all the luxuries of life. Why does the Lord give us so much? I'm sure with it comes the responsibility to help those in need, and with giving comes blessing.

We had a little inconvenience in coming home; waiting in the airport for six and a half hours wasn't the nicest thing, but the flight was good and we give thanks for another safe trip. As we were getting off the plane in Singapore, our thoughts were how nice it would be if that was the Gerald R. Ford International Airport in Grand Rapids. Well, not this time, but we look forward to that in a couple months' time, the Lord willing.

India—April 10-May 1, 1998

India, a huge country with over a billion people. Where would our little niche be in this vast place? In 1992 Grandpa made a trip to India with Pastor Jai Mahtani. Grandpa kept in touch with the people he met and also established some new contacts. The purpose of this visit was to conduct a teaching seminar, to visit the Presbyterian Theological Seminary (PTS) in Dehra Dun to determine if some of the Myanmar pastors could have some training there, and to personally meet some of the people with whom Grandpa was working through correspondence.

What a fantastic trip! Where do you begin when you have so many interesting stories to tell? I guess the best place to start is at the beginning.

The trip began on Friday, April 10, leaving Singapore at 7:00 a.m. Being Good Friday, which is a holiday in Singapore, our friends Goh Kheng Joo and Hooi Im offered to bring us to the airport since they didn't have to work. We were using up some of our MileagePlus vouchers from United Airlines for the flight from Singapore to Delhi, India, which gave us a long day (ten hours) in Hong Kong waiting for the connecting flight. Angelia Teng, a church member from FERC who accompanied us on the trip, flew on Air India, which was a direct flight, so she left late in the afternoon and was waiting for us when we arrived at 12:30 a.m.

Reservations had been made at the York Hotel in Delhi and we were also assured that there would be a driver waiting for us. Here's where we encountered our first difficulty, and thankfully, it was also the last one. There was no one at the airport holding a sign reading YORK HOTEL or KORTERING. We had been forewarned not to catch a taxi off the road in India, so we booked a prepaid cab in the airport. After riding a while, the driver stopped, but there was no York Hotel in sight. We said very distinctly, "York Hotel," but he shrugs his shoulders and says he doesn't know where. We don't have a clue as to where we are or where we're going and think, "What are we in for anyway?"

From that point onward, three different "autos" drove right alongside us. The drivers of the autos talked with our driver in a language that we could not understand. We began to wonder what they were conniving about and where they were going to bring us. Finally we arrived at the York Hotel and we breathed a sigh of relief, but the frustration wasn't over yet. There were men standing around the door and the conversation went something like this: "No, no room. Sorry, fully booked. Come along, I'll show you to a room."

"But we have a reservation. There is a room for us. They already have our credit card number."

"Sorry, sir."

"I would like to speak with the manager."

"Already gone home. No one here. Come with us. We'll show you where you can stay tonight."

All this time they were blocking the door so we couldn't get in. The three of us began to ponder what we should do. A few minutes later Grandpa noticed another Western couple entering the building so he was determined we were going to go in too. He became a bit bolder and wasn't going to let those men stop us. One thing that had slipped Grandpa's mind was that the registration desk was on the second floor so those managing the hotel could not see what was going on outside their entrance. It was around 3:30 a.m. by that time and you never know what those characters might be up to, so it wasn't a pleasant experience. We got inside, made our way upstairs to registration, and found they did have our reservation and our room was waiting for us.

MISSION TRIPS: INDIA—APRIL 10-MAY 1, 1998

What a grand initiation to India! Is this what it was going to be like for three weeks? We thanked the Lord for bringing us safely through and for providing this place for us to stay. We found out that there are plenty of people in India who will manipulate, lie, and cheat. We had to learn the lesson right away and be on our guard.

The hotel was nice, located on Connaught Circus in the heart of Delhi. There was a balcony outside our door, and it was fun just to stand up there and watch the throngs of people and the traffic below—a real circus. We stayed at the hotel for four nights and each morning we enjoyed our breakfast on the balcony. I'm sorry I can't capture all the sights, sounds, and smells of India in writing, but the noise here was horrendous.

After a few hours of sleep, a good shower, and breakfast, we ventured out on our Saturday exploring. We found out that the train depot was within walking distance, and we wanted to inquire about taking the train to Dehra Dun on Tuesday. A local travel agent approached Grandpa; he was out on the road trying to drum up some business. If it weren't for him, I don't know if we would have been able to cross that road. The locals know just how to do it and either are more brave or take more risks.

I never saw as many people at one time as I did at the train depot and what a sight to behold! People all over, some are sleeping right on the ground, others are taking some lunch, queues are long, and there is a special place on the second floor for foreigners to book tickets, which helped to thin out the crowd for us. Grandpa observed that there weren't as many beggars and touters around as there were when he went to India in '92. (A touter is a person who will harass you to buy his product, and he doesn't take no for an answer very quickly.) We found out we could get the train to Dehra Dun but it was completely booked for the return trip.

Our next possibility was to book a cab. The travel agent spotted us once again on our way back to the hotel and took us to his office. He was a pretty smooth talker but the most he could get from us was, "We'll get back to you if we're interested." There was also a travel agent at the hotel and when we inquired of him, we found the cost of hiring a cab to be much cheaper. The first man said there would be an additional charge of 400 rupees (Rs) per person for tax; the hotel man said the tax is per car and it was included in the price. We decided on the taxi and asked if we could possibly have an English-speaking driver. We're learning a lot—fast! Don't believe everything the first person tells you.

We had a delicious lunch at the York Hotel Restaurant and were all set for a stroll around Connaught Circus. There were many guys in the park with their shoe-shining equipment so for the fun of it, Grandpa had his shoes polished. And while we're waiting anyway, they might just as well do mine too. What a funny experience. Both Grandpa and I had old shoes that we fully intended to replace, but those men wanted to repair them as well. The heels on Grandpa's shoes were worn down so he cut a piece and glued it on to make it level. They don't ask ahead, they just do it, tell you later, and expect you to pay. While he's busy working on the shoes, another guy comes around and starts massaging Grandpa's feet and legs, and the crowds begin to gather around to watch the whole ordeal.

All of these "workers" have their little notepads in which tourists have jotted down their comments about the good service, etc. along with their name and address. They hold the notepads out in front of you and turn the pages so you can see what others have written about their work, but of course, they aren't able to read any of it because it's not in their language. The job is finally finished and it's time to pay. What started out as a shoeshine for 10 Rs has now become 400 Rs.

"See how nice. Guaranteed for two years."

"But we didn't ask you to do it. Here's 30 rupees."

He refuses the money so Grandpa says, "Here it is. Take it or leave it," and starts to walk away.

Then the guy took the money and said, "Are you happy now?"

We thought that was cute and used that little phrase repeatedly throughout our trip.

Then the massager had to collect. Grandpa said, "You never asked

MISSION TRIPS: INDIA—APRIL 10-MAY 1, 1998

if I wanted it and I never told you to do it. I'll give you 20 rupees." That was a far cry from the 400 Rs he wanted. Do you know what he said? "Are you happy now?"

There was some touting and begging there and we decided it's just best to ignore them. But it's difficult; you'd have to have a heart of stone not to be touched by everything you see. These people are so desperately poor, many have physical handicaps, and begging is their only hope of getting something. One man we saw that afternoon was walking barefoot on the heels of his feet; the rest of his foot was two long toes.

I guess I'll interject here a little about the money in India. One U.S. dollar is 39 rupees (Rs) and one Singapore dollar is 22 Rs. Labor is very cheap in India. Many people put in a hard day's work for 50 Rs (U.S. $1.25) so when they get 30 Rs (U.S. 75 cents) for a fifteen-minute job of shoe-shining and repair, they are earning extremely good wages, even though it's hardly worth talking about for us. Throughout the trip we did find that there was no consistent basis for charging and paying. Everyone was out to get as much as they possibly could for whatever job, be it large or small. It just seemed so unfair, but seeing the poverty of the country helps to understand where they're coming from.

Rev. Steve Poelman from Ramachandrapuram (a missionary sent to India by the Cornerstone United Reformed Church in Hudsonville, Michigan) had told Grandpa about the Faith Academy in Delhi where he thought we might enjoy worshiping on Sunday. Faith Academy is quite impressive. They have a large school, enclosed premises, guarded. They have an excellent reputation for discipline and learning, so along with that comes a waiting list of well-to-do people who wish to have their children enrolled there.

The church is actually an outreach of the school. Most of the students at Faith Academy are Hindu and they and their families are encouraged to come to the worship services of the church. On Sunday they have a morning and an evening worship service, which are held in the hallway of the school. Church began at 9:15. We took a cab from the hotel (100 Rs or U.S. $2.50). In our minds we had pictured a large auditorium with a crowd of people. At the beginning of the service, there were about ten or fifteen people there, but slowly on the meeting place was filled up. The guest preacher for the Easter Sunday morning church service was the professor of Old Testament at the Presbyterian Theological Seminary in Dehra Dun. His message was on Jesus' appearance to the two men on the way to Emmaus.

We stayed for the lunch fellowship and visited at the table with Mr. Dorsey and Mr. and Mrs. David Fiol and the Fiols' niece from Florida. Mr. John Dorsey is the senior pastor of this church but as far as the church activities are concerned, they are more taken care of by the assistant pastor and Mr. Dorsey is more involved with the school. Mr. Fiol is the principal of the Grace Academy in Dehra Dun, India.

After that we had our first ride in an auto for 50 Rs, which brought us back to the hotel. (Autos are not cars in India. They are like a motorcycle but have three wheels and a small covered cab. They are used for hired transportation and we could sit with the three of us in one, but it was a bit squished.) We spent the evening at the hotel and did some reading.

For the next four days we had use of an A/C cab (air-conditioned) with our driver, Neggie. On Monday we saw the sights of Delhi. Delhi is the capital of India and the third largest city. There were three main places we visited: Red Fort, Tombs, and Jama Masjid Mosque. All these attractions date back to the sixteenth and seventeenth century, are very spacious and elaborate, and the detail in the construction is very impressive. Quite a contrast from all the poverty you see in India today. Our lunch that day was by Nirula's Restaurant, and in the afternoon we took the time to confirm all our reservations for the domestic flights that we would be taking on Indian Air.

Then Neggie drove us around showing us the government buildings, etc. These drivers all have some special places to bring you, and Neggie's was the Cottage Industries Exposition. We were shown some handwoven silk rugs from Kashmir and decided to purchase a small one (three by five feet) as a special memory of this trip. Grandpa and I had looked at rugs in Singapore and had hoped to buy one sooner

MISSION TRIPS: INDIA—APRIL 10-MAY 1, 1998

or later so now was a good time. It will always be a keepsake of our many years in this part of the world.

The trip to Dehra Dun was to inquire about the Presbyterian Theological Seminary. This is a Reformed seminary in northern India, and the ERCS is wondering if they can consider this school for some of the initial training of the Myanmar pastors. Neggie picked us up at 6:30 a.m. and it was a seven-hour trip. Angelia wasn't feeling the best but she hung in there and managed to keep up.

There were so many interesting things we saw along the way that my mind was busy all the time thinking about the sad condition of the people in India. There were large areas where squatters lived in makeshift shacks. They were crowded together literally like sardines in a can, some with hardly any protection at all. Sometimes we read of huge fires with so many people left homeless or killed, and it's so easy to understand when you see how they are packed in there. And when I thought of all these people without hearing the gospel, this song came to me:

> Far, far away, in heathen darkness dwelling,
> Millions of souls forever may be lost;
> Who, who will go, salvation's story telling,
> Looking to Jesus, minding not the cost?
>
> All pow'r is given unto Me,
> All pow'r is given unto Me,
> Go ye into all the world and preach the gospel,
> And lo, I am with you alway.*

And that's not all. I only have three words to say to anyone who I hear complaining: "Count your blessings." These people use "buffalo chips" (dung) for cooking fuel. Many times we saw women along the side of the road shaping these "chips" with their bare hands. Yes, I agree, Yuck! And how easy it is for us to complain even when we have all the modern conveniences in our clean kitchens.

---

* By James McGranahan (1886).

Grandpa was sitting up front with the driver. Angelia wasn't feeling well and slept most of the way, and I was thinking, thinking, thinking. So here's the challenge I came up with for the grandkids. Around Thanksgiving day the teachers in school ask the students to write down some of the things they are thankful for, and the children will write Christian parents, church where the truth is preached, schoolteachers who love the Lord, etc. These are all great blessings that the Lord gives us, but now how about listing one hundred things that we all take so easily for granted. We saw all these people who so easily could put all their worldly possessions in a small box! Tears came into my eyes, and I was thankful that I could so easily open my bag and pull out a fresh, clean tissue. Each one make your own list; it should be quite easy. I'm not going to give you something if you do it, but instead, for each completed list, $10 will be given to help some orphans. (I'll tell you about them later.)

The driving was something else. Neggie was a good driver and we all felt quite comfortable with him at the wheel, but the way they drive in India is terrifying. On a two-way road, they drive down the center, constantly blowing the horn. There are buses, lorries, cars, autos, animals, and people, all crowding the road. The driver weaves in and out, to the left, to the right, wherever there is room he will go. Perhaps these people understand some kind of unwritten law: if the driver toots the horn, then they have given warning, and if you don't get out of the way it's your fault, not the driver's. When we see something ahead, we'll slow down and be prepared to stop, but in India, when they see something ahead, they speed up and try to make it. Most of the time it works out alright because the autos and animals move slower, but it looks a bit risky when you see a big bus barreling down on you.

We did see some pretty bad accidents involving buses; one was with a truck that was broken in two, another was plastered up against a tree. An accident we saw on Tuesday wasn't cleared up yet when we came through again on Thursday. Never, never, never were we more conscious of the Lord's protecting care over us!

MISSION TRIPS: INDIA—APRIL 10-MAY 1, 1998

Our home in Dehra Dun for the next couple nights was Hotel Great Value. Angelia wasn't up to eating yet that night, so Grandpa and I had dinner at the hotel restaurant. It was chicken steak: delicious.

On Wednesday we visited the Presbyterian Theological Seminary (PTS). Dr. Mohan Chacko is the principal. He studied in the United States and met his Dutch wife there. Mrs. Chacko is the former Judy Deters from Holland, Michigan. They met at RBI (Reformed Bible College in those days but now it is called Kuyper College in Grand Rapids, Michigan). Dr. Chacko asked Grandpa to speak for chapel that morning (Philippians 4:8, 9). We enjoyed the tea break with the students (I met a girl from Myanmar) and then spent the rest of the morning with Dr. Chacko. His wife teaches English and music at the school, so she was busy, but they did invite us to have evening dinner with them in their home.

PTS is a Reformed school but they do have a problem with getting all Reformed men to teach there. Dr. Chacko takes all the theology courses. Sometimes they have guest instructors who teach for three or six months. We met a retired CRC pastor and his wife who are there now for short term. PTS is putting up a new building that will have a large auditorium (seating six hundred) and will include new offices at a cost of U.S. $150,000. They have many occasions for using a large auditorium—they prepare programs and invite many to come and then have opportunity to preach the Word. In a country as big as India with cheap labor, it's possible to have these large campuses (if you receive foreign help). Very different from Singapore, where you can't buy a large piece of land even if you had the money, and to erect large buildings like that would cost a mint.

They have apartments for the teachers and separate dorms for the men and women. They don't encourage dating between the students, and the reason for that is because of the Indian culture. In India they still have arranged marriages, or at least the parents have quite a say as to whom their children marry. If a boy and girl would be attracted to each other, they advise (a little stronger than that, I should say enforce) one or the other to discontinue their education.

In the afternoon we visited Grace Academy, a Christian school in Dehra Dun, where David Fiol (whom we met in Delhi on Sunday) is the principal. They have four hundred students from nursery through tenth grade. The facilities are nice and quite new. Mr. Fiol mentioned that it's always difficult to get Christian school teachers. This school was originally set up to accommodate children of missionaries and that is still their top priority. A number of these children are separated from their parents during the school year and live on the school premises.

Mr. Fiol's secretary showed us around to the various classes. The children were all so well trained and orderly. When we appeared at the door, they all immediately stood up by their seats and said, "Good afternoon, Sir. Good afternoon, Madam."

Dinner was in the home of the Chackos. They have two children, Maria and Jeremy. Maria is in the tenth grade at Grace Academy so will be graduating. The menu was scalloped potatoes (one of Grandpa's favorites), rolls, mixed vegetables, coffee, and cake. Ummm, good!

While Grandpa and I were having dinner the night before, it suddenly dawned on me: Anna Petter Grundy! She was a missionary in India! We got talking about that and I was telling Grandpa everything I remembered about her. Anna was a sister of my Uncle Andrew Petter. I remember when I was a child that Anna Petter visited by our house when she was on furlough. It seems to me she had a six-month furlough and was missing India so much, she couldn't wait to get back. She went out there single but married an Indian and adopted twenty or twenty-one children (I believe some were adopted before her marriage). We all were quite enthralled with her stories, and afterward my mother encouraged us children to give up some of our toys and dolls so Anna could take them along to the children in India.

Grandpa asked if there was anything written about her work in India. I didn't have any idea whether there was or not, but we brought it up with the Chackos and much to our surprise, they were very well acquainted with her work. One of the children, Esther Grundy, had studied at RBI when Judy Chacko was there. They knew Anna

MISSION TRIPS: INDIA—APRIL 10-MAY 1, 1998

Grundy had written a book entitled *Sunshine and Shadows* so Dr. Chacko called to the library of PTS and soon a copy was brought over to the house. The book is mimeographed. To be able to find a copy to buy is a dream but I sure hope I can locate one that I can photostat. We promised to call Judy's parents when we got back to Michigan to let them know about our visit. Her parents and some of the siblings have been to India to visit them.

On Thursday we headed back to Delhi. We got an early start (7:30) so the traffic wasn't quite so heavy at first and we arrived back at the York Hotel by 3:00. Angelia was feeling a little better but not completely over it yet. Along the way we saw more women making the buffalo chips. After the chips set in the sun to dry, they are stacked in a heap like a pyramid and you see these piles all over.

There were also women working in the fields cutting the grain by hand. The children in school uniforms looked very neat. We saw autos loaded with children and all the school bags were hanging on the outside of the auto. Several times we saw kids skinny dipping in small lakes or ponds. And we saw lots of "Dhobies." A Dhobi is a laundry person: they're doing the laundry by the river and beat the fabrics against the rocks and lay them out on the ground to dry. The women's saris are about six yards of fabric so you know what large pieces of material they're working with. For some people, this is their business and they might have clothesline to hang the wash up to dry.

It was to bed early that night because Friday morning's flight was at 6:15, which meant getting up at 4:00.

We're all ready for the next lap of our journey, which is a visit to the Poelmans in Ramachandrapuram (Rama). It's Friday, April 17. We left Delhi at 6:15 and flew to Hyderabad and then took a connecting flight to Vishakhapatnam (or like the locals call it, Visag). Pastor Steve Poelman, his wife Nalini, and their youngest daughter were at the airport to welcome us.

The Poelmans own a van and have a hired driver, but before we started out to Rama, Steve offered a prayer for the Lord's protection during the four-hour trip. This is their practice as a family each time they set out in the van, and we really appreciated the need and sincerity of it. Steve does some local driving but he isn't comfortable yet driving on the highway. The driver, twenty-five years old, is experienced and alert, but at times a bit risky. It's not exactly a ride where you can relax and doze off. If you shut your eyes, you open them immediately with the next jerk.

It was around 7 or 7:30 when we arrived at the mission compound, LCM (Life Centre Ministries) in Rama. Dinner was ready for us and after that was a meeting, at which time they welcomed us and presented garlands.

Rev. Poelman holds a pastors' conference for around forty men every other month for two days. This happened to be scheduled for the very weekend we were due to come. The only change he made was to switch it from Thursday/Friday to Friday/Saturday. Grandpa extended greetings along with a short message, and they asked Angelia and me to make a few comments as well. On Saturday there was a teaching session where Grandpa treated the subject of the covenant. After the conference was over, the men made their way back to their homes, traveling mostly by bus.

We had a wonderful weekend and a very enjoyable stay by the Poelmans. It's a mission compound that was started by Nalini's parents, Rev. Michael and Siromani Nanda, about twenty-five years ago. He bought the land very cheaply because it was undesirable, being lowland, but over the years he built it up and erected buildings suitable for the ministry. Steve Poelman from Wyoming, Michigan, and Nalini from Rama, India, met at Moody Bible Institute in America, and later Steve attended and graduated from MARS (Mid-America Reformed Seminary).

I have to tell you this little story. Rev. Nanda was coming to America. Nalini was faced with the problem of getting her father from the airport. A friend suggested she ask Steve to help her since he had a car. She didn't know him at all at that time but approached him about it and he was happy to help. Things went fast. I don't know just how long Rev. Nanda was in the States (probably three months)

MISSION TRIPS: INDIA—APRIL 10-MAY 1, 1998

but before he left to go back to India, they were married! In a culture of arranged marriages, no way could Rev. Nanda go back to his country and have a daughter dating in the U.S. without his arranging the marriage. When the Poelmans eventually got to India, they had another marriage ceremony on the compound.

Talli, sister of Nalini, lives with the Don VanDykes from Cornerstone URC in Hudsonville. The two sons of the Nandas are Victor and John. Both studied in the U.S. and took American wives and are back in India now. The wives had a difficult time adjusting to life on the mission compound and preferred to live in a larger city, so both couples with their children are settling in Visag. The background of the Nanda family is more in the line of Baptist, but Rev. Nanda has become thoroughly Reformed and he and Steve are in full agreement doctrinally. They are working with Victor and John to explain the Reformed faith to them so they can work unitedly as a family in sharing the gospel. Steve has an enormous amount of work, and his great desire is to be able to learn the language so he can communicate better. That requires so much time, effort, and experience, but he's working at it.

Steve and Nalini have three daughters: Surekha Joy is nine (her birthday is the same day as Grandpa's), Sarala Christy is six, and Sundhya Rose is three. The older girls remembered us from the day we met the Poelmans at Changi Airport in Singapore. That was eighteen months ago and Sundhya was only a year and a half, but her mother told her how I carried her and got her to sleep so her mother could take a rest. It was easy to attach to the kids. I guess we kind of reminded the children of Grandpa and Grandma Poelman who live in Wyoming, Michigan.

They had an American teacher for the children but Bonnie could not get her visa renewed and had to return to the States. Now they have a local fellow, one who was schooled at the orphanage and later graduated from higher education (I don't know what level). Steve is presently trying to train him to be his interpreter and this same young man is also teaching the children. It appears to be quite a challenge.

There is an orphanage on the compound with around seventy children. They are so sweet and lovable, well-behaved and mannerly. They greet you every time they see you. They have a room for the boys and a room for the girls. Each child has a small box (like a footlocker, about twelve by thirty by ten inches) that sets against the wall and in which they keep all their personal belongings. At night they lay out a little pad on the floor to sleep on. Some of these children are truly orphans whose parents have died, but others have been rejected. Honestly, you can't help but love them, they are so precious! Just giving them a little attention, putting an arm around them, brings out all the smiles and they come around again for more.

They have a school for the children. They would like to have more Christian teachers; they have one, but the other two are unbelievers. The dialect there is Telugu and the children are memorizing the Heidelberg Catechism in their language. Can you imagine how thrilling it is to see all these children standing up and reciting together in unison questions and answers from the Heidelberg Catechism? It's just like there is a whole world out there that we knew nothing about, and you see how the Lord is working in the hearts and lives of these children. Nothing short of *marvelous*!

The background of all these children is Hindu, but God in his own time and way is bringing some of these children to a saving knowledge of him. These children do not have toys; they just have to play and make their own fun if and when they have time. It's also important that they have some chores to do so each one must do their own laundry by hand; they sweep the sand, and in the evening sprinkle the sand with water to settle the dust.

The LCM also provides a home for widows on the compound. A widow is one who has lost her husband or who is divorced, and they are a despised lot. In Indian culture, when a husband died the wife was to cast herself on his pyre and burn with him, or relatives would throw her on. Without the husband, the wife is worthless. That is changing some now in that they don't necessarily end their life, but the scorn and rejection is still there. If they don't die with the

MISSION TRIPS: INDIA—APRIL 10-MAY 1, 1998

husband, they should wear only white clothing, no bright-colored clothing, no jewelry, no make-up, so they can be easily identified as a widow. They are unable to get any work. No one would want them to work in their house because they are cursed.

When the Nandas or Poelmans hear of someone who needs a place to stay, they take them in and create jobs for them to do on the compound. Consequently, there are many helpers around, which makes things a bit easier for Nalini as far as physical work is concerned: washing, cooking, etc. But in its place are many problems that have to be dealt with and counseling to be done.

Mrs. Nanda is the matriarch. She had heart surgery when she was in her thirties. The Lord brought her through, and it was a changing point in her life. She has literally given her life for the work. She's in her sixties now but not in the best physical health. She sits on the couch most of the day and is in control of *Grand Central Station*. Everyone, just everyone, consults with Mrs. Nanda. They love her and seek her counsel. She's patient and can give a listening ear. Even the mailman walks directly into the house and brings the mail to her. Delivery men (rice or whatever) come to her with their bills and she pays them. The little children come and talk with her, I even saw one giving her a backrub, and the women share their problems with her. There's very little privacy for the family and never a dull moment. Everyone walks freely throughout the house whenever they want to.

Nalini is a lawyer and although she was going to set it aside, they have decided that it can be part of their ministry. She offers her services for free to the poor and needy, working only in the morning. Her role will be to follow in her mother's footsteps. With her education and experience, she is able also to work through problems that arise.

Cornerstone URC is footing the cost of a new home for the Poelmans. Pastor Poelman is very forward looking and has included space where he can instruct students in the Reformed faith. The future plan is definitely to include seminary training. One thing Steve promised Nalini is a Western kitchen with conveniences built in. They realize the great need of their own family unit, and after they shift into the new house, they don't intend it to be a "free for all" but will try to keep their own family structure. They have to be careful not to sacrifice their own family for the sake of the work.

There's also another new building going up on the compound near the house. This will be for the orphanage with a dorm for the boys and one for the girls. Living conditions will still be simple, but Steve mentioned it will take some training to teach the children how to use the showers and toilets.

India showers are with a bucket of water and a small pan. You see people defecating and urinating anywhere and everywhere. Steve was telling us someone (I believe he said Winston Churchill) was asked what he thought of India and his answer was, "One huge toilet."

On Saturday afternoon Victor Nanda (Nalini's brother) brought us to the leprosy hospital. What a pathetic sight. These people are the undesirables and outcasts of society. But here is a Christian institution that is trying to minister to these people. Victor Nanda's friend lives with his family on the hospital grounds and brings the Word to these sick and dying. It's really heartrending, awaking each day not realizing any real purpose in life and merely existing. But we do know that God has a purpose for all this and makes no mistakes. His ways are perfect and just and good.

From the leprosy hospital we went to the house of an uncle of the Nandas. The uncle and his son are ministers in the Church of Christ and live in the village. We entered the village on the wrong road but, "Never mind, we'll get out and walk and the driver can come around and pick us up at the house." What an experience! All the village children followed us—we look like a strange species with our light-colored skin! They all reached out to shake our hands. While we were in the house, the children all gathered around by the door and watched what was going on.

Next stop was a fort where the king of the area used to live. The king has died and there is no longer a king; consequently the fort is not maintained as it has been in the past. There was a lot of activity there that afternoon. They were just finished shooting pictures for a

MISSION TRIPS: INDIA—APRIL 10-MAY 1, 1998

TV program. The Nandas are long standing in the community and are respected by everyone. Rev. Nanda, on many occasions, visited with the king and shared God's Word with him. We were introduced to the king's son and could look around the fort.

Grandpa and I had a guest room, which was in a separate building on the compound, and Angelia's bedroom was in the main house. Sunday morning we were awake in bed, but still resting, when we heard someone knock on the door at 6:10. They kept knocking, so Grandpa finally went to the door. It was one of the little children who noticed the light on the outside of our building was still on and wanted to shut it off. This is just one example of how the kids have their eyes open for something to do. They are so cute. By the way, the children are all up at 5:30 and gather together for devotions at 6:00 every day.

Grandpa preached for the Sunday morning worship at the compound on 1 Peter 2:2, desiring the sincere milk of the Word, with interpretation in Telugu. Most of those in attendance were the ones who live on the compound, but there are a few others who come from outside. Everyone sits on mats on the floor. The group is not organized into a church as yet. This is a goal that Pastor Poelman will work toward. Some of the widows are truly converted, but they all come under the preaching of the Word and are witnessed to. We were struck with how attentively the children of the compound listen. They sit right next to each other and you don't see them bothering one another. Certainly commendable.

We had lunch at the Poelmans and then set out on a forty-five-minute drive to Madiki, a village church where Pastor Peter Raju is the minister. Pastor Poelman brought the message. There were many elderly people at the service, and at the end when it was time to present their offerings, it was very touching how they all walked to the front and dropped their coins in the metal box, which has a small opening on top and was sitting on the table. Coins in India are almost worthless in our estimation, but they were giving even what little bit they had. The largest coin is 5 Rs, which is worth about 22 cents in Singapore. Fifty paise, a smaller coin, is about 2 cents.

Indian hospitality is to come in for a cup of tea so we stopped just briefly at the pastor's house after the service. The pastor and his wife are elderly and not well so it was important that they take care of the marriage of their son before they might die. The son is now married to a seventeen-year-old wife who is expecting their first child. The son will carry on in his father's pastorate.

Then we also had a quick stop at the home of Ezra Sastri, whose wife is dying of cancer. Grandpa offered a prayer for them and then the man himself poured out his heart in prayer. It's very obvious that the woman is suffering; she is extremely thin and longs for the Lord to take her home to glory. They are the parents of Lakshmi, a "widow" who is a rejected wife living at the compound; her husband left her when she was only twenty-one years old, and she is the mother of one daughter, who is now married. She has a couple brothers who do not show any love or concern for the parents even though they live nearby. Their attitude is that the daughter can tend to them. This is difficult because of the distance involved, but she loves her parents and so travels by bus to stay with them and care for them a few days at a time.

After arriving back at the compound, we had a quick bite to eat and then were off to another village, Chelluru, where there was a little service for about forty village children at the home of "America Grandma." She's called America Grandma because she has traveled to the United States several times and whenever there are children around, she has to get something ready to serve to them. We took several children along from the orphanage because they lead in the singing. It's cute; they really do well. They are teaching the songs they learn at the compound to the village children. Pastor Poelman spoke to the children in English and Nalini translated into Telugu. America Grandma came out and served her goodies right while Steve was speaking, which made it disruptive—something they will have to straighten out with her.

We had to stop in at the neighbors of America Grandma, who are Hindu. The Poelmans use every opportunity they have to befriend people and witness to them. It was a large place and it appeared like the whole extended family lived there: an elderly father, sons and daughters-in-law, grandchildren. These are all long-time acquaintances of the Nanda family. We were served a cup of tea and some biscuits there as well.

What an active Sunday! After a little dinner, we felt completely drained and soon headed off to our room. Steve sat outside with his brother-in-law, Victor, and talked Reformed theology until one in the morning.

Monday was an easy day. But "easy" on the compound is not boring. Just being there with all the people is extremely interesting. We had some time to sit and visit with Mrs. Nanda, and while we were there, one of the girls who used to live on the compound showed up, fell down on her knees by Mrs. Nanda, and sobbed uncontrollably. After she got herself together, she poured out her heart to her. Here I'm wondering if I have all the facts straight, but the story goes something like this: Suddenly one time she disappeared from the compound and didn't return. She was forced into an arranged marriage. I'm thinking she must have been troubled because she disappeared and the Nandas did not know her whereabouts and may have been worried for her. But thankfully the marriage is alright so far and she's happy. Later on in the visit, the girl's husband came in with their little son. Mrs. Nanda spent time talking with them and before they left, she prayed with them.

Later in the afternoon, there were a couple other things the Nandas wanted us to do. One was to see some land that brother John had purchased at Railugattu, on the edge of town, with the idea of relocating the compound. The Poelmans are not in favor of it because the compound is more centrally located and in a better area where it is now. It is well established and people are familiar with it, so it would not be wise to uproot it at this time.

Then we had a little stop by Pastor Elijah; he's a very old man and even though he still preaches, he's unable to stand up while doing so. Little visits mean a lot to these people, and they appreciate the time you take for them and also the prayers, even though they are not interpreted and not understood.

The final stop was at the government hospital. Emmanuel, the interpreter who Steve is training, knows a doctor at the government hospital so he asked the doctor to give us a tour. Oh dear, what a sight! You wonder how anyone can get better in those conditions. The doctor was more than willing to take us through and show us everything. We paraded through the various wards, saw the operation theater, and he even opened the door to the delivery room and, to our shock, there was a woman lying there waiting for an abortion. The bedding appeared to be filthy, but without proper laundry facilities, things can look grimy quite quickly.

Sitting in the courtyard was a patient, the husband of one of the women who attended church on Sunday. Perhaps both the husband and wife are Christians, I don't know. Grandpa prayed with them too. The woman herself has just recovered from eye surgery, thanks to the Nandas; Mrs. Nanda had made arrangements for this woman to see a better doctor in another city and the Poelman van was used to transport her there.

I haven't said anything about Rev. Nanda yet; he's slowing down and letting Steve take over the ministry but he is still involved with the running of the mission. What he was busy with when we were there was getting ready for the inspection of the facilities for their nurses' training. The exams had just been completed so most of the nurses were gone from the compound while we were there, but nurses' training is another aspect of their work. Previously Mrs. Nanda was a nurse, so she has had opportunity to witness to many, many people during her nursing career. It's just unbelievable what an influence this family has in the community. It seems everyone knows them and respects them. Their roots are down deep.

It's Tuesday morning and time for us to leave. We appreciated beyond words the kind hospitality that was shown to us by this loving and compassionate family. And they appreciated our including a visit to the compound as well. Steve was happy to have opportunity to visit with another Reformed man, to be able to talk heart to heart. They said repeatedly it was so good for him. And Nalini in some respects is lonesome. I had some nice talks with her. She's constantly on the giving end and has little companionship aside from her own husband and mother. They have a tremendous calling where they are and are happy and joyful in the Lord. We feel greatly blessed for the time we could spend with them and now will continue to pray for them. We will also try to keep in touch and see if there are other ways we can be of help.

The family went along to bring us to the airport in Visag. The Poelmans were going to spend a couple days at a little place they rent there, a retreat; the girls could go swimming and the family could relax together. The children wanted to stay at the airport until the plane took off. It wasn't easy saying goodbye to them. If and when they go to the States for a furlough, we did invite them to stop over in Singapore and stay with us a few days. Steve's parents are hoping to make a trip to India in the not-too-distant future, and the family is really looking forward to that.

We traveled to Madras on Tuesday and met Rajastephen and his wife, Shakila, at the airport there. Rajastephen made hotel reservations for us, so we took a cab to the hotel, and he and his wife came on his scooter. We only had the one evening there, so we took them for dinner at the hotel and visited in our room. Grandpa met Rajastephen on his India trip in '92. Since that time, Rajastephen has married. They told us that they only saw each other one time before they were married and had never spoken to each other. Now they've been married for three years and greatly desire to have a child. It looks like a happy marriage alright.

Rajastephen manages an orphanage. There is a chain of orphanages in India called Elim Christian Home, and he has around seventy children to care for. He would have liked to take us to their home, but there was no extra time available. It seems he is pretty well settled down in his work at the orphanage and doesn't intend to be a minister.

Wednesday was up early again. Our flight to Madurai was at 6:00. All of the above were side benefits of the trip to India. Now we were ready for the main purpose of the trip, which was the conference. Upon arrival in Madurai, there was a group of twelve there to welcome us, and once again we were garlanded. Pastor Stephen, the organizer, had left home at 2:00 a.m., went from place to place picking up the people, which took a couple hours, and then made the trip to Madurai: some two and a half to three hours. He said the people would feel hurt if they weren't invited to come along.

The place for the conference and the lodge where we stayed was in Theni (Allipagaram on the map). Communicating with the locals was impossible here. We never registered at the hotel. They had Pastor Stephen's name down and that was all they needed. They couldn't understand a word we said. The whole group went for a little lunch at a restaurant down the road. Four of the men came up to the room to visit a while and the others made their way back to their homes. Then we were left to rest a short time and had to be ready by 5:00 to go to another village.

What a night! I hope I can describe it as meaningful as it was! We caught the bus right in front of the Sri Vijay Nivas Lodge where we stayed. The men were with us; we could never have done it on our own. The bus was jammed and we stood up all the way. We got off the bus on the highway by Saruthupatti (patti means village) and had to walk into the village. The village roads are dirt and bumpy. As we walked along, children from the village followed us. You can't believe it, they just seem to come out of nowhere. There were at least fifty of them trailing along.

Our first stop was by Philip's house, one of the men who came along all day to the airport. He let all the children come into the house and they sat down quietly on the floor, smack up against each other. They had chairs for us to sit on and served us coconut milk. They cut off the top of the coconut so you can drink the milk out of it, using a straw, just like they do in Singapore. Grandpa gave a little meditation on the Lord is my shepherd, and Pastor Stephen interpreted it. The children all sat quietly and listened.

MISSION TRIPS: INDIA—APRIL 10-MAY 1, 1998

You know, it really makes you think—right away you have an instant audience. It's not often that some foreigners walk through their village, so they are attracted by these people who look so different. They think it's so strange and funny, and they want to feel that light skin and hear them talk. And then you're able to share the gospel with them. Is this how it was when the multitudes followed Jesus?

After we left Philip's house and were walking down the village roads again, the children were all crowding around as close as they could get, and the men who were with us took up little pieces of cane and shooed them away with a hitting motion. It doesn't make sense, does it; first you welcome them and talk with them, and then you drive them away. We walked around to several more homes of Christians in the village. These were only very brief visits along with a word of prayer.

I must include the little story about Philip's marriage. I believe the marriage was arranged. He had promised to marry the girl but then changed his mind and ran away. In their culture that is very bad and a disgrace. When he returned, his mother tried to persuade him, but when she was having difficulty, she asked Pastor Stephen to talk with him. The girl herself pleaded with him, "Marry me! Marry me!" After Stephen spoke with him, he decided yes, he would marry her. They're married and now he is a village pastor.

After our visits, we returned to Theni on the bus and were told to be ready early on Thursday for our outing to the mountain villages. A taxi was hired for the drive into the mountains. Angelia, Grandpa, and I sat in the back and three men sat in front with the driver. We had an excellent driver for the day so felt very comfortable riding with him. The place we went is called Cardamom Hills. It was spectacular! Reminded us of the winding roads in Rocky Mountain National Park. As we got higher and higher, we finally came to Kodaikanal, a little tourist village like Estes Park.

We found out how deeply Pastor Stephen's roots are in this part of India—he absolutely knows people everywhere! He was brought up in the area and walked from village to village sharing the gospel. He's a man who has befriended many people, is highly respected, is not pushy nor thinks highly of himself, but has a very gentle and kind spirit and will talk with anyone. He himself is thoroughly Reformed, but he is very patient with those who are still willing to listen and learn.

We stopped for breakfast in a very neat restaurant. (Much to our surprise, this was the only place in India where we had to use a squat toilet.) After breakfast, we went to the bank. There was this whole long line of foreigners waiting to change their money into Rs. Stephen escorted me right up to the counter, talked with his friend there, the friend took my passport and money and handed it over to the teller, and suddenly we realized that we had jumped the whole long queue and were waited on right away. From there we went into an office to meet another friend, the president of the bank. We would have loved to spend one or two hours browsing in Kodaikanal, but there were more important things to do.

Years back there were two women missionaries who served in the villages there. One, a Miss Baker, was from Canada, and the other was from England, a Miss June B. Ward. One was a missionary and the other a school teacher, and interestingly, they met each other on the boat, and the teacher joined the missionary and they worked together. They gave their lives for their calling and donated buildings that still stand today and are used for Christian worship. The people who knew them talk very lovingly about them, how they ministered to the people and showed compassion to them, always bringing them the Word of God. Without a doubt, they had quite an influence in the community. Both of them are living yet. Miss Baker is back in Canada and Miss Ward lives in Portland, Oregon.

One stop was by Kirupa Karan's home. He was with us a lot, a short man, very quiet but get him around his people and in his language and he could really talk. Pastor Stephen was telling how they were trying to find a wife for him. Here was this man from the hills who needed a wife and they didn't know who was suitable. Then they find this wonderful girl from the plains for him, they marry, and she becomes a real hills lady. They have four children.

MISSION TRIPS: INDIA—APRIL 10-MAY 1, 1998

They live in a three-story house. The first floor is just one small room, which is used for worship services. On the second floor is the kitchen. The wife cooks over a little opening where charcoal is burnt. The power was off (not unusual at all) so they lit some candles for light. When we were in Kodaikanal, the men picked up some very tasty cakes and served them to us at this house along with a bottle of pop. On the third floor is where they sleep, and you can also go on the rooftop and look over the village. In each home we visited, prayer is offered for the family.

Lunch for the day was by Pastor D. Monoharan in the village of Kavungi. His wife, Meena, cooked for the Canadian missionaries and also learned to speak the English language from them. They have one acre of land for vegetable farming, and after a dry spell of six months with no rain, it rained hard the day we came. They were so happy and thankful and said we brought the rain with us. The wife prepared a delicious dinner of rice, potatoes and carrots, chicken with gravy, sago (a warm dessert), and bananas.

I guess this was the day for telling all the stories about marriages. This pastor's mother had found a girl for him to marry but he didn't like her. Finally, in desperation, the mother asked Stephen to talk with him and find out what the problem was. The reason was that he liked the girl who would eventually become his wife.

Finally I asked Stephen, what about his own marriage? Stephen already was a Christian and married a Christian, but his family is Hindu. He said his family did not attend the wedding. His father was more open to accepting Stephen's wife, but his mother didn't accept the wife until their first child was born.

The hills were beautiful, a lot of terraced farming where we saw potatoes, carrots, cabbage, peas, etc. It looked lush and bountiful. They were harvesting the carrots and had large tubs filled with carrots and water and were swishing it around with their feet to wash them.

There was a short stop by a lookout. Grandpa and I got out to look around, and Grandpa was busy taking some pictures when a family came up and asked if they could take a picture with me. We run into this more often; people like to have a picture taken with a foreigner. I started up a conversation with them.

"Are you all one family?"

"Yes." There was an elderly mother, two of her children with spouses, and grandchildren. They had rented a van and hired a driver for a day's outing.

They asked where we were from. "We live in Singapore but we are Americans."

The one lady says, "I used to work in Singapore on Orchard Road!" (Singapore downtown.) Small world, isn't it.

Across the road from where the picture was taken was a mountain. Next to the mountain, along the road, there were about eight men bowing down. My remark was, "Look at all those men praying by the mountain." Coming from a country and being in a country with so much heathen worship, I thought that was a reasonable conclusion—you never know why or what people worship the way they do. Angelia said, "I don't think they're praying, they're peeing." Oops, okay Grandma, it's time you get a little India smart! But they were down on their haunches so it certainly looked like they were bowing down. That was our good laugh for the day.

There were several other stops to make at people's homes, and then it was time to head back. It would be another three or four hours before getting to Theni. It was a wonderful day enjoying God's beautiful creation, something we did not expect to see in India, and you all know how Grandpa and I love the mountains, so it was a very special day for us and for Angelia too.

Friday morning, April 24, marked the beginning of the conference. They had arranged to hold the conference in a building not far from where we stayed. We were able to catch a little auto to get over there. The men who attended the conference slept there as well. Meals were good.

Quite a few people attended the conference, so they had to eat in two shifts. They just sat in two long rows on the floor, their meal was dished out on a banana leaf in front of them, and they ate with

MISSION TRIPS: INDIA—APRIL 10-MAY 1, 1998

their hands. We were given a small table with chairs where we could eat our lunch. Our lunch was also served on a banana leaf and yes, we did eat with our fingers too. I was quite surprised at how well it went. They might have smiled at us because I know we picked up some of our food with our left hand, which is a no-no. The right hand is used for eating and is always kept clean while the left hand is used for cleaning oneself.

We found out what a conference is like Indian style. We are used to beginning on time, 9:00 or 9:30, sing a few songs, and get on with the teaching. Their conference begins at 10:30 and they sing until 11:00. They love to sing and really get into it. One man played a keyboard and another had some instrument that he tapped. They had it amplified and the men and women sang their hearts out, clapping along with the music.

Teaching session was from 11:00 to 12:30, after which they had lunch and a resting time until 2:30. Then they sang again for another half hour and the afternoon session was from 3:00 to 4:30 or 5:00. The subject treated in the morning was covenant friendship with God. The afternoon session began with questions, and it came close to being chaotic. We realized it appears more that way to us because we don't understand the language. "Therefore, if I do not know the meaning of the language, I shall be a foreigner to him who speaks, and he who speaks will be a foreigner to me" (1 Cor. 14:11 NKJV).

Someone asked a question, and rather than translating it for Grandpa and letting him answer, about four or five others butt in and try to answer and give their view. This went on for a little while and then Grandpa called a halt. He had had enough and explained that the questions should be asked directly to him, interpreted, and he be given the opportunity to answer. I thought Grandpa handled it very well; he was patient and accepted the fact that things are done differently in India. All was good though. We heard the next day that they had carried on with their discussions after the conference and into the evening.

Y. Paulraj came along with us to the lodge to talk with Grandpa about his desire to study for the ministry. Grandpa has been corresponding with him for quite some time, so we were happy that we could finally meet him, face to face, on this trip. He is a fine young man, single, and twenty-five years of age. You can read more of his life story in chapter 12. His heart's desire is to prepare for the ministry and to bring the gospel to "my people." It's not difficult to feel his sincerity; he has such a genuine love for his family not only, but also for his country and his people. It was neat to see his submissive attitude, quiet trust, and contentment in whatever way the Lord leads. His face beams with happiness, grateful for the Lord's working in his life and his heart's wish to serve the Lord full-time.

After he left, Stephen came, and that was the general pattern for the whole weekend. People coming and going. It sure was interesting. They had a lot of activities planned and took full advantage of all the time we had there.

Before going to the conference on Saturday, Angelia, Grandpa, and I went to the little restaurant down the road. We were getting used to the people staring at us, watching how we eat, etc. The workers in the restaurant would actually stand right by our table and gawk—it was really funny. They have a certain way of mixing their coffee and cream by pouring from one container to another and we were trying to get the knack of doing it ourselves. They got quite a kick out of that and were happy to do it for us. After we had gone to the same place for three days, they were getting used to having us around.

Saturday morning's session began with some comments on how the conference was to be conducted. There would be no interruptions. People would be given opportunity to speak, and only one person at a time. Everything was more orderly that day.

Pastor Jayachandran came for the Saturday session. He traveled six hours by bus. Grandpa has corresponded with Jayachandran for years, and when the conference was arranged, Grandpa wrote to him again and invited him to come down. Pastor Stephen and Jayachandran had never met before, but it was quite something to see how quickly they clicked. Right away they could sense in each other the love of the Reformed faith; there was doctrinal unity between the

MISSION TRIPS: INDIA—APRIL 10-MAY 1, 1998

two men. Paulraj came over to visit with us again after the conference until it was time for us to check out of the lodge.

Then we had to get settled in our place for the weekend. Saturday and Sunday nights we stayed in the guest house of the Christian Hospital in Periyakulam. Dr. George, a medical missionary, has the Christian Hospital. The room in which we stayed was small but we could manage; we wouldn't be spending a lot of time there anyway. After Dr. George had his medical training, his burden was to set up his practice in South India where he would also have opportunity to witness to his patients. From this came the Christian Hospital, which includes a general hospital, an eye hospital, and a maternity hospital.

Dinner that night was in the home of Susai in Periyakulam. There are four generations living in that home: Susai's elderly father, Susai and his wife, their daughter Roselin, and her two-year-old son. Roselin's husband was on heroin, unknown to them, involved with some gang, and committed suicide. Thankfully, Roselin has a loving family, and she herself is a very cheerful and happy person. They have a large room above the house that they adapted for a kindergarten for thirty children. Roselin has one other woman helping her with the K, and Roselin's mother cooks lunch every day for all those children! Wow, that's fantastic!

Again many people from the village stood in the doorway to get a look at us. Their homes aren't like ours, close the door and it's private. Over there, everything is open and people are free to walk in, come and go as they please. That night two neighbor girls (Hindu) came over with a camera and wanted to have a picture taken with us and then came back again with a pad of paper to get an autograph. Again we had a delicious meal. To tell you the truth, I am just amazed and overwhelmed with how these women can prepare such beautiful and tasty meals in their simple kitchens. It's all in the training and adapting with what you have, and it's proof positive that we can get along with a lot less. (It made me think again about the ingenuity of the Native Americans with their cliff dwellings in Mesa Verde. People are innovative and learn to adapt, no question about it.)

We had to be on our way. We reached the Christian Hospital by 7:00 for their evening chapel service, to which the patients are invited to come. James, the hospital chaplain, was already singing for the few people who were there, but more women kept coming. On the spot, James informed Grandpa that he could speak for fifteen minutes, and also on the spot, Paulraj had to translate. It went well. Grandpa spoke on Psalm 46:10, "Be still, and know that I am God." We found out afterward that most of the people in the audience were Hindus.

After the service, we visited with Dr. George in his office and he invited us to his home for lunch on Monday. The Christian Hospital is small but they are able to do some surgeries. More severe cases are referred to other hospitals. In addition to running the hospital, he also puts out a quarterly religious periodical.

Sunday morning we worshiped at Stephen's church. Before I tell you about that, I should tell you about Stephen's family. Stephen's wife, Leela, had heart trouble, and before she was able to have heart surgery, she passed away two years ago at the age of forty-two. Dr. George is a good friend of Stephen and cared for them through the time of his wife's illness. Stephen has five children: S. Joy, twenty-three; S. Kerzia, twenty-two; S. Kerena, twenty; S. John, eighteen; and S. Presena, seventeen. The "S" in each of the names stands for "daughter of Stephen" or "son of Stephen." Stephen himself is C. Stephen, which would mean his father's name begins with "C." Y. Paulraj's father's name begins with "Y." They don't have surnames but are identified by whom they are the children of.

Since the wife passed away, Joy has stayed at home and cared for the family. But that's not all; listen to this! There are children whose homes are in the hills without a school nearby, so Stephen has a hostel for thirteen children as well. They all live there. I'm sure there is some help from the children, but I wouldn't want to minimize what this young girl is doing, managing all those children, seeing that the laundry is done (by hand), meals are prepared, etc.

When the medical bills for the wife mounted, it became necessary for Stephen to sell the family home and get a cheaper place. The

MISSION TRIPS: INDIA—APRIL 10-MAY 1, 1998

living quarters are small and in back of the building, and the large room in front, where they have the worship services, also serves as the hostel for the children. They all have their footlocker boxes lined up against the wall, the same as by Poelmans. Stephen is now in the process of arranging a marriage for Joy. Kerzia is a nurse and teaches nursing students. The youngest daughter has just recovered from a two-month bout of typhoid fever. She was very ill and her life was in danger, so they are very thankful that she is well once again.

About the hostel children: the parents pay 200 Rs per month for their keep at the hostel, if they can afford it. Stephen shared with us particularly about this thirteen-year-old girl at the hostel whose parents are poor and are having a difficult time paying this amount. It would be a great help if this girl could be sponsored by someone. She has two more years of school left. 200 Rs times 12 equals 2400 Rs per year, divided by 22 equals SGDll0 divided by $1.60 equals U.S. $68.75 per year or U.S. $137.50 for the two years! Later that week, someone was trying hard to sell us a pair of ruby earrings with a Star of India. I told Grandpa I'd rather sponsor an orphan or help this girl than to have another pair of earrings.

Back to Sunday morning's church service. Grandpa preached from 1 Peter 2:1, 2. Stephen did the interpreting. The people in attendance were his children, the children from the hostel, and also men, women, and children from the village. While Grandpa was preaching, a man walked in, picked up a child, and walked out. Evidently this child drifted in out of curiosity, and the father didn't want him there. After the church service there were people with special needs and sicknesses who asked for a special prayer. This happened a lot in India.

We had dinner by Stephen's house; it was rice, chicken, and a banana. Stephen's parents were there also. After the lunch, we had to walk down to the parents' house, which is in the same village. On Sunday, the village town is full of garlic. The harvesting of garlic is done once a week, and Sunday is the day it is brought into town, sacked, and sent off to market, or perhaps shipped somewhere (maybe Singapore). Stephen's brothers and sisters with their spouses were all at the parents' house and much to our surprise, they had garlands for us. They served a bottle of pop and cookies and gave each of us a souvenir handkerchief.

We went back to our room at the hospital, tried to catch a quick nap, and were ready again by 4:00. We stopped in at another interesting home. At the conference we met a doctor of acupuncture, his wife, and their two children, who live with the doctor's grandparents. This doctor is the son of his father's first marriage. The doctor's mother died when he was young, and he was taken care of by his grandparents. The doctor's father remarried but the son (doctor) continued to live with the grandparents. The couple (doctor's father and his second wife) had two sons who are grown up now, and just recently, after they had been married for twenty years, they had a baby daughter. The father works for a shipping company, so he is gone from home a year or two at a time. When the father gets to Madras, the family (doctor's stepmother and stepbrothers) will meet him there to spend some time with him. Anyway, the acupuncture doctor wanted us to stop by. If I remember right, I believe the grandfather was a dentist. They have a little chapel room built off from the house.

It was time again for the chapel service at the hospital. Grandpa spoke from John 14:27 on peace. Angelia and I were sitting in the back of the chapel (everyone sits on mats on the floor, but along the back of the chapel are three steps where we sat) and there was a young boy sitting there who just stared and stared at us. I assume he was a patient at the hospital. He kept sliding closer and closer to Angelia, and when there was a blackout, Angelia thought he might try getting at her bag. It was getting a bit uncomfortable, so I motioned to him to sit down a step lower, which he caught on to and did.

And then the strangest experience of all. After the service they asked for Angelia and me to come to the front as well. So Grandpa kind of motioned for us to come, not knowing what was in store for us. What was happening was these patients wanted us to offer a special prayer for them. They were dividing the group up with each one of us having a group. Angelia snuck out. I prayed with my group, realizing that many are unbelievers, so the prayer was more that if they are God's elect, that he would work in their hearts to convict them of their sins, bring them to repentance, and give them the joy of salvation in Jesus Christ, and then also for patience in time of suffering, etc. When I finished, Ebenezer, one of the conference men who spent quite a bit of time with us, said, "Not so long, just a short prayer." I thought I was praying with the whole group, but all these women with their newborn babies, and others with diseases, wanted their own special prayer.

I'm still trying to sort it out. The prayer was similar for each one; if they were able to understand what was being said, I'm not sure they would be satisfied. We wondered, Why? What is it? What do they think? Do they think we are some holy people and perhaps we can bring some healing or blessing to them? Only the Lord knows. If it is his will that their hearts are touched by the Word, then the seed has been sown.

It rained hard during the service and our shoes had been left outside so they were full of water by the time we got out there. We had our dinner that night by the woman (the stepmother of the doctor of acupuncture) with the baby daughter. We found it a bit strange that in the homes to which we were invited for meals, the people did not sit down and eat with us. It felt so funny just to be sitting there with the three of us and whoever accompanied us, eating alone and the people waiting on us. But this again is Indian culture: they are very hospitable and kind and want to be sure that you have plenty, keep the water glass full, etc.

Monday morning. We had about a half day left before leaving for the airport in Madurai. We had breakfast in the home of James (the chaplain at the Christian Hospital), his wife Naomi, and their two young daughters. Although they are in the process of building a new home, their present place is the smallest home we were in. You have to duck down to get through the doorway, the first room is a tiny kitchen, and the other room (small) is for everything else.

We sat around a table with six or seven people. (Roselin, the single mother who runs a kindergarten, was there also to help Naomi.) They brought on a feed like you wouldn't believe, and it was delicious! (It made me feel like the meals I prepare for the Tuesday morning prayer breakfasts in Singapore aren't much.) We each had three poori puffs (an Indian bread) with the special potato sauce that goes with it, Bombay toast (known to you as French toast), rice cake (idli) with white sauce, papaya, and then there was some special drink too that was really good. (We had had enough to last the entire day, and we still had lunch coming up by Dr. George from the Christian Hospital. Oh, dear!)

Our next stop was by Paulraj's house to meet his family. Interesting. You enter from the village road, and there is a courtyard with rooms off from the courtyard. The oxen are kept in the courtyard. The parents were hoping we would come on Sunday, and now it was Monday morning, and the father felt so bad that he had to go to work and wasn't able to meet us. His mother expressed how happy she was to meet us and how thankful she was for her son and her wish that he may pursue his desire to be a pastor. A very sweet woman, still quite young, in her forties. Paulraj would interpret for us what his mother was saying. Her marriage was arranged when she was born, and she started living with her husband when she was twelve years old! Her first child, Paulraj's sister, was born when she was fifteen! She was twelve; the husband was twenty-seven when they married!

We had to stop in by Stephen's neighbor. That was supposed to be on Sunday but Stephen forgot. He would be hurt if we didn't come. The neighbor wasn't well at the time; he just had eye surgery the week before but he was in church on Sunday morning. He is just beginning to show interest in the Christian faith but the rest of the family are Hindus. He is a trader in garlic.

Next we had to meet Dr. George at the hospital. We had to wait a few minutes because there was an emergency surgery that morning. A man came in with a piece of metal embedded in his abdomen. While we were there, they wheeled him out, or should I say, tried to wheel him out. Actually, it was dragging the gurney across the floor;

the wheels were no longer round but worn down flat. When they got to the door, two men picked up the top portion of the bed and carried him off to another building.

Okay, Dr. George was ready, so his driver came around with his station wagon to take us to his house. His house was not elaborate as you think of doctors' houses, but it definitely was the best we saw in India, comfortable, nice, and clean. His wife and daughter prepared a beautiful meal of rice, chicken, mutton, meatballs, and dessert. Dr. George ate with us (Stephen, Angelia, Grandpa, and myself) and visited afterward in the front room with us. Everyone else was in the background: his wife, daughter, son (also a doctor), daughter-in-law, grandchild, and maid. Dr. George is an interesting person, very committed to sharing the gospel, and also to the medical profession and his desire to help people.

En route to Madurai we had to make one more stop at a pastor who wanted to attend the conference but couldn't because there was another conference the same weekend from his denomination. By his place they have their home and a separate building for the church. Recently they had some difficulty with their neighbors over property. It seems the neighbors were infringing a bit on their property, and when they were approached about it, the neighbors (Hindus) became angry and beat the pastor and his wife. The pastor had to have fourteen stitches on his head.

We hired a taxi for the trip to the airport, and the three men who went along took the taxi back to the village. While we were waiting there, Philip and Pastor David Monoharan came by yet to say goodbye. They had traveled down by bus and were going to take the bus back home again. Too bad the taxi had just left—they could have caught a ride.

All our contacts were finished and we were on our own. We had arranged to stay in the same hotel in Madras where we were before, and the hotel van would be there to pick us up. Sure enough, there the man was with a sign reading "Kortering." Super! It was already 9:30 and the next morning's flight was at 6:40 so it was another short night.

On Tuesday we flew from Madras to Delhi and then had a connecting flight to Agra. All our flights on Indian Air were good: left on time, arrived on time. In Delhi we only had fifty minutes to make the connection, but it worked out fine.

Having stayed at a Great Value Hotel in Dehra Dun, we chose Great Value in Agra. It wasn't as nice but still acceptable. The restaurant was small, only four tables, and whenever we ate we were the only ones there.

Tuesday afternoon we took a little walk in the neighborhood of the hotel and were instantly besieged with touters; you get your fill real quick with that. You'd like to say, "Leave me alone." The only way to escape was to get into a vehicle. We got an auto to take us for a ride past the Taj Mahal and Red Fort without going into these places. We planned to do that on Wednesday. The driver was an older man, probably in his fifties, and he showed us around a bit. We arranged for him to drive us around all day on Wednesday, and he showed up just as planned at 8:00.

After an omelet breakfast, we were on our way for sightseeing. At both the Taj Mahal and Red Fort, we engaged a tour guide. We decided it would be quite meaningless just seeing these places without any explanation. The construction of these places is massive. The Taj Mahal took twenty-two years to build and they had twenty thousand workers! Many precious stones are embedded in the marble. Somehow these things just seem so out of place in such a poor country. Agra itself is a city just like the rest of India. You would think that they would capitalize on all the tourists coming in and improve it. They do have plenty of souvenir shops, jewelry, and rugs.

The driver knew a good restaurant where we could have lunch. After driving around some more and making a few more stops, we had him bring us back to the hotel around 3:30. Angelia and I finished up what little packing we had to do and spent some time reading while Grandpa was using every free moment he had in Agra getting his report ready on his handy little palmtop computer. That was really worthwhile—nice to come home and have it all finished!

Look at me sitting here, keying all this stuff in by the hour at home.

Thursday morning and our sights were on home once again. We left for the airport around noon and arrived in Delhi about 4:30. Then we were in for a long wait: our flight on United was scheduled to leave at 2:15 a.m. and Angelia's was still later, at 3:40 a.m. So what do you do in an airport? I think Angelia and I looked through the one and only gift shop three or four times. We had to wait in the lounge area until three hours before flying off and there wasn't even a restaurant there, only a coffee stand and sandwiches.

Angelia had a direct flight to Singapore and arrived home at noon on Friday. We had a ten-hour layover in Hong Kong and finally arrived home at midnight. We were very much surprised when we saw quite a group from CERC at the airport to welcome us back home at that hour of the night. Pastor Cheah Fook Meng and Lee Choo gave us a ride home. There was yet another surprise for us: Hooi Im (a friend from FERC living near our place) and her maid, Anik, had come to the house and mopped all the floors. Dear me, what sweethearts! It was so nice that we didn't have to do that first thing Saturday morning.

Home, Sweet Home

What a wonderful time we had! Thanks be to God for his loving protection and guidance over us! As we prepared for the trip, there were some apprehensions as to how we would be able to handle everything. As plans were made, we experienced every step of the way that the Lord was opening the doors for us to go so there was no question left in our minds but that it was his will for us to make the trip. We saw a lot more than the average tourist sees when going to India. We got a good feel of life in India, being with the locals, etc. Certainly it was a trip we will always remember.

The Christians with whom we came in contact are a delightful people. We found them to be loving, friendly, hospitable, willing to share with us what little they had. How we wish that we were able to speak their language so we could communicate better with them and get to know them in a more personal way. The bond of faith unites so quickly and strongly that it's difficult to say goodbye. They are happy and do not complain about their poverty. I'm wondering how many of us could exist on their level. These people can come out of their village homes looking so clean and neat. The Indian women look very attractive in their colorful saris.

India as a country is dirty. There are garbage heaps along the roads everywhere with pigs wallowing in the filth. Surprisingly, the stench is not overwhelmingly obnoxious. The main roads are paved, some wide, some narrow. The village is all dirt and sand and the children are dirty from their play. It's not uncommon to see small naked children running around. People, children and adults, relieve themselves whenever and wherever they please. It's crowded: people, people, and more people. You don't know who you can trust so you just live cautiously wherever you are, hanging on to your bags and making sure that your group stays together—you wouldn't want to lose anyone in the people jam. But the countryside and the mountains are beautiful, God's wonderful creation, and it's refreshing to behold that in India as well.

Money: in a poor country, money just doesn't seem to make sense. By our standards, it's worth so little. For U.S. $100, we received 3,900 Rs. There are people who work hard all day long, toiling under the hot sun, and receive 1,000 Rs a month. Then there are others, like the shoe polishers, who want to charge 400 Rs for a few minutes' work. They don't need a lot of customers to earn their keep that way. The tour guides at the attractions set their price, and tourists are willing to pay it because it sounds so cheap. The auto driver in Agra was willing to take us around for the whole day for 150 Rs. He did a good job so we gave him 200 Rs, but that's only about $9.00 in Singapore and much less than that in the U.S. When someone works hard, you just feel you want to give them some extra. The most touching is how the Christians give for the Lord out of their meagerness: truly precious in the Lord's sight.

Now we're back in a country of wealth and abundance, but our lives have been greatly enriched. Along with the many material riches the Lord gives us comes a responsibility to use it all for his glory. May we ever be mindful of all God's children wherever they are in the midst of this world and be ready to help them in their needs.

India, 2000

Wow! What a lot of preparation went into this trip! First there was the uncertainty of whether we would also be going to Calcutta, then waiting as long as we possibly could to hear from Pastor Pallab from Nepal, and then trying to get reservations at such a late time. Our travel agent stuck right with it: final reservation made on Saturday morning, tickets delivered around 2:00, and we left for the airport at 6:15 on Saturday evening, not exactly our style of traveling.

Once again we are very thankful for this opportunity. Grandpa is looking forward to teaching the seminar and we're eager to meet up with some of the friends we already know and also to make new acquaintances.

We were hoping to leave on Monday, but all the flights were completely booked. We really didn't have the choice of delaying the trip a day or two because all the arrangements were already made for the conference to begin Monday night. Consequently, we are spending a Sunday in a hotel in Madras. We already listened to a message by Pastor Mahtani on "Ready to Give an Answer," and we'll listen to one by Pastor denHartog this evening.

What a different Saturday night! We both love a quiet Saturday night to prepare for Sunday, and here we were flying off to India. The trip from Singapore to Madras on the twentieth and the return flight to Singapore on the twenty-ninth are both on Singapore Airlines. The trip went well, excellent service and a delicious meal. We even had an ice cream bar for dessert on the plane, and I think Grandpa could have handled another one this afternoon; he said, "Wasn't that a good ice cream bar last night?" All last week we were scheduled to fly on Air India, and it wasn't until about 10:30 on Saturday morning that we found out we could go on Singapore Airlines.

This weekend we're staying at Hotel Mars. We faxed our reservation in and asked that they pick us up from the airport with their courtesy car. Our plane landed around 10:00 p.m., and we waited and waited before we could get our luggage. When we finally got outside, there was no sign of the hotel van. There were literally hundreds of men waiting to get riders. Grandpa bargained with one to take us to Hotel Mars for 100 rupees (Rs) (U.S. $2.30). Grandpa thought we were getting a taxi at that price, but this guy grabbed our two small suitcases and trotted off with us following. We walked and walked to about the farthest corner of the airport parking lot, where he led us to a tut-tut (a small three-wheel vehicle with a motorcycle engine and a two-passenger seat in back).

It was funny; Grandpa must have been tired or something because he wasn't about to pay 100 Rs for a tut-tut. He was going to make the man take our stuff out, but what would we have done, walk all the way back carrying our luggage? Finally we settled for 70 Rs. This was so out of character for your grandpa. I jokingly said to him on the way to the hotel, "What are you trying to do, bleed the poor?" The guy was pretty happy when we gave him the 100 Rs.

We were given a room without a window. Who needs a window when they're sleeping anyway? That's not too bad, but you like to have some daylight during the day, and we couldn't stand the thought of spending Sunday in a dark and dingy room, so we asked for a different room. We have a large room now, comfortable and light. Nice? That's a matter of opinion, but more than likely it's the best place we'll have on this trip.

MISSION TRIPS: INDIA, 2000

Sunday night we listened to our second service with Pastor denHartog preaching from Deuteronomy 6:3–9, the sermon he had in Loveland on my way back to Singapore last year.

Then we were going to go down for dinner and found we didn't even have a key for the room. They had moved us in the morning and didn't give us the key. Grandpa went down to inquire but they couldn't find the key either. We had three Indian men in our room scouting around to find the key. What a riot! They opened every drawer, checked the wardrobe, picked up our piles of books, etc., and even checked the portable refrigerator, inside and underneath. They were finally convinced, and while one man went to find another key, the other two men stood around inside the room.

It's a wild guess when it comes to ordering food. The only familiar item was fried rice. They accommodated us and went easy on the spices, but it was still plenty hot for me. Near the end of our meal, we saw a rat scurry across the floor. Oh well, the food was good, and India is no place to be squeamish.

It's Monday morning and we feel refreshed after a good night of sleep. We realized that what we had Saturday night in a windowless room was in reality the Lord providing the very best for us. It gets light in India at 5:00, and at least yesterday we were able to sleep until 7:00. The air-con went off last night, so we were thankful for the ceiling fan, which kept the air moving.

On Monday we left the hotel at 10:30 a.m. to catch the flight for Madurai. The trip went well, just a fifty-minute plane ride. It said "snack" on the schedule so I'm thinking a cookie, a roll, a sandwich, or a donut, but we're in India so we must adapt to Indian style snacks: rice, vegetables you can't identify, and some dessert made with coconut milk. Taste buds need a little adjusting.

We arrived in Madurai and there to greet us was Paulraj, his sister and brother-in-law, Silvi and John Ravichandran, their threeyear-old son Theophily, and Rev. Steve Poelman along with five men with whom he works. A van and taxi were hired to take us to Kumily where the conference will be. What a trip! And how would you go about describing India? Here I'd say, "A picture is worth a thousand words," but it would have to be a video.

When we go to Myanmar, you see much poverty, but India is different. Besides the extreme poverty, there are so very many people. The villages are just swarming with people. The people just flood the streets since their homes (shacks) are so very small. The villages have all kinds of little shops that set right alongside the road. Add to that cows and herds of goats walking down the roads and all kinds of vehicles, small and large, slow and fast, and you get quite an idea of the chaotic situation. No wonder all the truck and bus drivers are constantly laying on their horns.

But we saw more than the villages. We also saw beautiful India in the country. The ride to Kumily was close to five hours! Not in an air-conditioned van but one with the windows open, not the most comfortable seats, and a scorching temperature of over a hundred degrees. I thought, "You now have fully cooked, well-done grandparents." Even though you can see poverty in the country too, the view of fields and trees is beautiful. We stopped at a coconut stand along the road for a drink. They cut off the top of the coconut, give you a straw, and you can drink the coconut milk. Before coming to Kumily, we had to cross a mountain pass that was simply spectacular, although at times it can be a little scary because the roads are narrow and taking those bends with big vehicles, you wouldn't want to meet anyone.

And then we came to the spot where the conference was to be held. What a different world that is! Nothing less than purely delightful! Here we are, perched up on a mountain top, away from all the busyness of the village, where the temperature is at least twenty degrees lower and you can feel the nice mountain breezes.

This retreat is called Holiday Homes; it is owned by the government and rented out for retreats. The men are staying in a dormitory, which is a large, long room with about twenty beds on the one end and chairs set up on the other end for our meetings. We are staying in a little chalet right next door to the restaurant. It has two rooms with twin beds. Rev. Poelman has the one room and we have the

MISSION TRIPS: INDIA, 2000

other. The shower is cold water, although there is a water heater but it's only for a faucet. The drain is a bit slow so the floor stays wet a long time. If you want to use the toilet, you have to take your shoes and socks off first. But there are no complaints from us. This place is great, much nicer than we expected to have.

Paulraj made all the arrangements for the conference. Pastors from the Church of South India (CSI), including his brother-in-law, Pastor John Ravichandran, were invited, as well as men whom Pastor Steve Poelman was training in the Reformed faith. This seminar was an introduction to the doctrines of grace. Grandpa started out with a brief history: Pelagius, Augustine, Roman Catholicism, Luther, Huss, Calvin, Arminius, the Synod of Dordt. It's a big day with a number of sessions of one and a half hours each to teach the five points of Calvinism.

I just so thoroughly enjoy listening each time Grandpa teaches. It is so orderly and clear, and since I wish I could retain it all better, these refresher courses are good for me. I often think of the family because I know you would enjoy it too and it's such a thrill to see these men listening so intently.

Pastor Poelman was given a little time the next day to introduce his course entitled "The Everlasting Covenant Seminar." It's an intense five-day teaching course, which he has prepared in a booklet and transparencies. He was only able to start scratching the surface of it, but if these men are interested in holding a five-day seminar, he'd be willing to come down and teach it to them.

We had all our meals at the restaurant next door to our chalet. The food was good; for the most part it was vegetarian, although this noon we had a little beef for the grand finale. We were surprised because the cow is holy in the Hindu religion and they don't kill them, but Paulraj told us some states are stricter than others, and in South India they are allowed to have beef.

I forgot to tell you, shortly after we got to the retreat, we had to walk down to the office with Paulraj to register with our passports and visas. It was already quite dark, and as Grandpa went down the steps in front of the chalet, he missed the last step and fell on the path. The path is rough and he scratched his left wrist and broke his watchband. (I don't know if that calls for a new band or a new watch, but we're thankful it wasn't broken glasses or a broken arm or leg.) He had a scrape on his knee too, but the trousers survived without getting damaged.

It's Wednesday afternoon, 2:30, and the conference has just ended, so I have some catching up to do on my reporting.

The people love to sing, especially in their own language. When we sang in English, the volume was considerably less than when they sang in Tamil. They had a guitar and a keyboard, the keyboard was connected to an amplifier, and they had to have a little beat and rhythm when they sang; it was all very reasonable though. The men were all very orderly, nothing rowdy, very neatly dressed, and also friendly and pleasant.

About half of the men could speak English. Pastor Poelman's group of men speak Telugu so they could only understand the English of Grandpa and Rev. Poelman, as all the interpretation was in Tamil. You really marvel at the wonder when the apostles were able to speak in the different languages at Pentecost. It's just overwhelming to think of being able to learn these other languages and be able to speak them fluently. Just like the Chinese language, Mandarin, which has four different tones, so you can have the same word meaning four different things depending on the tone (our ears aren't sensitive enough to hear the difference), so these languages will have other complications.

Paulraj seems to be a very promising young man. At this point, he just reminds us so much of Rev. Titus in Myanmar—so eager to learn and so excited about the Reformed faith, he just drinks it all in. He was the interpreter so he really worked hard the whole time. He's twenty-eight years old now and has a lot of energy and zeal. Grandpa will be meeting with him this evening to discuss his future training. He is planning to attend Rev. Poelman's seminar next week.

On Wednesday night we took a walk from Holiday Homes to Kumily village. We stopped in only one gift shop to look around.

MISSION TRIPS: INDIA, 2000

On the way back we stopped at the home of one of the men who attended the conference. They couldn't speak English so the conversation had to be interpreted back and forth. The eighteen-year-old daughter, Sheba, was very cute. She was so shy; she hid her face on her mother's shoulder many times during the little stay there. When we wanted to take a photo, she had to quickly change her dress, and then it was cute, she wanted her mother to get up a minute so she could squeeze behind the chair and stand between us. They are so elated just to be able to have you visit in their home.

It's Thursday today and we were ready by 6:30 this morning for our little outing. We rode in a jeep with twelve people. Good thing we didn't have to go very far. They took us to Thekkady Tiger Reserve, which is a large lake surrounded by a forest reserve where you can watch for wild animals. We went for a two-hour boat ride, and although we didn't spot any tigers, we did see quite a few elephants, wild boars, bison, antelope, and many, many birds. We had such a nice, relaxing time. We were so surprised to see so many people there already at 7:00. The likelihood of seeing more animals is early in the morning or in the evening. It's 104 years ago that they built the dam, and we saw where these monstrous pipes go down the mountain to a power plant to supply electricity.

We came back from the outing and had our breakfast around 10:30. We left Holiday Homes at noon and now we are in Uthamapalayam. We're staying at the E.A.J. Rest House on Cumbum Road. We are once again in hot country and can we ever feel it, but it's a dry heat so we aren't perspiring as much as in Singapore. This is a cute little place along the main road with about eighteen very small guest rooms. You enter the room and there are two twin beds right next to each other and up against the wall on the other side. The pathway is the width of the door and there's about that much room at the foot end of the bed as well. Then there's the bathroom consisting of an Eastern toilet, some buckets, and a couple water spigots; no sink, no mirror. I'm thankful it is all nice and clean. And yes, we're managing just fine. No air-con either but there is a ceiling fan. Good thing we can slip the suitcases under the bed or we'd be stumbling over them. Oh yes, the pillow is as hard as a brick. It made me think of Jacob's pillow in Genesis 28:11.

Friday was a day to go out into the mountains and enjoy God's beautiful creation. Paulraj hired a taxi to take us. He went along and so did Selvam, one of the attendees at the seminar. This young man is presently working as a bus conductor and is very familiar with the route we would be taking. The views were magnificent! There were so many beautiful flowers along the roads. Don't think of roads like Rocky Mountain National Park; these roads are for the most part one lane. They sound the horn when approaching a bend and keep driving. I guess these drivers are used to the method because sometimes they also hear a horn and then know to get over.

There were acres and acres of tea plantations. What a nice sight that was. It just looked like a carpet with all those green tea bushes! We saw them harvesting too; there were around seventy women picking the tea leaves by hand. They carry a large bag on their back, and we noticed the bag strap was put on their head like a headband.

I had a slight headache in the morning and it kept getting worse. I took a couple pills after lunch, but they didn't help. It was a full-class migraine, and it wasn't much later that the vomiting began. The plan was to stay away overnight and come back on Saturday. We decided to go back to the town where we would stay overnight, get our room so I could rest, and continue on our way on Saturday. We were quite impressed with the first place they brought us, but that was fully booked already. It turned out that everything in the town was fully booked, so we had no choice but to come back to the village.

It was providential that we came back when we did. If we found out at 7:00 or 8:00 that no room was available, it would have been tough coming down in the dark. But what a ride it was anyway! Think of having a terrible headache and taking all those switchbacks; it was miserable. We saw something interesting on the way down. Men were spreading wheat on the road. They want the cars, trucks,

MISSION TRIPS: INDIA, 2000

and buses to ride over the wheat in order to sift it. We were back here by 7:30, Grandpa walked down the road for a little dinner, and I laid down. After a full night of rest, I am feeling fine again today (Saturday).

Paulraj came to our place at 10:00 and we sat under a shade tree in the back. It's all sand back there, some piles of broken bricks, some sand heaps, a little junky but that's more or less expected here. It was kind of cute, the old Indian lady who is a servant here (servant doesn't mean hard worker, she sits around quite a bit and scuffs along slowly when she moves about, but it does look like she did a fair amount of work in her life) was sitting on the sand heap drawing with her finger in the sand and then she laid down for a little rest. All she had to do was take the long scarf portion of her dress, lay it out, and she had somewhere to lay her head. It was good that we did come back last night; there were so many important things to discuss with Paulraj.

Paulraj is planning to get married. "My parents really would like to have me get married." So he was thinking and praying about it and his mind went back to Kasthuri. He was just beaming when he spoke of Kasthuri that day. There were a couple interesting things that were important to him when he considered Kasthuri; first, of course, he desired a godly wife who would truly be a help to him in his future work of ministry, she had to be younger than he, and her family must be poorer than his family. Paul's family is poor; the house is very small so if it's not raining, he sleeps outside.

We were picked up around 5:00 Saturday afternoon to go to Paulraj's house and meet the family. It was to be about a one and a half hour drive, but along the way they decided to show us the Vaigai Dam in Periyakulam because we missed out on seeing a dam on our little sightseeing trip. It was a very long dam, and along the whole front of it they have constructed a park, the largest park in South India. A section of it is the zoo. We saw one antelope in a cage and a few monkeys and then they said it wasn't worth going through because there weren't many animals. All that was in the monkey cage were a few monkeys and some trash. Wow, after being used to

Singapore's zoo, the manicured landscaping, the cleanliness, this was trashy. Parts of the park were nice though. There was a large section of land with a topographical model of South India. You could see the state and city boundary lines, mountains, rivers, etc. There were a few play areas around and then a lighted walk with steps leading to the top of the dam where we could see the lake.

We reached Paulraj's home at 7:30. Word must have been out that an American couple was coming because as soon as we got there, people started pouring in: the father's sister, cousins, even a cousin with his new wife, married on Wednesday, and neighbors. First they served us with a bottle of 7UP. Then a cousin, who is a photographer, took a bunch of pictures. Next was dinner. The custom here is to serve guests first, so a small stool was placed in front of each of us and we were served chapati and idli (Indian breads). Good thing we were familiar with the foods so we knew how to eat them, because everyone was sitting around watching us and ready to put more on our plates if we wanted it. And something else I must tell you—we were eating all week with our fingers, no silverware! Imagine that! When we were about finished eating, they served a plate to the men, and when the men finished, the women ate what was left over.

They had a gift for us, a replica of the Taj Mahal enclosed in a glass case. I'm sure that was selected with the greatest of care and now we'll have to be careful to get it home in one piece. They also gave me a garland of jasmine flowers. We stayed until 9:15 and arrived back at our abode at 10:40. Paul told us there were things the parents wished to talk about with us but there wasn't opportunity because so many people were around. I guess we'll just have to handle that through Paul.

It is Sunday today and we were picked up at 8:00. We went first to Paul's sister's house for breakfast and had potato poori and an idli. After breakfast we went with an auto to Annamalayanpatty, about fifteen minutes away (an auto is a three-wheel scooter with a seat in back for two or three persons and another person can share a little space of the driver's seat). Grandpa preached in a Lutheran church

MISSION TRIPS: INDIA, 2000

there. It was a long, narrow church building and the people all sat on the floor. We were quite surprised, the people just kept coming (150 to 175) but my guess is that 85 percent were women and young people, 10 percent children, and 5 percent men. When we asked about this later, we learned that the men have to work in the fields, earning only 50 Rs a day; if they don't work, their family doesn't eat. I had a chair to sit on (there were only a few chairs around).

I just have to tell you about this cute girl sitting close by me; she was probably about thirteen years old. She kept turning around to look at me. I smiled at her, and she smiled back. Then throughout the whole service she kept looking back too. I just looked at Grandpa but could see her from the corner of my eye. Pretty soon she was fingering my skirt, and all this time she was moving closer and closer to me. Then I thought my purse, which was on the floor, was in her way, so I picked it up and put it on my lap. The bottom of the purse was a bit dusty so she tried to wipe it off. Then before long, she was resting her head against my knee. She was such a sweetie with her dark skin and gleaming white teeth. I was looking forward to after the service when I could show her a little special attention, but then I had to go up to the front and I didn't get to see her again.

Grandpa preached from the last verses of Romans 8, "Who shall separate us from the love of Christ," etc. After the service there were some announcements. Then we saw something we had never seen before: poor people who don't have any money to put in the offering will take some vegetables from their garden to church. Members of the church will buy these vegetables and the money is placed in the offering. The widow's mite?

Then they called me up to the front. They had to introduce Grandpa and me, we each had to make a few comments, and then they garlanded us with a shawl. After that we met with the women's fellowship. Grandpa made a few remarks on "Be careful for nothing; but in every thing by prayer" etc. from Philippians 4:6. There were several prayer requests: just last week a father of three children died suddenly of a massive heart attack, a fourteen-year-old boy already had surgery to remove one eye and now is having problems with the other eye. After the meeting, several women came forward and requested special prayer for themselves. One lady has a diseased foot, another had a heart problem, etc., etc.

Finally it was time to leave the church. We walked to the home of the lady whose husband died. There is one son, nineteen, who is studying to be a teacher. During the school year he is away from home. She also has two daughters. The responsibility of the family will fall upon this young son, and his situation will be much like Paulraj's, but in the meantime according to their culture, the oldest brother of the man who passed away should assume responsibility for them. Then we stopped by John Ravichandran's sister's home for a short visit, and finally could go back to our room for some rest.

Paulraj came at 5:00 so we could spend some more time discussing things with him. There was going to be a prayer meeting at John's house that night, but we had to make a few stops on the way. The first stop was at the home of Christian doctors, a husband/wife team who run a clinic. Everyone around here seems to be a relative or a relative of a relative and likes to have you pay a visit in their home. The doctors talk to their patients about Christ when they treat them. From the conversation we learned that they are charismatic, although they didn't know the word when Grandpa used it. It was only after he mentioned faith healing and speaking in tongues that they said yes, that's what they believed in. It was neat how Grandpa talked with them, quoting Scripture to show them that this was not what the Bible teaches.

Then we had to pay a short visit at the home of the pastor of the church where Grandpa had preached. He had already gotten feedback that the people really appreciated the morning message. Finally we got to John's house, thirty minutes later than scheduled.

I'll first tell you about the situation there and then I'll tell you about the meeting. John Ravichandran is the brother-in-law of Paul, married to Paul's oldest sister. John and his wife have two boys, three and nine. John is a pastor in the CSI (Church of South India). Many years ago there were missionaries from various denominations in India. When all the missionaries were ordered to leave India, the churches combined to form CSI and CNI (Church of North India). The situation is changing now again with various denominations in India. John and many of his minister and missionary friends are interested to learn more of the Reformed faith.

John has two married sisters and one married brother. In the house where they live, the parents, two single brothers, and John's younger sister's family live on the ground floor. The two brothers are twins, twenty-eight years old. When they were two years old, they both had polio. They received injections, but too much was given, and both sons now have the same affliction: their legs haven't grown, perhaps they have in length a bit, but they are very short, and the legs are as thin as a small child's. They are unable to walk and get around on their hands and knees. They are very agile; they come up to a chair and can just hoist themselves up on it. From the waist up they are quite normal, only short.

They're both good-looking, graduated from university with a degree in economics, first in their class, but their real interest is in Christian music. They play several instruments, didn't take lessons but play by ear, and give performances for which they are paid. They both attended the seminar. They are handicapped, but it was neat to see them interact with everyone; they certainly don't hold back. What an evidence of God's sustaining grace in difficult situations. They're both so happy and cheerful.

John's family has two rooms upstairs and an open porch area. It's on the porch where they have the prayer meeting.

The village is made up of many relatives. John's father has five brothers. When sons marry, they settle in the village where they were born, whereas the daughters will move to their husband's village. With descendants of six brothers in a village, there are lots of cousins. I know my mother would say, "Oh, how gezellig." (That's a Dutch word meaning pleasant and cozy lifestyle.) The group that gets together on Sunday night is mostly relatives and a few other neighbors. There was a lot of picture taking. John's mother was standing next to me; she is so short, she could fit under my arm. Cute lady.

Grandpa spoke last night from 1 Peter 1:3, "Begotten us again unto a lively hope." Then he closed with a prayer, but afterward others came forward for their own special prayer. We're still trying to figure that out. When Grandpa prays with them individually, they aren't able to understand the language, but when he prays with the whole group, it is interpreted. This was also the case on our previous visit; it means something special to these people when you pray with them alone.

We saw something interesting in the village on Sunday. A man goes around through the village doing ironing. He has a cart that he pushes down the streets and stops by the homes to iron. The bottom of the iron is about three inches deep and inside are hot coals to heat the iron. That way it is completely portable and he doesn't need electricity. He was doing up a shirt at the time and you could tell he had plenty of experience; it looked very neat.

Four times I was given a lei of jasmine flowers. I expressed appreciation and delight each time I received them. They do smell very nice so it's true that I do like them, and perhaps knowing that, they gave more to please me. They don't last very long at all. Many of the Indian women put them in their hair and the flowers would just last for the evening. I had one Thursday night when Paul's sisters came to visit, Saturday night by Paul's house, Sunday night at the home prayer meeting, and this morning when we went to someone's house for breakfast before leaving for the airport. I guess I forgot to mention that they also garlanded Poelman, Grandpa, and me at the conference. They purchased leis of roses on the way up to Kumily. They were kept in the bag overnight and presented the next day. It was so funny, when they put them on us, all the petals started falling off, and the floor was covered with all these petals. We couldn't keep them on because of this but they sure did smell good.

We were invited to John's cousin's house for breakfast before

MISSION TRIPS: INDIA, 2000

setting off for the airport on Monday morning. His wife prepared such a big meal, and I tried to put that into our setting and could hardly imagine preparing a meal like that at 8:00 on Monday morning. We had potato poori, idli, cubed beef, one-egg omelet, some Indian crispy bread, and coffee. It was all so very delicious, and after their feeding us like that, it sure feels strange to leave so quickly.

After that it was time to get on our way back to the airport in Madurai, about a three-hour drive. All the drivers we've had have been excellent; they really have to be sharp. We didn't have a real long wait in the airport itself, but once we got on the plane, we had a two-hour wait without moving away from the building. Did you ever hear of a plane not being able to take off because the runway was too hot? It didn't matter to us because we had a long wait in Madras before taking off for Singapore. Finally we were able to leave, and we arrived in Madras at 4:00 p.m.

Our flight out is scheduled for 11:20. We weren't able to check in until 8:00, and talk about a bare-bones airport, this one is! We were sitting in this waiting room, Grandpa working on his report and me figuring out the financial report, when the lights and fans went off. The lights came on again quite soon, but we sat several hours without fans and about roasted.

It's 11:00 and they still haven't announced boarding, so it looks like we might get a bit late. Okay, all is set, and we're on our way around midnight. We arrived in Singapore about 6:00 a.m. and were home by 7:00.

India and Singapore—two different worlds. From a dirty, poverty-stricken country to a clean, rich country. But in both countries God has his people, and we are so grateful that we may know them and love them in the Lord.

And so another trip is completed. We truly are thankful that the Lord has kept us healthy and has given us safety in our travels. Do continue to pray for God's children in India and Myanmar. They do not have much of this world's goods, but they have true spiritual joy, which is of much more value.

India, 2002

We are soon to venture off on a trip to India, the Lord willing, for a seminar to be held at Holiday Homes in Kumily, Kerala State. Cory Griess arrived by our home in Singapore early on Wednesday morning, January 9, and Elaine Bos came early the next day. On Thursday morning we went to the India High Commission to apply for our visas. Pastor Cheah and Mohan will also be along on this trip. Visas were subsequently approved and tickets were picked up on Friday. We're all going to travel light, just a backpack for each and then a few boxes of things to distribute.

On Monday morning, January 14, Kam Loon from FERC fetched us and Pastor Cheah came by as well. We were all at the airport shortly after 6:00. We didn't encounter any problems at Changi Airport; we checked in our three boxes and had plenty of time to have a bite at Burger King before making our way to the boarding gate. Kam Loon read a psalm and prayed with us before saying goodbye. At security they just weighed a couple of our backpacks and we were on our way.

The first lap of the journey was Singapore to Madras (Chennai is the new name for Madras). We had a little waiting time in Chennai and then carried on to Madurai, where Paulraj, Kasthuri, and Paul's brother-in-law, John Ravichandran, were waiting for us. They had hired a small van for the four-hour trip to Kumily.

It's impossible to adequately describe the sights and sounds of India. What a ride and what an eye-opener for Cory. Just the week before was the first time he was out of the United States, and now in a third-world country! The shock wasn't so great for Pastor Cheah and Elaine as they had both been to Myanmar before, but India is different. It's neat having Mohan with us. Mohan is an Indian-Singaporean; he's been to India many times, understands much more of the culture, and can understand and speak Tamil, which is a tremendous advantage.

MISSION TRIPS: INDIA, 2002

The ride was so very interesting, you hardly dare to blink your eyes and a few extra eyes would be handy—can't you just picture us turning our heads this way and that whenever someone points something out. "A picture is worth a thousand words" is so true! To the people there, this is where they live and their activities are the everyday way of life, but to us it is all so strange. The villages are crowded with people, people, people, some of whom are going about their work, others walking here or there, and others just sitting or hanging around.

To add to the confusion, the traffic is atrocious. There are no lanes on the road; you just go wherever there happens to be room. That's one thing yet; besides that they drive quite fast. Drivers use their horns constantly. Actually it's quite interesting, after observing them for some time you catch on that they really are considerate drivers. Sounding the horn signals a person to step out of the way without their having to turn their head to look; it signals another driver to please give a little more passing room. It's funny how they hurry up to pass something and we're all holding our breath wondering if the driver will make it. There is so very much to see in the villages and everything spills out into the road: cows, herds of goats, sheep, autos (three-wheeled), trucks, buses, and people.

We were riding along and noticed a small dead pig on the road and birds pecking at it. There was also a live pig making his way across the road, and our driver braked to avoid hitting it. The motorcycle behind was following too closely and rammed into the back of our vehicle. The driver of the motorcycle wasn't hurt badly, but he jumped around for a while holding his leg. We were really surprised when men just came from everywhere, all jabbering away and talking through each other. They were actually trying to settle things among themselves. We all stayed inside the van to avoid bringing attention to ourselves: see Westerners and they would probably demand more rupees. The deciding factor was whether the motorcycle would still run, and it did, so the settlement was 100 Rs (U.S. $2). Everyone was satisfied, and we were on our way again. This is what you would call a community trial with justice on the spot. Elaine and I observed that the driver slowed down a bit after that.

We did stop at a stand along the road to get a stretch and a drink of coconut milk. They cut the top from a coconut and give you a straw with which to drink the milk. It was like a little family enterprise with women and children handling it. They didn't want us to take a picture because "the last time when someone took a picture of us, we had some bad luck in the family."

The seminar was held at Holiday Homes in Kumily, which was the same place as the seminar in 2000. There are two bedrooms in each chalet, so we shared a chalet with Elaine, and Pastor Cheah, Mohan, and Cory shared another chalet. The meals were served in the restaurant, which is a part of the "resort." The men attending the seminar slept in the dormitory, which is one large room with many single beds. During the day they shoved the beds to one side of the room so we could hold the seminar in the same room but on the other end.

Each session of the seminar began with singing. They love to sing; they are enthusiastic and sing loudly. John Ravichandran's twin brothers played the keyboard and drums, and those are amplified as well. They sang mostly Tamil songs but there were a few English choruses. The men don't hesitate to get up and sing a solo.

There were approximately thirty men present at the seminar. Some of the men are pastors; some are church workers or helpers. Pastor Cheah had the opening devotions on Hebrews 11:13–16. He developed the idea of the life of a pilgrim as a journey, with the eye of faith set upon our heavenly home. There were two teaching sessions that day: Grandpa had the first session in the morning on the importance of the church and Pastor Cheah had the second session in the afternoon on the gathering of the church. The rest of the afternoon was set aside for Q&A.

On Wednesday Mohan used the book of Habakkuk for devotions. For chapter 1 he explained "Wondering and Worrying," chapter 2 with "Watch and Wait," and chapter 3 with "Worship and

MISSION TRIPS: INDIA, 2002

Witness." Other teaching sessions were on the keys of the kingdom and assessing a faithful church. In addition to this, Paulraj gave a critique on the charismatic movement.

While at the seminar, we did catch on to some definite Indian culture. The first time we were in India, we were appalled at all the interruptions. It was the same way this time, so they really are not being rude but rather it is just accepted behavior in India. (True at the seminars, but it was also the case with the motorcycle episode, everyone talking through each other.) There were a few Pentecostals in the group who were not shy; we appreciate it if they come to listen and learn, but when they become argumentative, it distracts from the message of the seminar. For the most part, however, the men are all eager to learn and appreciate the instruction.

Paulraj was the interpreter, and it was a struggle for him not to become involved in the explaining. This was true especially in the Q&A. There would be a question from the men, and Paulraj would want to step right in and answer it, rather than simply interpreting the question for Pastor Cheah or Grandpa. Finally this had to be pointed out to him so the pastors could have the opportunity to answer.

The food at the seminar was good, sometimes a bit hot on the spice side. A couple mornings we had toast and omelet. Some Indian foods we had were poori (an Indian bread that comes with a potato sauce, which you scoop up with the bread—this one soon became a favorite), idli, chapati, and chicken biryani. We were always careful about taking only bottled water. Many times we were served milk coffee, and hindsight tells us that perhaps they didn't bring the local water to a boil when making the coffee, and who knows, it might have been raw milk besides. As a precaution, we always stay away from any milk products in third-world countries, and we only eat fruit that can be peeled.

One night we walked to the village of Kumily to do a bit of shopping. As we walked along through the town, we went past the shop where I bought some things two years ago, and the man standing by the door recognized me and asked us to come in. We all bought some souvenirs in Kumily. Sometimes we give familiar U.S. names to foreign places, for example, Kumily is Estes Park in Colorado. This gives you a little idea of what it is like.

The seminar finished up on Thursday, and after some of the men started on their way home, we still were able to go to the Thekkady Tiger Reserve (our second time there but the first time for the others). They take you for a boat ride on a reservoir and you're able to see different animals that come out of the forest. That particular day we saw elephants, wild boar, bison, jackals, sea otter, and lots of beautiful birds. The guide on the boat said they spot about six tigers a year, so it wasn't surprising that we didn't see any. The ride was from 4:00 to 6:00 and the weather was ideal for it.

We had dinner at Holiday Homes, the spiciest meal of all (all our mouths and lips were burning and tingling). After dinner we set off yet to Uthamapalayam (John Ravichandran's village). Along the way the driver stopped in a village to buy something, and while we were waiting in the van, a man came up to the window where Cory was sitting in the front seat. You learn that you just have to ignore that kind of stuff; more than likely they are looking for a handout. When he didn't get any response from Cory, he walked around to the other side of the vehicle, reached in and took the water bottle that was setting on the dashboard, took a drink, and set it back.

Our place for the next few nights was Deen Lodge in Uthamapalayam. Pastor Cheah and Mohan were there for only one night and shared a room. Elaine and Cory each had their own room and Grandpa and I had another room. We did not splurge on lodging here. The rate was 150 Rs per night (U.S. $3). The rooms are small: there is room for two twin beds, but they must be shoved right up against each other or you won't be able to open the door. The bathroom has a squat toilet and a spigot and bucket for showering. You find out quickly that you can manage quite well with very little. Just a short walk from the lodge is a restaurant called Singapore Mess. The food is good and also cheap.

MISSION TRIPS: INDIA, 2002

On Friday morning we had our breakfast at the home of John Ravichandran. The family lives above the house of John's parents and brothers. They have an outside stairway with a rooftop porch before you enter their home. They served the breakfast on the porch. We were just amazed at all the work they went through to serve this meal. They definitely gave it their very best! Everything was delicious; the poori, dosai, vada, idli, all these things are served with different sauces and are very tasty. The Indian breads are very nice. It still puzzles me how they can prepare all this wonderful food in their limited kitchens (any one of us would feel handicapped in their kitchens) and they carry it all off very efficiently.

After the breakfast, Pastor Cheah and Mohan left for Madurai by car and then flew to Madras. Mohan met a brother-in-law in Madras and then they had some family business to tend to in another city in India. Paulraj had arranged with a friend in Madras to show Pastor Cheah around for the day since the flight to Singapore wasn't until 1:00 a.m. on Saturday. Prior to this, Paulraj was going to confirm their reservations, so he had their tickets. When he handed the tickets back to them, they didn't check which one they had. Pastor Cheah was going to check in for his flight from Madras to Singapore and the date was incorrect: January 23 instead of January 19. Then they noticed the name was wrong as well. He had no choice but to buy another ticket. They had to get in touch with Mohan and inform him of the problem so the friend in Madras could meet Mohan at the airport on the twenty-third and hand him the correct ticket.

Grandpa had some studying to do on Friday morning, so Paulraj, Kasthuri, Cory, Elaine, and I hired a car and went for a ride for a couple hours, stopping at different places and seeing local things. This was the first time any of us had seen a rice field close up. Women were weeding the rice, so we stopped to have a look. We often have to chuckle at how we can miscommunicate. Elaine was looking at a field of rice and asked Paul if the rice grew underneath and his answer was "yes." I was looking at a different field and could see the kernels of rice growing much like wheat, so I asked if that was the rice on the stalks and the answer to that question was "yes" as well.

In the villages there are men who go around doing ironing. They have a table on wheels so they can move from house to house. The iron has a base of about three or four inches high filled with charcoal for heat. It's amazing how neatly they iron the shirts and fold them.

Another stop was at the school where Paulraj's sister (John's wife) teaches. That was so very cute—those children just melt your heart! Cory has a digital camera and he just instantly wins over the children by showing them the pictures he takes. She had the children sing a little Christian song for us that they learned in the English language.

Indian women carry a lot of things on their heads. We saw them carrying large baskets filled with greens, probably some kind of vegetable. There were some baskets setting on the ground, so Cory gave it a try and the local people got quite a charge out of that and laughed.

We saw a real India laundromat by the riverside. It was quite an operation, and I sure don't know how they keep all the bundles of laundry separate from each other. What a back-breaking job! There were women scrubbing and beating the clothes against big rocks. There was a huge pile of laundry that had been wrung out and was ready for hanging up or laying on the grass. There was a small shack where a man was busy ironing. All around were children running and playing. As soon as they see a Westerner they think of it as an opportunity to get something. They came up to us, holding out their hand, and asked, "Pen?" "Soap?" "Shampoo?" "Rupees?"

Next to the laundry business is a brick business, another back-breaking job. And these people work so hard for so little. To us their clothing looks cumbersome for the kind of work they are doing.

It was neat seeing so many new and interesting things that morning. When we got back, Grandpa joined us for lunch at the Singapore Mess.

Friday night was spent at the home of Paulraj's parents in Periyakulam. They were intending that we would all stay there overnight, but we could not imagine how all of us could sleep in that small house. First of all there are the parents and two sisters who live there, John's family (husband, wife, and two children), plus Paulraj and Kas would be there, and then the four of us. We told them we preferred to go back to Deen Lodge, and we could take the van back by ourselves after visiting; they would not have to accompany us back.

What an eventful night we had! First they dressed Elaine and me up in beautiful saris. A sari outfit comes in three parts. It has a snug, short blouse, which makes for a bare midriff (the midriff can be covered with the sari but most often is bare both in India and in Singapore), an inskirt, and the sari itself. The sari is five meters of fabric and there is a certain way to wrap it around, pleat the front, and still have a section of it to throw over the shoulder (safety pins come in handy to keep everything in place). Kasthuri knows just how to go about the whole procedure, and she had fun dressing us up. Elaine's outfit is in mauve and mine in a beautiful forest green. Grandpa and Cory were dressed in a dhoti (a man's skirt). What a lot of admiring, laughs, and picture taking. I just cannot imagine how the Indian women find them to be comfortable, it's just so much material wrapped around, but being new material, it was a bit stiff; probably it would soften up after washing it a few times.

Next we had to go upstairs to the rooftop for a special program that was prepared for us. Paulraj's youngest sister has a little ministry with the village children. About twenty-five to thirty children come each day for about one or one and a half hours (early evening, 5:00 or so). She tells them Bible stories, teaches them songs, does some crafts, etc. She had small groups singing special numbers, a few children who did cultural dances, little recitations, etc. It was really sweet and some mothers of the children were also there. I do believe it was a big event for that little village. Other people were watching the whole thing from their rooftops.

Then it was time for the dinner. We sat on a bed with a small stool in front of us and Cory sat on the floor. In India the host family does not eat with the guests; they give all their time to serving you, filling your cups with more coffee, and bringing on more food.

Everything was prepared very nicely: chicken biryani, chapati—a generous meal. After we finished eating, the rest of the family ate their meal. We stayed for a short time after the dinner, and then it was time to get on our way again. The ride to Uthamapalayam would take at least an hour.

Paulraj's parents are in the process of arranging a marriage for his twenty-three-year-old sister. It is being arranged through a third party, a man who lives across the walk from them. This man knows the prospective groom's family and the prospective bride's family. Paul and Kasthuri were planning to come to Singapore in early February, and they were hoping to have the marriage solemnized before their departure from India. The sister and family have not met the man and all they know about him is what the neighbor told them. To us this arrangement sounds very scary, and how could you be excited about committing the rest of your life to someone you haven't even met? It sure seems like they have to have a lot of trust in the neighbor who is making the contact.

They are in the process of working out a dowry. The bride's family gives the dowry to the groom's family. An offer was made, but before we left India, we were told that the amount was not accepted, so they had to continue to work out an agreeable sum. This would cause the delay of the wedding at least until Paul and Kas return from Singapore (August 2002), or possibly the wedding might be called off altogether, and then the parents would have to seek out another suitable man for her.

Saturday morning we had breakfast, did a bit of laundry, and waited for the others to come and join us for another little sightseeing tour. Grandpa was able to join us this time, and John, Paulraj, and Kasthuri also went along. We saw more interesting things again. Our first stop was at a huge statue of the Cali god. Cali is a fierce god who punishes; it looks very frightful. We had a cup of tea at the little roadside stand that was there.

They took us to a tea plantation where there was also a tea factory. There was some connection between the driver and a father or uncle who worked at the factory, so we could get in and have a tour. It wasn't a modern factory by any means, but they get the job done, and even though it's old, it still is efficient. We took a walk through the tea bushes on the mountainside and also saw coffee plants, pepper plants, and cardamom growing there.

We saw another river laundromat on this outing, a big operation like the one before. Then we saw a place where they were working with gravel. We had to move back quite a way because they were going to blast the mountainside. After all the waiting, we were surprised that it wasn't all that much. Women were working, picking up gravel and carrying it on their heads. The men with us said these women probably earn about 30 Rs a day, which is U.S. 60 cents.

It was nice to be on time for Saturday night. We took our dinner at the Singapore Mess again and had a relaxing evening.

Sunday morning: breakfast at Singapore Mess. Grandpa prayed that even though this was a very different Sunday for us, the Lord would use even our praying as a witness in this restaurant. After we finished eating, a man approached our table and asked what brought us to India and if we were doing missionary work. We weren't in a hurry because we didn't have to be ready until 11:00 so we talked with him for a whole hour. The man is a Muslim but is interested in understanding the Christian faith, and it was evident that he had done some reading and was searching. He had lots of questions; he couldn't understand how the Christians have one God but talk about three persons. We all thought he was a worker at the restaurant, so we were surprised that he could take so much time, but then he told us that he had just come there to eat.

There wasn't a service for us to attend on Sunday morning, so we arranged for Paul and Kas, John's family, and his parents to come to Deen Lodge at 11:00 after their service, and we had a little service of our own outside in the shade behind the lodge. They furnished us with some lunch that they brought along from home.

Grandpa preached in a village church in the evening. We made several stops on the way to the village. One was at the Crow temple.

We learned that each Hindu god has a means of transportation. The transportation of the god at that particular temple was the crow. The temple was quite run down and there were some elderly unkempt people milling about, perhaps beggars. A couple interesting things in the courtyard: there was a tree with many small cloth cradles in it, and we were told they were placed there by childless couples who desire to have a child. In another place there was a branch with many strings attached: single girls who desire to get married put them there. They say that the cloth cradles help them to conceive, and after girls put the string on the branch, they manage to get a husband. We saw a crematorium, outdoor style, which was just sand pits in which they placed the dead body and burned it—quite different from the crematoriums in Singapore.

There was a fairly large group who came for worship that Sunday night. The service was held in a Church of South India (CSI), and John was in charge of it; actually he is responsible for about seven of these small churches. There were two old men, one with a drum and another with some kind of horn instrument, who were playing before the service, quite loudly. Grandpa preached that night on Daniel in the lion's den. After the service they presented us with leis, and pictures were taken.

The origin of the CSI church is quite interesting. You can read about the CSI in the previous chapter. There are many theological differences among the pastors in the CSI. John Ravichandran is a CSI pastor, but he and many of his pastor friends desire to grow in an understanding of the Reformed faith and appreciate all the instruction that is given at the seminars.

Monday morning we had to prepare to leave Deen Lodge and Uthamapalayam. We stopped in Periyakulam for breakfast by Paul's parents before making the trip to Vellore. That was our final goodbye to them for this trip. Each time we see them, they give us some flowers to put in our hair, and this time was no exception, so Elaine and I had flowers on the trip to Vellore.

Riding along, we saw many children dressed in uniforms going to school. Some children were brought to school in a horse-drawn carriage (reminded us of the Amish).

We made a stop in Trichy. There's a temple there, but to reach it, you must climb about 360 steps. We all did. That makes for a hot climb, but it was a nice lookout over the city. We rode past another crematorium where they actually had the fire burning.

It was about lunchtime; Paul's family had packed some lunch for all of us, so the next thing was to find a spot where we could eat. As we were riding along, they noticed a path and drove in. Some of the men walked on ahead till they came to a driveway and asked the people who lived there if we could eat our lunch in their yard. They accommodated us and brought out mats for everyone to sit on. There was a water pump in the yard, which came in handy for washing up a bit.

After that break, we made our way to Vellore and to the home of Paul and Kas, arriving there on Monday evening. Paul and Kas have a small apartment that is attached to a larger house. People were going to move into the house, but Paul asked if they could wait until the end of the week and if we could stay in the house for a few nights. The owners agreed, so that was our accommodations for the week. The house was completely empty. Paul and Kas rented some mattresses, pillows, sheets, and pillowcases. It really worked out well: Elaine had her room, Grandpa and I another room, Cory had the kitchen, and the living room and dining room was the walkway to the bathroom. Showers were with bucket and cup, but we were used to that already. It's really a nice home with a big front porch.

By the time we were settled, everyone was tired and ready for bed. Although we hadn't taken dinner, no one was really interested in it either, so we skipped dinner that day. We didn't suffer though; there had been some snacking in the car along the way.

Some Christians live across the street from Paul and Kas, and each morning at 5:00 they broadcast some kind of religious program over a loudspeaker and it is loud! The first morning it woke all of us up, the second morning some of us heard it going on but it didn't keep us awake, and I guess eventually we'd get used to it and it wouldn't bother at all. After our first night, we did keep the windows closed so the mosquitoes wouldn't get us and that might have helped to block the noise out as well.

Tuesday morning we went to Paul and Kas's place for breakfast. She prepared such a nice American-style breakfast for us; she must have gotten up early to get it all ready. She even had some bananas—they went to buy them yet on Monday night after we had settled in. After that she brought out their wedding photograph album. We spent some time looking through that while Paul, Kas, and John went away for a short while and took their breakfast outside.

We took a little outing that day to see a fort in Vellore. There was a museum and also an old Anglican church (built by the British) where they still hold services. From there we went to see a waterfall. We thought it was going to be close by but actually it was quite a ride. We had to hike to the falls. It was a nice hike, not a smooth path by any means but certainly manageable. When we got to the lake, we waded across so that we could sit in the shade. There were some guys in the water, letting the falls go over them. Cory plunged in too and had fun, after which the other men with us did the same. Cory looked pretty white compared with all the Indians there. After returning to Paul and Kas's house, the men from Uthamapalayam started on their way back home.

On Tuesday and Wednesday evenings, Paul had to speak at the village church of one of his minister friends on the whole subject of charismaticism. We all attended the meetings but couldn't understand one word of what was being said, but at least we were there to give loyal support. It was very evident that the people really appreciated the messages, and there were many questions that were asked. The people were very friendly and they liked to gather around and shake hands. The second night many of them wanted our signatures, like we were some kind of celebrity or something.

On the way to the meeting on Tuesday night, we took something to eat at a little restaurant outside a grocery store. Cory had been

MISSION TRIPS: INDIA, 2002

so hungry for ice cream. It's funny how a person can be especially hungry for something when they know they shouldn't have it. Ordinarily going without ice cream is no big deal, but when you have to go without it, it becomes a big deal. Grandpa and Cory broke down and had an ice cream bar that night; it probably wasn't all that great but they thought it was excellent.

On Wednesday we shopped for Punjabi sets that are also called Churidar sets. A Churidar consists of three parts: pants or "ooni," the dress, and the shawl or sash. This is very typical wear and it seems to us that it would be more comfortable than the sari. Cory bought a couple and Elaine bought one.

In the afternoon we went to visit Rajastephen. He has an orphanage, and since there are several from the U.S. who are helping with the support of the orphanage, we really wanted to see firsthand what the set-up was like over there. We had met Rajastephen on a previous trip to India and have been in correspondence with him on a regular basis. In the past it has been very difficult for him to make ends meet.

He was caring for seven to ten orphans in his home. His sister runs another orphanage with more children but for her it is more of a business venture. Rajastephen's home is different: he and his wife function as parents for these children and give them the love, help, and support they need. There was a church in a neighboring village that needed a pastor and asked if he could come and help them. He agreed to that, but a couple things changed their situation on account of it. One thing was that he could not transfer the children to another school in the middle of the school term, and the other thing was that the living accommodations were not large enough for the children to live with them. He had no choice but to put the children up with his sister until such a time that he could take them back and get them in school in the village where they live. We didn't make arrangements ahead of time that we were coming to visit them; we preferred to "drop in" to get a true picture of the situation.

It so happened that Rajastephen had just gone to visit the children the day before. He told us how the children were so happy to see him again and were sad to see him leave. He promised the children that he would work on making arrangements to take them all back to live with them. Rajastephen and his wife had been married for ten years and finally were blessed with a son of their own, who was about four months old at the time we called on them. They are living in a very small apartment; the owner downstairs was kind to bring up some plastic chairs so that we could sit together on the roof of the porch. As far as we can tell, Rajastephen is completely trustworthy.

We had a nice visit with them and feel we can certainly carry on with helping them, not as a denominational thing with church collections, but more on an individual basis by those who would be interested in helping these poor people. He desires to have up to ten children to care for, the reason being that many of the expenses (rent, etc.) stay the same whether you have three, five, seven, or ten children. Food is inexpensive so if you feed a few more, it doesn't make that much difference. With income for only a couple children, it's difficult to pay the bills, whereas if there are more children with a little more income, the bills are manageable.

Elaine and I needed a little instruction for hand washing. There we were with soap and buckets of water, scrubbing away (boy, did our clothes ever get dirty!), and then Kas came and said, "Here, let me help you." She laid the towel or garment on the "toilet" floor (a bathroom is called toilet), took her bar of soap and rubbed it on, took a brush and scrubbed it, and then picked the garment up and beat it on the floor. She let Elaine and me do the rinsing. We found out that towels aren't the easiest thing to wring out by hand.

Thursday morning Kasthuri prepared breakfast for us again, and this time it was a delicious Indian breakfast. Paulraj had arranged for a friend to come over and visit with us that morning. The friend had quite an interesting story. His Indian caste is Brahmin, which is the highest caste. He was born into a rich family, the parents being doctors. He had to make a report one time in school, and it puzzled him that the person he was writing the report on lived from a certain year to another year, BC. That didn't make sense to him. How come the numbers of the years went down instead of up, and what did BC stand for? He asked the teacher what that meant, and the answer he received was that was the way the Christians made up the calendar.

He continued his search for a proper answer by studying and reading. It more or less consumed him, and his parents thought he was losing his mind and had him committed to a mental institution. He was given shock treatments and counseling, but he kept telling the doctor that what he had learned about Christ gave him true inner peace and he believed it with all his heart. The Hindu doctor told him that was simply an illusion, people only imagine that they have peace and joy in Christ. This man insisted that Christianity was different from Hinduism and that Christ is the only way. Finally the doctor advised the parents to just leave their son alone and let him go ahead in his faith as he is very sure of what he believes and will not change. This, of course, ostracized him from the family so he became an outcast.

His personal commitment is to speak to at least one person a day about Christ. He has worked in a catering service but now he desires to take a course in tailoring. He does have a bad leg as a result of some accident. A charismatic was taunting him about his faith and said if he had strong faith, the leg would be healed. His answer was that he receives the leg the way it is from the Lord and doesn't need their miraculous healing; he also felt he could serve the Lord better with his lame leg than if his leg was good. He is able to get about, can walk, can ride his bike, and is able to witness how the Lord has blessed him even through these difficulties.

After he left, we headed to town to change some money, and what a hassle that turned out to be. Paulraj thought we could just go to the bank and change however much we wanted to—"No problem"—but it didn't work out quite that easily. At the bank they said tourists generally change U.S. $200 or $250, and no way were they going to change a larger amount for us.

Paul has acquaintances everywhere, and about that time, he ran into a pastor who was Kasthuri's guardian in Vellore before they were married. This man had some connections with someone else where he could change the U.S. money into rupees. The whole process took quite a while so there was time to look around some more, we took pictures in for developing, and Cory could get a CD cut of the pictures he had taken so far so at least he had a backup of everything. Finally the man came back, but then we had to find a safe place where he could transfer the money from his bag to my bag. That place turned out to be his wife's office at the hospital where Kasthuri works, so even though we didn't get a grand tour of the hospital, I did get to see a little of it.

The pastor of the church where Paul spoke the previous two evenings was going to meet us at the house at noon. We were running just a bit late after all our waiting and got back around 12:30. We just had a short visit with him for about forty-five minutes or so. He expressed his great appreciation for the friendship he has with Paulraj and his desire to have more instruction.

It was time to pack up in the afternoon, as we had to catch the train for Madras at 5:00. We hired two autos to take us to the train depot. The train ride was a neat experience; it took about two hours. We arrived in Madras and there were more friends there to greet us. The connection was a man who was brought up in the same house as Kasthuri by this Rev. K in Salem. You will remember Rev. K as the man who was her guardian and who arranged for all her education. The name of the man who met us is Ramesh and he is in charge of the El Shaddai Children Ministries.

They took us to a hotel, but it was fully booked. From there they called around until they found an opening at the Pandian Hotel. The lobby was nice and the rooms were acceptable, although our air-con didn't work and sometimes there wasn't any hot water for showers. We took our dinner in the hotel dining room that night and also ate breakfast there the next morning.

We were picked up fairly early on Friday morning to go to El Shaddai. They had just relocated to a different place so were having some dedication service. Part of a dedication ceremony is to heat a pan of milk, so Elaine had the honors of lighting the stove and

MISSION TRIPS: INDIA, 2002

placing the pan on the burner. Later they used the milk to serve us "milk coffee." We haven't figured out what the heating of milk might symbolize, so that remains a mystery. Grandpa made a few comments and led in prayer, after which Ramesh acquainted us with the work they are doing among the Hindu children and the opportunities they have to witness to them. Sometimes they are asked by schools or groups to prepare a program on a certain theme, and they write up the program and present it.

Elaine and I had the day to spend in Madras and then we were going to fly out to Singapore at 12:50 a.m. on Saturday. There were a couple other El Shaddai workers (a man they called Jones and a young woman of twenty-something named Shanty) who showed us around for the day. Kas came along too, and Jones's brother was the driver.

Our first stop was St. Thomas Mountain, where supposedly the apostle Thomas was killed and a bone fragment encased there. As you might guess, this is Roman Catholic territory. There is also a cross there that they say Thomas carved, and for many years in the 1500s, they claim that cross bled only on December 17. When I see all this worshiping of "things," it has a striking resemblance to Buddhism. It reminds you of the catechism where it is called "an accursed idolatry."

The next stop was a prawn factory where they breed tiger prawns. The man scooped up a cup of water from the huge breeding tank and it was just loaded with tiny fish—there must be millions of prawns in that tank!

We went to the beach by the Bay of Bengal and waded in the water. Our clothes got a bit wet but we knew they would dry up quickly in the hot sun. We ate dosai at a little roadside restaurant—if there was any restaurant we would have apprehensions of, it would be this one, dark and gloomy and far from being clean, but we felt dosai would be about the safest thing to eat.

We stopped at a cottage industries store where they sell all these fancy Indian crafts at fairly high prices. Elaine and I each bought a nice candy dish, but aside from that, we just looked around.

Back at the hotel, we took showers, did our packing, and then went down for dinner, and while we had dinner, we sorted through our pictures. They were going to pick us up at 8:30 to take us to the airport, and by the time we got back down to the lobby and paid our bill, they were there. We said our goodbyes and then had a long wait until our plane was due to take off at 12:50 a.m.

Security at the airport was intense and taking a long time, going through all the handbags, carry-ons, etc. We noticed that with some they were very thorough and then toward the end, they were whipping through them a little faster. We had to walk from the final searching table out to the plane, and when we reached the plane stairs, Elaine didn't have her boarding pass. Little panic attack there but she hurried back and found it lying on the ground. We had a good flight home and managed at least to get a little sleep that night.

The trip to India was a very enjoyable and enriching experience. We were certainly mindful of the Lord's protecting care over us throughout the entire trip and are thankful for the opportunity the Lord has given to fellowship among his children in that land. Now we look forward to the arrival of Paulraj and Kasthuri in Singapore to take up their studies at Asian Reformed Theological School (ARTS). As our work in Singapore draws to a close, it is a tremendous blessing that we can see the beginning of this training in Singapore and also further developments of training in Myanmar. Thanks be to God!

I'm going to turn this over to Grandpa so he can add a paragraph or two about the weekend spent in Hyderabad before he and Cory returned to Singapore.

Hyderabad

When Cory, Paulraj, and I flew into Hyderabad on Friday evening, it struck us that the city seemed clean. It was a bit difficult to be certain because the old wreck of a car that was used to

MISSION TRIPS: HYDERABAD

pick us up had such a dirty windscreen that a person could not be sure. Besides, the six of us (Gilbert, the contact person in Hyderabad, took with him another fellow from the fellowship and the driver) were so squeezed into the small car that we were a bit hard pressed to turn our necks to actually see anything. After about a thirty-minute ride we arrived at our hotel. We agreed to drop off our backpacks in our rooms and come down for dinner, which we ate with the other fellows. There was a restaurant attached to our hotel.

Since we were all strangers and this was the first time we saw each other face to face, it was a bit stiff, but conversation soon turned to the plans for Saturday, Sunday, and Monday, the time we would be there. Once that was settled, we headed off to our rooms. We had the luxury of each one having his own room; I thought that after two weeks of travel together, we might appreciate a bit of space. Besides that, the deluxe singles were only 250 Rs a night (about U.S. $5).

But, what a hotel it was. When I got a chance to look around a bit, I couldn't believe my eyes. It was dirty, holes in the carpet, sheets a yellow-brown color that actually had dirt on them. The bathroom smelled awful, the toilet was filthy, and it made me wish we had squat toilets. There was one thing that worked, the TV of course, and that with cable. It reminded me of seeing television in the mud houses in the village.

Since it was late already, I tried to sleep. No way, not only was it dirty, it was noisy. We had rooms on the street side, with nothing but honking of horns, yelling, and street noise all night long. First, I didn't dare use the pillow, so I tried to cover my ears with my shirt. Then I just gave up and turned on the TV, thinking that maybe a little noise in the background would relax me enough to sleep; that didn't work either. I doubt I slept much all night.

Why did we put up with such a mess? When I wrote to Gilbert and asked him to book hotel rooms for us, he responded by giving us choices. He preferred this one, since it was closest to where he lived; the other one was more than twice the distance away. How can you say to a man who booked rooms for you that you refuse his choice of rooms? Missions is cross-cultural you know; that means you have to be all things to all people. So all three of us made no noise, just quietly groaned, and put up with it for three nights.

You might ask why he booked such rooms in the first place. I sure wondered while I laid, restless and sleepless, night after night. The answer came Monday morning. It was time to check out, we had finished breakfast, and we were about to spend the day with men from the fellowship. Since Grandma wasn't with us, I had the distinction of being the treasurer. So, money in hand, I stood waiting for the fellow to complete our bill.

While this painfully slow activity was taking place, lo and behold, there came about twenty men down the steps in the very same hotel. They were dressed with white shirts, wearing ties and business suits of all things. I mused to myself, "They stayed in this hotel?" What is going on here? That raised my courage considerably as I asked Gilbert when he arrived, "What are all those well-dressed men doing here?"

"Oh," he said, "I forgot to tell you, they booked the entire first and second floor of the hotel. Those floors have just been completely renovated. When I booked for you men, the only rooms I could get were on the third floor." They of course had not been renovated; he didn't have to finish his sentence, we knew very well. There was a convention in Hyderabad for pharmaceutical salesmen. They were all carrying their black cases.

The saints of the Christ Reformed Fellowship made up for the lack of creaturely comforts. They were a delight to get to know. All day Saturday, we explained to them who we (ERCS and PRC) are, and they explained their history. It led to some theological discussions, of course, and that laid the groundwork for better understanding and how we can interact with each other. On Sunday, I preached for the group and there were about four visitors from the Hyderabad Reformed Church who also joined. These men were in the process of leaving their church, pastored by Rev. Prem, due to some indiscretions that he had said and how he counseled some of them. The group that worshiped together numbered about fifteen souls.

MISSION TRIPS: HYDERABAD

There are the usual stories of personal conflict and sorrow. Gilbert's wife left him because he did not approve of her father's charismatic ways. His father-in-law is one of the most famous charismatic preachers in South India, and he bluntly told his daughter to leave Gilbert, as he represented the devil who tried to oppose him. Gilbert is taking extension courses from Asian Baptist Theological School, which is headquartered in Singapore.

There are other stories of personal struggle. We met a delightful man, Bibu, who is a brilliant fellow, studying to be a lawyer. Just to illustrate high tech in a rather poor setting, he has a computer program that allows him to scan in a book page, and the computer reads it back to him orally. That blows my mind. There was another man, Praveen by name, who teaches in a local university. He is well-read in Reformed theology and wanted to discuss issues such as common grace, free offer, supra-infra, etc. I am not sure how spiritually mature he is; he is academically very sharp.

So the visit was worthwhile; even though we had to bear with dirt, we enjoyed sweet fellowship in the Spirit. They want very much to have us send them books; Gilbert would like a computer for his studies and writings. They asked us to come again and hold a teaching seminar for them, and for others in the area who are interested. The Lord obviously has given the ERCS an interesting contact to be developed.

Hyderabad is an interesting city as well. It is the capital of Andrha Pradesh, an intellectual center, and developed economically. There is interesting history and culture, the old city, which holds one of the oldest mosques of India, and the new city that is quite modern. The population is divided equally between Muslims and Hindus, which makes for interesting cultural and religious interaction. We even had pizza on Saturday night; that is quite something for India.

Let me tell you my final story. Cory and I were having fun with Paul. Since this was the first time he was away from Kasthuri since they were married, we thought he ought to bring something special back for her upon his return. What better thing than roses? So in the airport at Hyderabad we tried to find some roses. Cory went off to try to buy some in the area of the airport. While we were sitting there, a vendor came by and we bought some from him. In the end we had about ten small roses, properly wrapped up.

Paul dutifully carried them on the plane and Cory got his camera ready to preserve the event. It was so funny. Paul handed them to Kasthuri as if they were made of ice, he literally dumped them in her hands, and she made absolutely no response, just took them and sort of brushed them aside. Later he said to her, "It was Cory's idea." In the end we are not sure whether we did him a favor or not. The only redeeming evidence is that Paul wrote in an email to me, "Am eager to come to Singapore, see you, blah-blah, and to learn more from Cory about romancing."

Though Cory was sick the last four days in India, he was a good sport, kept a firm upper lip, and bore with fever, chills, diarrhea, and all that good stuff. I'm glad he came home with me, seeing he needed medical attention. He responded well to the two days of "drip" in Gleneagles Hospital and soon was feeling much better.

India, 2006

With thanksgiving to God, we were once again privileged to visit India. We thought our trip in 2002 would be the final one to India, but since, in God's providence, we were once again in Singapore for an extended stay, the way was also opened up for us to travel to India. The purpose of the trip was to visit with Paulraj and Kasthuri in Vellore and with Rajastephen in Molasur. The visit was brief, and there was no need for us to visit tourist sites we had already seen.

We traveled with Jet Airways this time. Until recently Jet Airways was only a domestic airline within India, but now they have

MISSION TRIPS: INDIA, 2006

reached out with international flights throughout Southeast Asia. Their service will be in keen competition with Singapore Airlines, which holds an excellent reputation. We were not disappointed; the service was superb, and meals were excellent and also presented very nicely—cloth napkins, nice silverware, good dishes. The plane was a 737 with two rows of three leather seats each across the plane, and it wasn't cramped, plenty of leg room and we didn't have a third person sharing the row with us (that would be nice on the long journey from Singapore to the U.S.). Both on the way to India and on the way back, the plane was less than half full.

Paul and Kas, along with a few men (Franklin, Prem, Smith, Arockiam, and Sampath) from the Protestant Reformed Fellowship, and their son Jason, were at the airport in Chennai to pick us up. They had hired a larger vehicle from Vellore for the whole day, so the driver was waiting for us there. The culture there is to adorn their guests with a lei of roses, so they hung these beautiful leis on us. They're gorgeous and they smell so nice, but the sad thing is that the petals drop off so quickly, so the enjoyment of them is short-lived. The vehicle was not air-conditioned, so conversation was difficult while traveling with all the outside noises and the wind blowing at you.

The time difference between Singapore and India is two and a half hours (Singapore's time ahead of India's). Indian money is called rupees (INR or Rs). One U.S. dollar is 42 Rs; one Singapore dollar is 26 Rs. A calculator is a necessity when you are there. The weather was nice, quite hot in the sun, but they told us the hottest season is more April to June. Paul said that in Vellore it gets to 115 degrees Fahrenheit. Their house gets so hot during that time that they purposely keep themselves wet: he makes his shirt wet and when it dries up, he makes it wet again. They sleep on the floor (cement), and besides making their clothes wet, they also make the floor wet.

We stayed at the Millennium Hotel Complex on Katpadi Main Road. Accommodations were adequate but nothing fancy, pretty much in line with what we had before when visiting India. Sometimes we had hot water, sometimes we didn't (even when we had to shower with cold water, it wasn't icy cold). The cost was 495 Rs a night (U.S. $11.75). On the fifth floor is the Spice Garden Restaurant; we really liked that place, good food and good service. We went there quite often when different ones came to the hotel to meet with us.

They do not serve breakfast, so we had to go to the restaurant of the hotel next door for that. One time that restaurant did not have gas for cooking, so they told us about a café a little further down the road. The waiter, John, by that time was getting to be quite friendly with us, and he apologized up and down for not being able to help us that day. It turned out the café was quite to our liking, very local and it's nice to be in that environment. The café breakfast for the two of us was less than 50 Rs. We always took poori for breakfast. For poori you get two pieces of an Indian bread (Indian breads, by the way, are very delicious) and some sauce that has small pieces of potato, onion, and other things in it. You rip off a piece of the bread, scoop up some of the sauce with it, and put it in your mouth.

All eating is done with your fingers, and actually, for that kind of food, I do believe fingers work better than forks. All the restaurants have sinks where you can wash your hands afterward. Their coffee is good too; they have their own way of making it with sugar and milk so it's more on the sweet side. We enjoyed it for the week but now are back to our black coffee.

On Tuesday we went to Paul and Kas's house and met his parents (whom we had met before) and Kas's parents. Paul's father toiled very hard with a yoke of oxen and a cart during his working years, taking any job he could get to haul things (feed, dirt, households, etc.), so when we met him several years back, he already looked like an old man (he's around sixty-five years old now). Now he is retired, living in the home there with Paul and Kas, and he actually looks much better and healthier. Kas's father has had a stroke, and although he can walk and get about the house, he cannot speak. He does greet you with a very happy smile.

The four grandparents help with taking care of the children and do some of the cooking and cleaning up, etc. We could not converse

MISSION TRIPS: INDIA, 2006

with them because of the language barrier, so after meeting them briefly, they went into another room while we sat around a table in Paul's study to visit. That's when Paul told us the study could get extremely hot in the summer. They live in a small home, the ceiling is quite low, and the heat just bears down on them, even to the point of getting blisters on their shoulders. Paul and Kas have two children: Jason is three years old, and Joan is one year old.

Paul's parents have a home in Periyakulam, and during the hot season they go back to their own home to escape the heat for a month or two. They even take Jason along with them for that time.

In the Indian culture, the son is responsible for the parents and family. When girls marry, they marry out of the family and become responsible along with their husband for the husband's parents. Paul has three sisters; two are married, and each one along with her husband cares for the husband's parents. This explains why Paul's parents are there in Vellore with them, although they are well enough to live on their own.

Kas's parents are living with them as well. Kas has one brother who should be responsible for the parents, but he is a drunkard and does not take that responsibility. It's quite unusual that the parents of both of them live together with the family. Paul comes from a Christian family whereas Kas is from a Hindu family. The blessing of having the parents there is that they are hearing the gospel, they are there with family devotions when Paul explains the Scriptures, and they also attend the worship on Sunday.

Tuesday evening we went to a meeting where we were introduced to the leaders of the fellowship and some of the other people who attend. There is a Roman Catholic church just a block down from where Paul and Kas live. The living quarters are on the ground floor and the meeting place is upstairs. They are willing to have the fellowship use the upstairs for their evening meetings. I'm not sure if they pay rent or if it is rent-free. It's striking that there is nothing that makes it look Roman Catholic: no images, no pictures, just an ordinary room with a pulpit and chairs.

Wednesday Paul and Kas spent the day with us at the Millennium Hotel. The management is very accommodating and brought in a couple extra chairs for us to use and also served us some coffee. The purpose of the visit was to discuss the ministry in Vellore and the place of Ministry of Mercy (MOM). We had our lunch at the Spice Garden Restaurant. Just to give you an idea of prices here, we had a very nice dinner and it cost 300 Rs for the four of us: about U.S. $7. With the prices so cheap, we can easily add tips to it. It's a joy to see how grateful they are when they get some extra cash, and along with that the service gets even better and they cater to us. This restaurant is too upscale for most of the locals, very understandable when you know what kind of wages they earn.

I'll just tell you briefly where they're at in the ministry in Vellore. In February 2005 they rented a small upstairs room in a building, where they set up an academy called Sola deo Gratia. They printed out leaflets to advertise the academy and distributed them. The Lord blessed that work. Paulraj basically taught them all the subjects he had studied at ARTS in Singapore, using the notes his instructors had prepared for him. It's interesting that the men who attended these classes (which met three evenings a week for about five months until their funds ran out) really embraced the Reformed faith. Most of them come from a background of Hinduism, but before coming to the academy they were already in other churches—Baptist, Methodist, Pentecostal. What each one expressed in their own way was that the Bible really became alive for them when Paulraj taught them. They marveled at all the doctrines taught in the Scriptures, how the Scriptures harmonize, there are answers to all their questions, the preaching is different from what they were hearing before, etc. Our impression is that Paul is working hard and doing good work in explaining the Bible.

After having a Sunday evening Bible study for several months, they decided to begin a Sunday morning worship service, which is held in Paulraj's house. It is crowded (there were at least fifty people there the Sunday we were with them) but they sit on the floor and don't leave any walking room between the people, so you can crowd in quite a few that way. What I observe is that these people are very eager to learn and they are not argumentative. It's truly amazing how the Lord prepares their hearts to receive the Word, they can tell it's the truth because it is exactly what the Bible says, and they are drinking it all in.

The urgent need of the Protestant Reformed Fellowship is to have a more suitable place of worship. This will have to wait of course, until they receive more support. There are different possibilities: rent a larger home for Paul and Kas where they would have a large enough room to accommodate the Sunday worship service, or in addition to where they are living, rent another place for worship. If they have a separate place, they could arrange more meetings there, but it's also true that there would be times when the rented place would not be in use. If they could live in the same place, there would only be one rental payment to make. They will prayerfully wait for the Lord's direction in this regard.

Wednesday night we went to a Bible study. They have three weekly Bible studies in different localities (all within Vellore) so the people don't have to travel. These are small groups of about eight to twelve people. Before going there, we went to several homes of people who would be attending the Bible study that night. Paul explained the situation of the family living in each home: all of them are poor, several are young widows, some are working but the wages are very inadequate. The Bible study was held on the rooftop of one of the homes. It's really quite nice, since the sun is down by that time so it's comfortable and you just might feel some nice breezes as well. That night Grandpa spoke on Ezekiel 37 and Paul interpreted. Afterward they served coffee and biscuits.

On Thursday morning Rajastephen came to Vellore by bus. Paul and Kas joined us for the morning session. Grandpa met Rajastephen for the first time in 1992 and since that time has corresponded with him. Up until this time he really hasn't had opportunity to instruct him except through writing and sending books for him to study. Rajastephen understands and believes the doctrines of grace, but Grandpa always desired to have a teaching session with him on covenant and infant baptism, so that was the subject for that day. It would have been nice to have some of Paul's men there as well, but they were working. We took our lunch at Spice Garden once again and then continued after lunch until 4:00.

Rajastephen is very receptive to instruction and eager to learn. He understands and speaks well in English, so it would be nice if he could receive more instruction in the Reformed faith. We don't know what the Lord has in store for the future, but it certainly would seem to be a field for mission work.

Thursday was a big day. After meeting all day with Rajastephen, Grandpa gave a lecture on Reformed worship in the evening. This meeting was held in the meeting room of the Roman Catholic church (the upstairs room I told you about). There were about thirty-five people in attendance. Undoubtedly, with the church backgrounds of these people, this was all new material for them, but you wouldn't be able to find a more attentive group. You can tell they are listening alright by the questions they ask later. This lecture was interpreted by Paulraj, but some of the people do know a little English.

On Friday we went to visit by Rajastephen. The same vehicle we had on Monday was hired for this trip. We had to travel for about one and a half hours to get to his place. The home is in Molasur, Kancheepuram District, Tamil Nadu, South India. Rajastephen originally is from Salem, the same village where Kasthuri grew up.

Before I get into the story of where he is at now, I do have to tell you some interesting background. Rajastephen had an arranged marriage. His wife was a nurse in the hospital, and her colleague's husband arranged for Rajastephen to meet seven women. In one day's time, he visited the homes of these seven girls to meet them and their parents. He chose a girl named Shakila, and the next day he tried to speak with her on the phone but she refused to talk with him. They married without meeting up with each other. In our Western culture we learn to love and then get married. Their culture is to get married and then learn to love. (The very next week one of the girls he had met committed suicide. She was eight years his senior, which was one of the reasons he could not consider her, another cultural thing.)

Shakila's education was two years beyond 10th Standard (comparable to our high school) and then a three-year nursing program. Rajastephen received a B.Th. degree from Berean Baptist College in Bangalore, India. He was ordained about three years later in a Baptist church. Rajastephen and Shakila have two sons: Jerry, age four and a half, and Renny, age two.

Rajastephen's father was Hindu and his mother was Roman Catholic. They were converted before their marriage and the parents brought up their children in the Baptist church. He has one brother and five sisters. He remembers his mother as a very prayerful woman. About four years ago the doctor advised an internal pacemaker for the mother, but there was no way the family could afford such a device, and she passed away shortly after.

The family was involved in orphanages all along, so it follows quite naturally that Rajastephen's interest lies in that as well. He and his wife worked in an orphanage in Chennai (formerly called Madras) until he took up the pastorate. His sister runs a large orphanage for 150 children in Salem as a business venture. Rajastephen's approach to orphanages is different from that. After returning to the village as a pastor, they began taking orphans into their own home, providing a place for them to live not only, but also nurturing them as parents and making a real home for them. This continued throughout the years; we tried to help them when we could, but it was nothing on a regular basis. Then one time, some young people in the PRCA who were interested in helping to support some mission work contacted us, and this seemed to be a nice project for them to get involved in. Ed Bos took over the management of it: corresponded with Rajastephen, held informational meetings and got sponsors for the orphans, and continues to forward the funds to Rajastephen at regular intervals so he knows how much he can plan on. This has worked out very well over the years. In addition to this, Rajastephen's sister does contribute some support for his family (approximately 2,500 Rs per month). Up until this time they have lived in a rented home with twelve to fifteen boys. Some months ago they were faced with a crisis: the landlord wanted them to vacate the premises by June 2006. It's difficult to find a suitable and large enough place to rent for that many people. Rajastephen shared this concern with Ed, who in turn shared the problem with the supporters. It was decided to help Rajastephen buy a piece of land on which to construct a home for the children. The home is presently under construction so we were able to visit there, see what is going on, and also get some details of the situation to share with the people who are involved in supporting this project. Byron Center PRC has also shown some interest in this work and has provided money for all the boys to have their own Bible, and in addition to that, they were able to purchase ten cots. In the present home there is only room to set up three of the cots, but eventually they hope that each child will have their own cot to sleep on. Before telling about the building, I'll write regarding the operation of the children's home. With that many children, it's necessary to have a schedule.

AM		PM	
5:00–5:30	Arise	4:30–5:00	Household chores
5:30–6:00	Prayer time	5:00–6:00	Games
6:00–7:30	Bathe, cleaning	6:00–7:30	Tuition
7:30–8:00	Homework	7:30–8:00	Prayer time
8:00–8:30	Breakfast	8:00–8:30	Supper
8:45	Prayer and off to school	9:00	Bedtime
9:00–4:30	At school		

The prayer time consists of singing, Bible reading, and prayer. For the evening prayer time Rajastephen prepares a ten-minute message for teaching them the Bible and also emphasizing Christian living. This is done every day. The boys attend a government school where there are about seventy children in each class. This education is of a lower quality: with that many children in a classroom it is impossible to maintain good discipline and to give any individual attention. Rajastephen's son Jerry attends a private school where there is a Christian teacher. The tuition fee in the private school is 150 Rs per month so it is too costly for all the children to attend.

A cook and a warden are employed, and they live in the home with the boys. Rajastephen's family lives in a small apartment nearby. Shakila is the one in charge of "Tuition" (meaning tutoring the boys and giving them extra help with their schoolwork).

The family worships together with the boys, the cook, and the warden, and Rajastephen preaches for them. Presently they are in an area that is predominantly Roman Catholic, making it very difficult to reach out to others. The new property is located in a different area, which is being developed, and their desire is to witness in that area so others may come to know the Reformed faith. On Saturdays, Sundays, and holidays, a few of the boys accompany Rajastephen when he goes outside the village to witness and give tracts. In that way he is also teaching them how to speak with others about Christ.

We were favorably impressed with the running of the home. The children were all very neat and clean and well-behaved. They had prepared a short program for us with recitations and singing. We couldn't understand it but we did ask what the meaning of it was. They read from their Bibles and the older children helped the younger ones with finding the passage. The children range in age from around four years to fifteen years. The older children are responsible for doing their own laundry and ironing. Each child has a small suitcase in which they must keep their clothing and any other possessions they have. The cook is teaching the older boys how to cook and several of them are quite keen to learn. There are no toys around; the games they play are outside games in the yard, mostly football (soccer). One of their former boys did go on for more studies and continues to keep in touch with them. He is involved in some aspect of Christian work.

The land that has been purchased is 4500 square feet with a cost of two lakhs (one lakh is 100,000 rupees or U.S. $2,400). They feel very blessed to have made this purchase when the price was low. Rajastephen has since been offered six lakhs for the piece of land they have. (He said if he had bought twice as much land and was able to sell half of it now, they would have enough to pay for their building.) The land is paid for. The reason the value of the land has increased is because they are located near Chennai and a new Nokia plant is going up in their area, which will result in more jobs.

The proposed building will consist of a large dormitory room, which will also serve as their sanctuary for church services on Sunday, a dining hall, a kitchen, a small guest room with attached bath, a storage room, and an inside toilet. The plan is to put the roof over the entire building and construct three rooms. The other rooms can be added as they have the funds available. For now they plan to do the main walls so the rooms are ready and they can move in. The bathrooms will probably be the last things they do; they are accustomed to taking their showers with a bucket of water and a scoop, and it will continue that way until they can install a proper shower.

Because they are building a children's home, the supplier of building materials is willing to give them credit, interest free, which must be paid up as each phase is completed. The supplier is also giving them a better price and adding some additional things. They have engaged a Christian builder who is also charging them less. In all these ways the Lord is providing for their needs.

While we were there, they had a little ceremony for the setting of the doorjamb. This is very typical in the Indian culture. A Christian will hold this ceremony asking for God's blessing upon the endeavor and the purpose for which the building will be used, for the safety of the workers during construction, etc. It might be similar to the laying of a cornerstone in our culture. The Hindus hold ceremonies of this nature as well, which to us is superstition, but to them it is reaching out to their gods. The builder in this case is a Christian, but Hindu workers are employed. So before the setting of the doorjamb, a prayer was offered to God while the Hindu workers set aside their work for a few moments and, out of respect, stood quietly while we all prayed together.

MISSION TRIPS: INDIA, 2006

The roof of the building will be flat and made of cement. In this way a second story could be added in the future and the orphanage would be able to accommodate up to forty children. The building will include electricity. When they move in, they will have to buy their water. Eventually they would like to have a well and pump (necessary before they can complete the bathrooms with showers and toilets). They must go down at least four hundred feet for the well, so this would involve additional cost.

We saw the construction in progress. Men mixing cement by hand and earning 150 Rs a day (U.S. $3.50), an elderly woman trying to eke out a living by hauling bricks on her head (she went to the brick pile, stacked nine bricks on her head, walked over to where they needed them, and carefully laid them down) all for 100 Rs a day and doing this under the hot sun.

They did serve us a nice noon meal of biryani (rice with veggies and typical Indian spices), served on banana leaves and eaten with your fingers. The boys sat quietly on the floor during their meal, and I inquired if they always ate that quietly. The answer was, "No, no, no, usually there is a lot of talking going on."

It was an interesting day there, and on the way back to Vellore, we stopped in by a Dr. Benjamin, with whom Paulraj has contact. Dr. Benjamin came to Vellore and attended a couple of the meetings we had. His wife is a professor in the college there. They have a nice home but in no way extravagant. In India everyone just throws their trash down on the ground, and we were rather surprised to see that right next to the doctor's home was a vacant lot completely littered with trash.

On Saturday we were able to use the room of the Roman Catholic church for an all-day seminar. In the morning the topic was the marks of the true church, and the subject for the afternoon session was offices of the church: pastor, elders, and deacons. At noon they brought in packet lunches of rice with scrambled egg mixed in. This seminar was intended for about seven men, but somehow word gets around about a meeting, and more and more come to listen. We had the evening free, which was a good thing as we were getting a little weary.

On Sunday morning we had a worship service at Paulraj's house. There were about fifty people in attendance for the service. Grandpa preached from Matthew 27:34, "When he had tasted thereof, he would not drink." Paulraj was the interpreter. After the closing prayer, the congregation prays in unison Psalm 103:1–2, the benediction is given, and a doxology is sung. When the service was over, they presented us with a garland of roses and expressed their thanks for our coming to India and for the work Grandpa did while there. They had a gift for us of three flower-decorated metal containers that fit inside each other, and one family gave us a picture frame.

The people started to leave, but there were several who wanted to share something about their life with us. To say it more correctly, I think Paulraj wanted to acquaint us with the difficulties they were facing. There was no asking for money, it was more to ask that we be prayerful for their circumstances, which we definitely continue to do. The people are poor, they work long hours for such a little bit of money, they have medical needs that are difficult to pay for, and there are family situations that are hard to manage, for example, there was a young widow with small children and out of necessity she has to work; she earns so little and has to leave her children unattended.

The Lord has placed these people upon our pathway, and you just cannot walk away from it without being affected. The Lord has given us so much, and since we have the means to help, without even changing our luxurious lifestyle, it certainly is our Christian calling to help them and certainly what the Lord would want us to do. Matthew 25:34–40 comes to mind. "Verily I say unto you, Inasmuch as ye have done it unto one of the least of these my brethren, ye have done it unto me" (v. 40).

> Withhold not Thou Thy grace from me,
> O Lord, Thy mercy let me see,
> To me Thy lovingkindness show,
> Thy truth be still my stay;
> Let them preserve me where I go,
> And keep me every day.

MISSION TRIPS: INDIA, 2006

>Let all who seek to see Thy face
>Be glad and joyful in Thy grace;
>Let those who Thy salvation love
>For evermore proclaim,
>O praise the Lord Who dwells above,
>And magnify his Name.
>
>Although I poor and needy be,
>The Lord in love takes thought for me;
>Thou art my help in time of need,
>My Saviour, Lord, art Thou;
>Then, O my God, I pray, I plead,
>Stay not, but save me now.[*]

Lunch on Sunday was by Paul and Kas's house, and then we rested in our hotel room in the afternoon. The core group of the Protestant Reformed Fellowship wanted to meet with us in the evening: they had many questions to ask. On Saturday I asked at the Spice Garden Restaurant (that place isn't busy at all) if we could have a table for up to twelve in a nice corner spot in which we could have a meeting. They gladly accommodated us, and it worked out very well.

They had their questions lined up alright: Give a brief history of the Reformed church. Is it possible for them to unite with the PRCA? Are there any things that we have observed that they should change? What is important for them to know and do in organizing a church? etc. This meeting began at 5:00 and lasted until 9:30; very enjoyable.

On Monday Paulraj and Kasthuri came to the hotel and visited with us in our room. Again the hotel staff prepared coffee for us and brought it to the room. The purpose of the visit that day was to have an interview with them and learn more of their background and how the Lord has led them all this way. The content of that interview is given in the chapter entitled "The First ARTS Student." We had our final lunch at Spice Garden Restaurant with Paul and Kas. After

---

[*] No. 112, 2-4, in *The Psalter.*

they left mid-afternoon we had a little time to relax and also to finish things up and do our packing.

Tuesday morning we had to be ready by 8:00. We had an "auto" to take us to the train station for our trip to Chennai. An auto is the local taxi and even that is expensive for most people. It has a motorcycle engine, one wheel in front and two in back, a small seat in front for the driver, and a bench in back for the passengers—comfortable for three people but they can jam in quite a few more if necessary. There is a roof over it but no doors. They can sure scoot around but don't go very fast. It's an idea for a self-help project because a person can make a living (read that as survival) with it.

Paulraj figured it would make more sense to take a train to Chennai rather than hiring a taxi and have the taxi go back to Vellore empty. He arranged for us to have an air-con car on the train, so it made the traveling very comfortable and easy. We went there with the five of us: Paulraj, Kas, Jason, Grandpa, and I. It's really neat when traveling in a foreign country to have a local arranging everything for you: they seem to have all the necessary connections so everything goes smoothly.

For the afternoon activities in Chennai, Paul's brother-in-law's company supplied an air-con car and driver for a reasonable cost, and the brother of the brother-in-law met us at the airport and went along for the sightseeing. Now that's deluxe treatment for India! We went to a large shopping mall first where we picked up just a few items, and a treat for the afternoon was an ice cream cone. Little Jason was enjoying it to the max—he did really well with handling it himself until he bit off the bottom of the cone. That white ice cream around his mouth against that dark skin was as cute as could be.

Then we took a ride along the beach where the tsunami hit. That has to be the largest beach we ever saw, both in length and width. Although it was cleaned up everywhere, you could certainly imagine what devastation the tsunami brought. Across the road from the beach are rows and rows of rebuilt thatch homes. These homes are nothing more than small huts; you can hardly believe that a family could live in one. It's mind-staggering to think of raising a family in those conditions, and yet for many people, that is all they have.

That night we had a room in the St. Thomas International Centre. Yes, it's Catholic, but here again, there was nothing around that appeared Roman Catholic—no images, etc. We were able to take our dinner and breakfast there as well. We had an air-con room, but Paul, Kas, and Jason were given a non-air-con so they had to use the mosquito netting. This center is perched on top of a hill away from the noise of Chennai and is located close to the airport, so it was an excellent choice of a place to stay. We hired a taxi to bring us to the airport in the morning, and then the driver brought Paul, Kas, and Jason to the bus depot so they could make their way back to Vellore.

All in all, it was a very enjoyable week, especially to see how the Lord is blessing the ministry of Paulraj in that area. It's so refreshing to witness the enthusiasm and excitement of the people when they embrace the Reformed faith and feel sure in their hearts that this is indeed the truth because they can see clearly it is what the Bible teaches. They are just so eager for all of India to hear it but realize this will take time and a lot of hard work.

"The harvest truly is great, but the labourers are few: pray ye therefore the Lord of the harvest, that he would send forth labourers into his harvest." Luke 10:2

Philippines — May 20-31, 1999

This visit to the Philippines was made with Rev. Daniel and Sharon Kleyn, from Edgerton, Minnesota. The trip went well, and we had a delightful time with them.

Traveling went well for all of us. The Kleyns left already on Tuesday, the eighteenth. Their flight was through Denver and San Francisco on United Airlines and then on to the Philippines on

Philippine Air. They had a strong tailwind so were able to skip the refueling stop in Honolulu and arrived in Manila about two hours early, 3:00 a.m. instead of 5:00. One of their pieces of luggage was missing: the one with all their clothes and personal items in it. The congregation of Hull, Iowa, had made up some gift packs to distribute to the people in the Philippines, and all of that arrived alright. The Kleyns are young and able to roll with the punches; no complaining, and you wouldn't think they have a bit of jet lag, they just hang in there and are going strong. After trying to locate the luggage, they went to the hotel and tried to get some rest.

Our flight left Singapore at 9:40 a.m. It was a direct flight from Singapore, and we arrived in the Philippines at 1:15. No time change, easy trip. The Kleyns were back at the airport to welcome us.

That evening six men came to the hotel to visit with us. Five of the men were from Worldwide Church of God, and they have a Bible study group, called Berean, which meets once a week. They are open to the Reformed faith and are studying, so they had lots of questions. The sixth man was a pastor from Scotland, Reformed Baptist, who was going to be their guest speaker that very evening, so instead they invited him to come along and meet with us.

The first night we stayed at the Shalom House. It's a hotel in Manila for missionaries. Our room was Shechem and I believe the Kleyns' was Cana. Our wake-up call on Friday morning was at 3:30! We had to fly out at 6:30 but wanted to check at the international airport first to see if the luggage arrived. No luggage yet, and we were going to be on our way to Naga, and from there to Daet. That meant no luggage for the Kleyns at least until Monday when we would get back to Manila.

We arrived in Naga around 7:30 a.m. and were welcomed by a group of men at the airport. We went by jeepney truck to Nabua (an hour's drive and we stopped for breakfast on the way). We reached Pastor Nelson's church at 9:30. Grandpa was going to speak that morning on church government, but it was mostly women who were there and not too knowledgeable yet, so the subject changed

MISSION TRIPS: PHILIPPINES—MAY 20-31, 1999

to "What It Means to Be a Christian." They served a lunch after the meeting and then we had to be on our way again.

It was a long ride of three and a half hours, so for comfort's sake, they took an air-con van, but the driver kept turning the air-con off (probably afraid of overheating) and we about cooked. We were fanning ourselves most of the time. But who are we to complain? About five local men rode along, and they sat packed like sardines in the back of the van along with all the luggage. They were hot too. We did take time along the way to stop for drinks.

Before going to the hotel, we stopped at a mall so the Kleyns could buy a few necessary items—shirt, blouse, underwear, disposable shaver, etc. They were able to take some shampoo, deodorant, toothpaste, and toothbrushes from one of the gift packs. Very convenient.

Our home for Friday and Saturday was the Dolar Hotel. We each had a large room with table and chairs and also a sofa. Friday night was a gathering in one of the homes. Pastor Kleyn introduced the subject of election, and then there was a time for Q&A. Before coming to the meeting we had a nice dinner at the Golden House Restaurant, and after the meeting they brought out a big feed, which we just couldn't do justice to. They presented a gift to us in appreciation. It was a set of three baskets joined together, I guess to put plants in and hang up. The baskets are very nice but they will be rather clumsy to haul around. I took mine apart and I have some large plastic bags along, so we'll just have to carry them on the plane.

When we got back to the hotel that night, the hotel staff apologized to us—there was dancing in the ball room right above us, raising money for the new building of a Catholic church. "You're welcome to take dinner in the dining room if you like." Grandpa understood that to be "on the house" for our being inconvenienced, but my idea of what they meant was just to take up some time while it was so noisy. Our day had started very early and everyone was tired so off to bed we went. The dancing lasted until 12:30, according to Grandpa; I slept right through it.

A group of men came to the hotel to visit with us on Saturday morning. The discussion was about direction for future work among the people there. We took the group out for lunch at the Golden House Restaurant. There were fourteen of us and the bill came to 1,216 pesos, which translated into U.S. money is only $33. There was a lot of food and a lot left over, which someone took along home. Saturday afternoon was easy. Sharon and I went out for a while, looking through a market that was nearby (it reminded me of the Colton Market in California), and we picked up some donuts and bananas for Sunday breakfast.

Saturday night we were by Pastor Tanierla's house with a group of people and Grandpa spoke on "Preservation of the Saints." We were half and half expecting that we'd get some dinner there, but it was mangoes and peanuts. Mangoes are in season now and very delicious. So after two dinners the night before, we didn't have any dinner on Saturday.

It was nice to meet up with the Tanierlas again, and I really conveyed to Deanna Tanierla on Deanna Klamer's behalf how happy she was to have a "Deanna" friend. I gave her a tablet of light purple paper, a ballpoint pen, and a small laminated card with her name and some Scripture verses on it. Deanna is a sweet girl; her birthday is September 4 and she's either going on fourteen or fifteen, I'm not sure which. I had a nice little chat with her again on Sunday.

She said, "May I ask you a question?"

"Sure you may."

"How should I address you?"

Some of her other questions were, "How do you feel when other people talk in their own language and you can't understand them?" and "Do you notice that people look at you a lot?" When I told her how they did look at us (a group of girls on Saturday afternoon, one had noticed us and must have told her friends because they all turned around, smiled, turned around again, smiled some more) she said so cutely, "They don't mean to be rude, because we really like Americans." She said it seems like all the foreigners she sees have curly hair and she wondered why they do that, why don't they just wear their

MISSION TRIPS: PHILIPPINES—MAY 20-31, 1999

hair straight? Cute, huh? Then she wanted to know about Deanna, about school in Singapore, etc. She really latched on to me and we took plenty of pictures. She had a camera too and had to have a picture with Sharon and me and one with Grandpa and me. She's a little sweetie, and we had a big hug when we left.

On Sunday morning the Kleyns came to our room at 8 a.m. for breakfast—we have a hot pot, which we take along on all these trips so we can make coffee and tea in our room.

Pastor Tanierla's father is also a pastor and he asked that one of the men take the Sunday School and the other, the church service. Grandpa's Sunday school lesson was on "What It Means to be a Christian" and Pastor Kleyn's message was on Philippians 2—he which has begun a good work, etc. After the service, they had some gifts for us too, a set of three purses made of banana leaves and a beautiful clock with an arrangement of shells around it. We sure have added the bags around here and between the two couples, we have to keep checking if we have all of them. Hope we can fit some of it in our suitcases after we give away some of the things we have taken along. Forgot to mention that a lady we met at the Friday night meeting also gave us something. She said she had a lot of frames made of coconut hair (made by prisoners) and asked if we would like some. (I had in mind a 5x7 frame, and I thought it would be nice if we each had one.) Saturday morning she brought them to the hotel. They're around 20x24 with a picture, made by her students, already in them. They melt small crayon pieces in a spoon over a candle flame, and using a paintbrush, they paint the picture which they had sketched. It's very nice and also very special. Once we're back home, we'll be happy we carted it all along.

There has been quite a bit of traveling along the roads and through the villages, and although we are used to seeing these sights, it's all a first for the Kleyns in a third-world country. Sure is nice that they have this trip together so they can share the memories. The people we have met are very friendly, open to the Reformed faith, and a delight to be with.

I got a little sidetracked there, better get back to Sunday. We had to get back at noon to get our stuff out of the hotel and take it along with us to the next place, which was by the younger Pastor Tanierla. Sunday school was at 2:00, with Rev. Kleyn teaching on Genesis 3:15. The church service followed immediately, and Grandpa preached on "Once I was blind but now I see."

We left that place around 4:45 and had to drive to Naga City in order to be on time for our flight on Monday morning from Naga to Bacolod. This was about a three-hour journey, and although for the most part roads are pretty good, there is a lot of repair work going on that makes driving a bit rough. To us it doesn't look like there is enough warning as to what's ahead, but we had a good driver, and the trip went fine.

Pastor Tanierla Sr. rode along to Naga City because he has a married daughter living there (the daughter is married to a Baptist minister who is older than her father). Grandpa sat in the front with the driver, Rev. Kleyn, Sharon, and I were in the middle seat, and Pastor Tanierla Sr. in the back. All along the way, he was asking questions about theology, counseling situations, etc., and Grandpa was explaining to him. (The driver might have gotten quite an education, if he was listening.) At one point Pastor Tanierla said, "Rev. Kortering, I'm tired of talking."

On Friday morning, Sharon lost her camera. Rev. Kleyn planned to take slides, but they really wanted prints too, so before they left Edgerton, they bought a new Samsung camera. That was the one she lost, and she didn't miss it until we got to Daet (three hours from where we were on Friday). She thought she left it in the church where we had the Friday morning meeting. She mentioned it to the men on Saturday, and on Sunday, the younger Pastor Tanierla made the trip down there to get it. He took his motorcycle to the bus terminal and then took the trip by bus. Although Sharon was very happy to have her camera back, she felt bad that he extended himself that way, especially because it was Sunday and besides that, he wasn't feeling well. He said he didn't want them to have any bad memories of their trip.

MISSION TRIPS: PHILIPPINES—MAY 20-31, 1999

We had a nice hotel on Sunday night in Naga and a good flight to Bacolod on Monday. There were a few people at the airport to meet us, and after bringing us to Sugarland Hotel and going over the schedule for the next few days, we had the rest of the day for ourselves, with the men going over their material and a time for Sharon and me to catch up with writing. We took our dinner at the restaurant in the hotel, relaxed, and had a lot of fun visiting with the four of us.

The meetings on Tuesday were at the Girl Scout Center just a block from the hotel. Rent for the day was 300 pesos, which is only about $8. We came back to the hotel for lunch and Grandpa took a quick rest before it was his turn for the afternoon session. Rev. Kleyn had the morning session on "What It Is to Be Reformed." In the afternoon session, Grandpa taught about church government. There were about fifteen people at the meetings.

After the meeting we walked to a place where we could check email, not far from the hotel where we were staying. Grandpa had fifty-seven messages to download and it took forty minutes. We quickly scanned from whom the messages came and printed out a couple from family and one that needed answering. Kleyns were away from home longer than we were so had more to download, and for some reason the machine they were using went extremely slow; ours was slow too, but theirs was slower. We were about ready to leave, but the Kleyns were still sitting huddled together by the computer reading a letter from their folks. It would have made a cute picture, but we didn't think of that until we got back to the hotel.

It was arranged that some of the men from the Convenors (a group of pastors from various denominations who meet together regularly and are developing in their understanding of the Reformed faith) were going to come to the hotel to talk with the men that evening. We were just down to the restaurant for dinner and were in the process of ordering when they showed up. We told the waiter we would just wait with eating until after they had their meeting. Sharon and I ordered a cup of tea and visited, while the men met. Dinner that night was around 9:00.

I have to interject something here. Grandpa and I also went to the Philippines in 1997. Since that trip was en route to the U.S. for our annual furlough, I did not make a detailed account of the trip. Time with our family was just too precious to be taking time then for a report.

In 1997 we had a seminar with the Convenors in Bacolod. One of the Convenors had a handwritten collection of poems that he authored, and since he did not have a typewriter or computer, I offered to make a computer document and get it printed out for him. Now on this trip in 1999, we had opportunity to give the finished copy of the book of poems to him. We had fifty copies made up in Singapore, so he would be able to distribute them among his friends. He was so very happy, it about made him speechless. He said, "This is the first thing that I have in print."

Then on Wednesday morning Baltazar Niangar, the author of the poem, showed me that he had proofread the book and sad to say, there were many corrections to be made. Not all were my mistakes; many were corrections or improvements he wanted to make over what he had written before. Grandpa felt sorry for me after all the work I did trying to make it as perfect as possible. The corrections are easy enough for me to make because it is all in the computer. I think it would have been smart, on our part, if we got five printed instead of fifty and had given him an opportunity for a second proofreading, but after he had gone through it once more before giving it to me, and I had made the changes he wanted, we both thought the job was complete. I learn fast—we won't print a quantity until we get a copy without mistakes.

The title of each sonnet is like an acrostic so if you follow the first letter of each line down the page, it's the title of the sonnet. To draw attention to that, he thought it would be nice to put the title and the first letters of the lines in a different print. Since the time he wrote them, he changed from believing in common grace to not believing in common grace, so a few poems had to be revised as well. Oh well, I guess we'll soon be able to put that behind us and forget about it.

MISSION TRIPS: PHILIPPINES—MAY 20-31, 1999

When we were in Daet, I noticed a portable typewriter in the window of a pawn shop. Just having gone through the experience in Myanmar, where we bought a portable typewriter for one of the congregations there, my attention was drawn to the typewriter in the window. When we got to Bacolod, Pastor Bal (Niangar) asked about the possibility of a typewriter. I just didn't have the heart to tell him that I had actually seen one for sale in Daet.

For the Wednesday morning session, Grandpa taught on children in the covenant. Grandpa is a good teacher (you'd expect me to say that, right?); I always enjoy listening to the messages. For the last session on Wednesday afternoon, Pastor Kleyn's assigned subject was, "Is the Christ of the Arminians a False Christ?" After he finished, there was time for questions on anything they wished to ask. Next was a meeting with a small group, which is loosely organized. Jay Nombre, who is single, along with two families desire to have a missionary labor there.

For the last night in Bacolod, we took the group out for dinner. It was a restaurant within walking distance of the hotel; it had an inside place where you could sit but also a large covered area outside with picnic tables. We left the ordering up to the locals and believe me, we had quite the variety: some things to our liking and other things we were at a loss as to how to handle it. There was a bowl of beef soup, intended to be passed around, that had a huge bone with some meat and a lot of fat, and about one-sixth of a head of cabbage, not broken up, so how do you attack that? At the end, the bowl was empty and one of the ladies was chewing off the bone.

After a couple hours of fellowship, it was back to the hotel for packing for the next lap. Our wake-up call on Thursday was at 5:30 and we had to be on our way by 6:00. The hotel provided transport to the airport, which was only a couple minutes away. First we had to fly from Bacolod to Manila, where we had a one and a half hour wait before our connecting flight to Cagayan de Oro.

When we arrived at the airport, no one was there to greet us so we were sure wondering what might have happened. We waited around for a while and then arranged for a taxi to take us to the hotel—good thing we knew which hotel to go to. We tried to contact the person in charge but there was no answer. We went and had our lunch and then stayed at the hotel until we finally were able to establish contact on his cell phone. What had happened is that Romegio Lapiz had gone to visit his sick brother-in-law in Davao City and would be back by Friday noon and he was unable to reach his brother, Loloy. Probably we will get more of the story later.

The outcome of the above was that we had the rest of the afternoon and the evening free, and we took advantage of that. We left the hotel around 3:30. Grandpa really wanted Rev. Kleyn and Sharon to experience some local color, so he suggested we take a ride in a power scooter. After we found a driver who could understand English, we asked him to give us a ride anywhere for about 50 pesos.

He took us for the nicest ride down to the sea where some kids were swimming by the shore, a few were riding on ski-jets, and in the distance there were tiny and flimsy shacks on stilts with fishing nets for kelong fishing; after a while, the net is dragged in with the fish. Further down the coast was a little village with all the huts the people live in. All in all, it was a neat time, and when we came back to the hotel, we paid him 200 pesos (about U.S. $5). I think it made his day and he was smiling ear to ear. That probably doesn't happen too often, and we were wondering what he would be telling his family that evening—something like, "Guess what happened today? I had four American passengers and they paid me 200 pesos!"

Next we started walking and strolled through a park and came across a couple guys polishing shoes. That reminds me of something else I forgot to tell you before. On Sunday we took a trishaw to church and Grandpa's foot slipped off the little step while we were riding, his foot bent backward, and the wheel went over it (I was kind of wondering why he was bent over and shifting about). His shoe was scuffed badly, but we were just thankful the shoe did not slip off and his foot did not get hurt—it was amazing to us that seeing it got twisted the way it did, he didn't have any pain in the foot at

MISSION TRIPS: PHILIPPINES—MAY 20-31, 1999

all! It would be tough to do what we are doing this week with a sore foot; certainly the Lord provided in this as well and kept him from getting hurt.

Back to where I started: his shoes really could use some polishing, and Rev. Kleyn's weren't a whole lot better, so they asked the guys: how much? "Thirty pesos." Okay. Those men did a super job (I've never polished shoes that well!). I'm sure it took them all of twenty-five or thirty minutes, each one doing a pair. We talked to them a little while they were working. The one man was thirty-six years old, had six children, and this was his work. (I remembered from India that they get you started by quoting a cheap price and then find reasons to make it higher and was wondering what their tactic would be.) They were doing a good job, so we were going to give them a little extra for all their effort and Grandpa handed him 50 pesos. Then the joke was on us, it was 30 pesos for each shoe! We had a good laugh and paid him the extra ten.

Grandpa thought the Kleyns should also experience riding in a jeepney, a truck with seats in the back. We had no idea where it was going, but we thought we could at least ride a ways and take a taxi back. Along came one that was quite empty so we got in. It was going to Bugo, the next town, and would reach the same spot where we got on in about an hour and a half. It was fun having the jeepney ride; it was raining part of the time, we saw some countryside, had a ride through the little town, and all that for a total of 100 pesos for four people (U.S. $2.67), cheap entertainment.

On the ride this morning, Grandpa noticed a sign that read, "Lady bedspacer." He wondered what that could mean, and they told him that meant an apartment was available for a woman.

The Filipinos are a friendly people. Sometimes when we are walking or are in a vehicle waiting for a traffic light, someone will wave and call out, "Hi, Joe," "How ya doin', Joe," etc. They tell us that is how the locals greet Americans. We think this might be a carryover from when the American soldiers were in the Philippines and called G. I. Joe.

After showers, we went down for dinner, which lasted until 9:45. While sitting at the table talking, Rev. Kleyn looked down at his shoes and pretended to fix his hair using the shoes for his mirror.

We had our best night of sleep. The room was quiet, but it still gets light early and we were awake by 5:30.

We had the morning to do whatever we wanted, since the person we had to meet would not be there until noon. We left around 9:00 and took a taxi to Eco Village. It was a nice ride, not very far. It was a good place to stroll around and definitely the neatest maintained place we've seen in the Philippines; the grounds were all neat and clean, the many varieties of flowers were beautiful. The first little stop was at an actual home, very sparsely furnished, and the people inside were busy with basket weaving and also had baskets available for sale. You have to be careful with souvenir buying so you don't get big and bulky things (I guess we have enough of that already with the gifts we received). They did have some pretty plates made from banana leaves, which are small enough to take along, so that's what I bought. It was terribly hot walking, so we were glad there was a place to get a drink. It was a nice outing, nice to be able to take in a little of the local sights, but I think the men would feel a bit more comfortable if they were able to have the meetings they were planning on.

It's now 4:00 p.m. We had a late lunch (saw a rat several times in the dining room—we might find a different place for dinner tonight). We're still waiting around for the people we have to visit. Hopefully we're able to meet up with them yet today because tonight some men are coming in from Davao City; tomorrow could get a bit complicated with two groups of men to visit with.

It is Saturday morning and again I can say how wonderfully the Lord guided all the events of last evening. Shortly after writing the above, the men arrived. Remegio had written Grandpa an email to find out the time of our arrival, but we didn't get the message until Tuesday night when we checked email in Bacolod. By that time he was in Davao City and not able to collect Grandpa's answer, so it was clearly a matter of misunderstanding, and we were relieved to find

MISSION TRIPS: PHILIPPINES—MAY 20-31, 1999

that relationships with them are very much intact. They left Davao City at 4:00 a.m. in order to reach Cagayan de Oro by the time they did. They must have been very tired, but they still extended themselves to meet with us. After meeting with them some three hours, we were informed that the other men intending to come Friday night would not be arriving until Saturday afternoon so now we have the morning with the one group and the afternoon with the other.

And then last night—what a riot! We decided to go to KFC, about two blocks away, for dinner. It was just starting to rain, but Grandpa and I both had umbrellas with us, so no problem, one for each couple. The rain turned to a downpour, and it was still raining heavily by the time we finished eating. It was Grandpa's idea to brave it since it wasn't letting up at all, so off we went. The locals know what these rains are like; many were huddled under the overhangs of buildings, but here these four Americans carry on.

Crossing the first street, there was a puddle too big to jump across so that's when our shoes first got soaked, but the next street was flooded and the water was flowing like a river (at that time about halfway up a car wheel). I took my shoes off and went barefoot. Sharon left hers on figuring they were wet anyway. Both Grandpa's and my shoes are still quite wet this morning, but they are the only ones we have along, so we'll just make the best of it today. Everything was soaked, right down to our skin. When we got to the hotel, they were preparing for handling the situation—the water was over the sidewalk and approaching the door. It was funny: the elevator walls are mirrors all around and we looked like a bunch of drenched bums.

It is Saturday afternoon as I write this, and we had an interesting morning. The Lapiz brothers, Remegio with his family and Loloy with his son Joseph, took us around to a few members of their church. Our first stop was by a single man who rents a small place for his home and business. The business is roasting chickens and pigs. He takes orders for special occasions, and you'd wonder how that could keep someone busy, but being single, I guess he can make a go of it. He said, "I just pray the Lord that I can earn some money to help support the ministry." (It is from him that the Lapiz brothers borrow money to pay for the rent of the meeting place when they run behind. They were three months in arrears at the time, but Rev. Kleyn was authorized to contribute $400, so now they are just a month behind.)

Then we stopped at another place that looked a little better off (a refrigerator in the kitchen and nice table and chairs) but there's more to the story. A mother was there, about forty-seven years old; her husband is working in Manila, driving a truck, and comes home twice a year. The good part is he will be coming home for good around July. They have three children; the oldest is a girl of twenty-five years, married to a Catholic and the mother of a ten-month-old daughter. The girl and her husband are also working in Manila, and the baby is cared for by her grandmother, the lady we were talking with. There was also an eighteen-year-old daughter who is studying medicine and will be supported through school by a grandfather. We didn't meet the third child, but there was also another girl there who is a domestic helper in the home.

Then we went to the homes of the Lapiz families. That has its own unique character. When the pastors were young, the parents had one house on that piece of land for their family of four sons and four daughters. The children all married and have families, and five of them have houses very near to each other on that land, so there are lots of cousins who can play together. The parents are still living; the mother is seventy-seven and the father is ninety-two. The father has suffered a stroke and lies on a straw mat on a wooden floor; it looks so pathetic, and it is the very same place and way he was lying two years ago when we first met them. The eldest daughter was in the house helping to care for him, and when Grandpa was going to pray with the family, she helped the father to sit up and let him lean against her legs. His hearing isn't good, and he's pretty much out of it, really just waiting to be delivered and go to his eternal home.

For three years Beth Lapiz (wife of Remegio) has had a cystic goiter that fills up with fluid and about every two months has to be

MISSION TRIPS: PHILIPPINES—MAY 20-31, 1999

drained. She should have surgery because the doctor says they cannot just keep doing this, but they really cannot afford to have the operation. Grandpa and I felt very happy and thankful for the emergency fund so we could give them the necessary amount for the surgery. Dorothy Lapiz (wife of Loloy) had a tooth extracted and now she has infection in her jaw so her jaw is swollen. They got antibiotics for her this morning, so hopefully it will get better. Both families have three children, and they are all such nice kids, well-behaved, polite, and easy to talk with. One from each family is in university on scholarship, which is a big help to the family.

Just seeing the compound where they lived made me think that that must be what it was like thirty-five years ago in Singapore with the kampongs. The homes are kind-of huddled together and everyone feels at home in all the houses with the children moving about very freely. People in Singapore who are in their forties now talk about those times as being so much fun with lots of freedom, and they miss it in contrast to the high-rise buildings they live in now. A bit of nostalgia for them.

We were only back for about ten minutes when the other men arrived from Davao. They joined us for lunch, and we visited for a while, mostly just getting acquainted with them. Then it was time for a little rest, seeing they had been traveling some six hours. We are going to meet them again for dinner and focus more on the work in Davao.

It is interesting; this Nollie is a Filipino but has U.S citizenship, having lived in America for twenty years. He does computer work in Davao for SIL (Summer Institute of Linguistics), which is Wycliffe Bible Translators. He will soon be fifty years old, plans to work for SIL until retirement, and then the family will go back to the U.S. Their oldest son is already in the U.S. attending university. They have three more children with them in the Philippines. There was a younger fellow with him named Vic, and he and his wife are expecting their second child.

We had a wonderful Sunday, very different and I just hope I can recall everything to tell you. They are now renting some commercial property in town for U.S. $200 per month. As far as the building is concerned, it is nice, but the environment leaves something to be desired, at least in our estimation, although I do think the locals are very used to it. They rent the second floor of this building. It has a large room that easily accommodates quite a large number of people. Pastor Remegio and his family live there as well. It has just a small kitchen in the corner, a small room that doubles as a study and a Sunday school room, two rooms for bedrooms, and since there isn't another room for their son, he has a bed in a corner of the large room.

The building is located on the corner of two busy streets, so there's a lot of traffic noise, and since there is no air-con, all the windows must be open to catch whatever precious little breeze there might be. In addition to that, there is a charismatic group that meets at the same time on the third floor, and they make a lot of noise too. Grandpa taught the Sunday school lesson on "What It Means to Be a Christian." He asks questions and tries to have them give the answers. He first talks about Christ as prophet, priest, and king while on earth, then about Christ as prophet, priest, and king in heaven, and then how we are prophets, priests, and kings. After the Sunday school, Rev. Kleyn preached on "Go Tell My Disciples and Peter"—Peter restored after having denied Christ.

We had six men with us at the hotel for a simple dinner: the Lapiz pastors, two other pastors, and the two men who had come from Davao. Loloy Lapiz's father-in-law is a seventy-one-year-old pastor and has two congregations by the Smokey Mountains, which are about a fifteen-minute drive from Cagayan de Oro if the traffic isn't too heavy. Two interesting stories about him. There is a garbage dump near to the area where he lives. The people are so poor there that they come as scavengers to the dump for food or anything else they might be able to sell (metal) or use. The gate opens each day at 3:00 and stays open for two hours. Because there are so many scavengers, people come already at 1:00 and wait by the gate so they can be among the first ones in. He goes to the dump and preaches to the people while they're waiting to go in. He invited Grandpa to come and do that the next time we come to the Philippines.

MISSION TRIPS: PHILIPPINES—MAY 20-31, 1999

This same man was going to retire from the ministry when he was sixty years old. After retiring, he became sick and landed in the hospital for eleven days. He was in a coma for about a half day, and his wife and family were expecting that he would die. He was given a blood transfusion, and he regained consciousness. He said the Lord taught him that you don't retire when you serve him. He promised that if he became well again, he would continue in the ministry, and now he has been active again for eleven more years.

We had one and a half hours in the afternoon to get revived before going back by 4:00. The evening was more informal, but while we were waiting for the people to come, we just gathered in a circle and they asked questions. That continued for over two hours, and then Grandpa said that Pastor Kleyn was prepared to give a short devotional and that would be a nice way to conclude the evening. He spoke on the verses from Philippians 4, "Be careful for nothing," etc. It was a nice message and very comforting. One of the questions that they asked Grandpa to explain was what we believed regarding the second coming of Christ. It was like giving an impromptu mini sermon. He explained it so well and orderly; I just wish I could retain it so orderly in my mind.

After Pastor Kleyn and Grandpa were finished with their part, both of the Lapiz brothers expressed their thanks for the time of fellowship and teaching. They were so warmhearted in their expressions of gratitude, saying they had learned so much and were greatly blessed with all the instruction. It was quite touching, and you could tell it came straight from the heart.

We stayed and chatted with the people for quite a while afterward. I was talking with Dorothy Lapiz. We had the gift packs that the ladies from Hull church had made up, and they were distributed earlier in the day. Dorothy was telling me how very happy their family was with it. There was a toothbrush in the bag, and their fourteen-year-old son, Michael, quickly took it. He was so happy; he right away put some toothpaste on it and started brushing his teeth. His old toothbrush was more than three years old. There were four bars of soap; the three children each took one "for a souvenir" (Joseph is twenty-one and Mary Joy is nineteen) and the other bar of soap they will use. "Of course, if we cannot afford to buy soap when we need it, they will have to give it up."

There was also new underwear in the bag. Michael was glad it would only fit him. He said he would wear it but he would not wash it. His mother said he couldn't do that; if he wears it, then they have to wash it. He said, "Then I won't wear it because I want to save the smell of America."

There were some pads of writing paper, and the children each got one and were so happy with it. I had taken boxes of tea bags along for the pastors' families. She told me that was the first time the children had tea; she had to show them how to use it. They have to use their money for rice and vegetables so aren't able to buy tea. She said if we had been there when they opened everything and had taken a picture, it would be so funny because they were all so very excited.

That is quite a story, but you know it is one thing to go there and witness all of this, but just think of what it must mean for these people—they can't walk away from it but must live with it day after day and year after year. You just wish you could go in there with a truckload of supplies to help them. Just pray that the Lord will always keep us grateful for what we have and willing to share from our abundance.

After walking back to the hotel, we had a little dinner, and then it was time to throw our stuff together in the suitcase. I noticed that all the shirts and blouses are really dirty after our sitting in the jeepneys and tricycles. But we don't have to wash them by hand (a little scrubbing maybe before going in the washing machine), nor by the river, as we saw some of them doing.

Our flight this Monday morning is at 7:30, so we were up by 5:30 in order to leave by 6:00. We had some time yet to spend with Rev. Kleyn and Sharon in the airport in Manila, reflecting on all the many experiences of the past twelve days. They were a very nice couple to be with, and it was good to get to know them better. It was quite an eye-opener for them to work in a third-world country, and

I can just imagine the many thoughts that must flood their minds as they think what it must be like to be a missionary in a land like that.

There are actually five different areas in the Philippines where there are contacts with people eager to learn the Reformed faith. A missionary would be very busy there giving instruction to church leaders and also traveling to the different areas. In a good way, Grandpa would be a bit envious of whoever that missionary might be, if and when the Lord grants that to our churches. He wishes he had another twenty years to do that kind of teaching.

We should be landing in about an hour or so, and it will be good to settle down again in our home even though it is only for a short time. Two weeks from today we leave for the church family camp, and four weeks from today for the USA! See you soon, the Lord willing.

We are thankful for the Lord's loving care and protection over us during the trip, for keeping us all in good health, and for granting us a safe return to our home. It was a busy couple weeks, but we enjoyed every minute of it. Our God is great, and we give him all the praise and glory.

Penang, Malaysia—October 19-25, 2005

This trip to Penang was made at the request of First Evangelical Reformed Church (FERC). The FERC is presently engaged with helping a fledgling group in Penang, Malaysia, in beginning a Reformed church. They call themselves the Penang Reformed Fellowship. It's a small, energetic, enthused group of only seven people, but they are committed to press on. They have been meeting together for about one and a half years but just started Sunday worship services in September 2005. Pastor Lau Chin Kwee, Pastor Paul Goh, and Elder Siew Chee Seng have gone to Penang to preach for them, and on the Sundays they do not have a pastor, one of the men of the group gives a message. Grandpa was asked to give two Reformation Day lectures in Penang and to preach on Sunday. We arranged to spend a week there to get acquainted with the people and have fellowship with them.

I'll first introduce you to the group members so as I refer to them, you'll understand who it is that I'm talking about.

- Paul and Ida Tan along with their three sons, Jonathan (fifteen), Timothy (thirteen), and Nicholas (seven).
- Sian Beng, a single man, thirty-five years old.
- Siew Chan, a single girl, works for Agilent and working toward a master's degree in economics.
- Jimmy and Karen, a very busy couple, both lawyers.

We took Singapore Airlines to Penang, arriving there at 5:00 p.m. on Wednesday. Ida first took us to the apartment where we would be staying for the week. Ida's friend owns the apartment and is willing to rent a room to the group for 250 ringgits (RM) per month (U.S. $75). No one else stays in the apartment so we were free to use all of it: front room, dining room, kitchen, bedroom, and bath. There are four units in the building, two units side by side, and each unit has two levels. We had an upper unit so actually the third and fourth floors of the building, thirty-six steps each time we left and came home. The apartment is comfortably furnished, not much in the kitchen but enough to get along since the only meals we had there were breakfast and lunch.

After we were settled, Paul and Ida picked us up, and we had a Chinese dinner in a restaurant nearby, along with their children and Sian Beng. After dinner they took us to a grocery store so we could pick up a few groceries.

On Thursday morning Ida came over at around 10:00 and we talked with her until noon. Ida was from a family of unbelievers and her husband Paul from a Roman Catholic background. Her father passed away a couple years ago, but prior to that time, she often spoke with him about the gospel. When she would go to visit him,

MISSION TRIPS: PENANG, MALAYSIA—OCTOBER 19-25, 2005

her father would say, "And what is my daughter going to read to me this time?" She would quote Bible verses to him: "If we confess our sins, he is faithful and just to forgive us our sins, and to cleanse us from all unrighteousness" (1 John 1:9). He struggled and said he didn't feel anything, but she continued to help him understand the Bible. He was sick at this time, and she would pray that God would not take him yet. Then one day he said to her, "Ida, you are right, I do believe God loves me and Jesus died for me." After that she was ready to give him up. Two of her sisters are "Christians," but she isn't so sure about them, judging from their life.

She told us more about the Penang Reformed Fellowship (PRF) and how it began. Originally Paul and Ida attended the Brethren Church. The Brethren Church does not have membership, nor do they have pastors; the elders do the preaching. When they left the Brethren Church for the Reformed Baptist, the people said, "Just come back to us anytime." Grandpa knows the pastor in the Reformed Baptist Church, Pastor Lau Sing Foo.

Pastor Lau Sing Foo came to Penang with his family and moved all his possessions there without even being called to be their pastor. She said they really didn't have anything to say about it; he was there, so they just had to accept him. His personality and his way of dealing with people caused problems in the church, but then he became influenced by the Primitive Baptists, and that occasioned the Tans and Sian Beng to leave the church. Being members of the RBC, the Tan children have not been baptized yet. Paul and Ida have studied infant baptism and covenant and have embraced the Reformed faith.

Ida is a group leader for International Bible Study. This involvement gives her many contacts, and she is always willing and eager to speak of the Reformed faith and to acquaint others with the PRF. She is the only at-home mom in the group, so she has more time to devote to reaching out.

Sian Beng picked us up for lunch at the hawkers (outside food court) on Thursday during his noon break. He usually takes his lunch at the canteen by his workplace, but during the month of

Ramadan (fasting month for the Muslims) the canteen is closed, so the people who are not Muslims go out for their lunch. We spent a nice hour with him.

Ida picked us up at 2:30, and we went with her and her son Timothy to the YMCA where the lectures would be held on Saturday. We saw the room we would be using and decided how to arrange things. Then we stopped at the florist to select some flowers so that Ida could arrange a bouquet for Saturday. After that we stopped for a Chinese dessert. It was custard made from soy milk; Grandpa's had chocolate chips in it, and mine had almonds. It's different, but we've had it before, so it didn't strike us as something strange.

There was one more stop yet that afternoon. We went to the home of Mr. Law and his wife Ruth. Ruth is a tutor in Mandarin for Jonathan and Timothy. Ida befriended Ruth and speaks with her about the Reformed faith. The couple attends the Methodist Church (Mandarin speaking). Without explaining to us what she had in mind, Ida brought us to their home. They were very gracious about inviting us in and offering a cold drink and biscuits (cookies). This turned out to be a very interesting meeting. The discussion was on the sovereignty of God and the subject of free will and man's responsibility. (We soon learned throughout all our visits that there are many who struggle with that topic.)

Mr. Law was actually an unbeliever when the couple married. He is retired now (fifty-five years old) and loves to read and study the Scriptures. He's especially fond of Rev. Stephen Tong, who preaches systematically through books of the Bible in the Mandarin language. Although Mr. Law speaks good English, he says he thinks better in the Chinese language. Grandpa is a bit familiar with this Rev. Tong; he is based in Jakarta, Indonesia, but he does a lot of traveling and speaks all over in this part of the world. Mr. Law brought out some of Rev. Tong's material, and we noted that there is a Penang contact by the name of Joseph Lim (we'll meet him later), who is involved in organizing lectures in Penang by Rev. Tong.

On Thursday night, Siew Chan picked us up and took us to a

MISSION TRIPS: PENANG, MALAYSIA—OCTOBER 19-25, 2005

Thai restaurant for dinner. It was great: we hadn't had Thai food since we left Singapore in 2002 or 2003. Siew Chan is in her late twenties; she's a quiet person, but being alone with her that evening, she could sure talk along. There are so many questions you can ask these people, so conversation flows easily. She lives only a few buildings away from where we were in the Lavinia Apartments. Her family lives in KL (Kuala Lumpur) so she just rents a room from a family. Besides working fulltime, she is studying for her master's degree, two nights a week and Saturday afternoons.

She is the only Christian in her family. Her roommate in college spoke with her about Christianity, and Campus Crusade had meetings there as well. For a while she backslid, and then a friend who attends the International Bible Study and knew Ida suggested that perhaps Ida would be willing to have a Bible study with her one-on-one. Ida and Siew Chan did meet for Bible study, and then Ida also brought her along to church. Siew Chan is learning; she plans to stay with the group, and they encourage her to come for the Friday night Bible studies. She did invite a couple of her colleagues to the Reformation Day lectures and also to church on Sunday. Siew Chan brought us home around 7:30 and then she had to get to her class.

Friday was a school holiday. Ida picked us up, along with Timothy and Nicholas, and we went to the Penang Botanical Gardens. The first thing she told us was that she had good news and bad news. The bad news was that the prime minister's wife had passed away that morning. Bawadi had been prime minister only for a short while, and his wife (sixty-five years old) was very well liked by the people. She was treated in the U.S. for breast cancer but wanted very much to come home for Harl Raja, which is November 1 or 3. She was at home in Malaysia when she died, and being Muslim, the burial took place that very day.

The good news Ida had was that there would be a national holiday on Monday out of respect for the prime minister's wife, and Paul was so very happy because then he could get to spend a whole day with us and take us to Penang Hill. This good news turned out to be a hoax—it had been on the news and in the paper, but it wasn't true. Here the kids all thought they were going to have a day off from school, and the workers were happy to have another day off from work, but the joy was short-lived.

I didn't tell you yet about Paul. He's a busy man. He is a project manager for a company that builds housing blocks (high-rise apartments). Penang is an island and he works on the mainland, so it takes him forty-five minutes to an hour each way, depending on traffic jams. Generally he's home by 7:00, but sometimes he has to work later. He has a good job, and they have a nice home quite close to the Lavinia Apartments where we stayed, so it was quite convenient for transportation. They have many pieces of antique Chinese furniture in their house, chairs and table with inlaid pearl, china cabinets, etc., all from Ida's grandmother.

One time when Ida was a bit down over the whole church situation, she asked, "Paul, have we counted the cost, what this means for our family, etc.?" She said when Paul left for work the next morning after they had been talking about it, he said to her, "Yes, I am counting the cost, but I'm really counting the blessings too."

The botanical gardens were very nice; they reminded us a lot of the botanical gardens in Singapore. We hiked a path in the gardens—talk about humidity, wow! We were really sweating! I guess if it were Grandpa and I alone, we wouldn't have done it. The path was wet and covered with leaves so you had to be careful not to slip on them and there were a lot of steps, but we made it alright, and I guess it was good exercise. After that we picked up the flowers from the florist, stopped at the Baptist Book Shop (they are trying to buy some offering bags), and then we stopped for a cup of coffee.

At 1:00 on Friday, Sian Beng picked us up. He took the afternoon off so he could take us for a tour of the island of Penang. After lunch at a hawker's, we set out for a very enjoyable afternoon. Sian Beng is really a neat guy. He was working at a job that was quite stressful; he had bought a house for himself and a car and was making payments on both. Then he thought there has to be more to life than work, work, work, and making payments. He decided to sell the house and go back to live with his mother and buy a cheaper car: "As long as it's dependable transportation and can get me from point A to point B, I'm content." He figured he could quit his job and take up to six months to find other work. It happened that a former colleague also quit his job and started up his own business, APL Tech Battery Industry (American Company), and called Sian Beng to work for him. Working conditions are much more pleasant, working hours are shorter, and pay is better.

Part of our afternoon tour was stopping at the house where he lives with his mother. That was really neat—they live in an old kampong (village). The houses are very simple with metal roofs. It is the house where he was brought up, so all his childhood memories are there. When these kampongs were first built, no one had cars, so the paths (streets) between the houses are small, probably six feet wide. Now people have cars, so they have to park them along the main road and walk in.

Sian Beng is one of seven sons; the father left the family when he was young, and the mother had to go out to work. She left at 5:00 in the morning and came home around 7:00 in the evening, doing laundry (by hand) for wealthy people. (She still does all her laundry by hand today.) Their grandmother who lived a couple doors away from them brought up the boys. She also brought the boys to church; one time Sian Beng tried to skip out of going to church, and that's one time he remembers well that his grandma gave him a good spanking.

The mother is my age, but what a hard life she has had. She is a Christian and attends the Chinese-speaking Methodist Church. She loves going to church on Sunday and meeting her friends there. Sian Beng takes her there in the morning, and then he has to leave soon after the PRF service so he can pick her up again and take her home. Sian Beng is such a humble person, warmhearted and happy, loves to read and study, and now that he has freed himself up some, he has more time to grow spiritually.

He took us for a tour around the island: winding roads through the hills, small villages with lots of character along the way, then the seaside and beaches with the beautiful hotels and resorts, where the tsunami hit the coastline, etc. We just thoroughly enjoyed it. It brought back lots of memories of things we have seen in Myanmar and India.

Next stop was dinner at the hawkers with Sian Beng and the Tan family (except for Paul as he got home late from work that evening) and then to the Tans' house. Usually on Friday night they have a Bible study, but this time it was discussing everything for the Reformation Day lectures and who was responsible for what (book sales, refreshments, microphone, ushering, etc.) Paul came home around 9:00, and then they had a short prayer meeting with view to the lectures the next day. Jimmy and Karen were at this meeting too, and so was Wendy, who was to play the keyboard on Saturday. One way they make sure that someone will come to the meeting is to give them a job to do; that was the case with Wendy. One of Ida's friends wanted her daughter-in-law to come to the lectures but knew she would have to be encouraged by someone other than herself, so she called Ida to see what she could do. Ida called this girl and asked if she could help out with ushering, so mission accomplished.

Saturday morning and Grandpa decided to take a walk. By the time he got downstairs, he thought, "Those clouds look pretty dark, oh, never mind, it probably won't rain before I get back home anyway, sure don't feel like going back up just to get my umbrella." He was at the farthest point of his walk and it started pouring. I imagined him stopping at the coffee shop and having a cup of coffee while waiting out the storm. He said by the time he reached the coffee shop he was so wet, he might just as well keep on going. He was drenched from head to toe; the guard at the entrance to the apartments shook his head and laughed at him. After a shower and breakfast, he spent the morning going over his messages.

One couple from Singapore, Ker Ming and Kwee Siew, came to Penang for the lectures on Saturday and for Sunday worship. It's encouraging for the PRF when ERCS members come up and show

MISSION TRIPS: PENANG, MALAYSIA—OCTOBER 19-25, 2005

interest and support for the work there. They also brought along some books from Singapore for the book table at the lectures.

Paul picked us up at 2:00. We met the others at the YMCA for an easy lunch of fried rice, and then by 3:00 we were at the meeting room upstairs. The first lecture was from 3:30 to 4:30, then a half-hour break, and the second lecture from 5:00 to 6:00. The schedule didn't work out quite that perfectly, but that was the general plan. The group did a good job of promoting the lectures and inviting friends and colleagues (mostly by Ida, but the others did their part too) so that there was a group of around seventy or seventy-five.

The subject was "The Great Revival. Our Common Protestant Heritage (1) How it all began (history of the Reformation) and (2) What are its teachings (sovereignty of God, doctrines of grace)." They were not able to use the word "Reformation" in advertising the lectures because this could be associated with the political party "Reformatzie," which is in opposition to the government in Malaysia, so instead they used the word "Revival." There were short periods of Q&A, but the people seemed to prefer asking their own questions personally afterward. We met Joseph Lim (the contact man for lectures by Rev. Tong) after the lectures, and he agreed to meet up with us on Sunday night. After all the guests had left and the packing up was finished, Jimmy and Karen wanted to take the whole group out for a nice dinner at the restaurant in the YMCA.

I sat next to Karen at the dinner so I had a nice opportunity to get a little better acquainted with her. She is twenty-eight years old, a very nice person, sincere and kind. She is more or less a property lawyer. She worked for about five years with going to court, but now has given that up, and she does all the background work for the court cases: still a lot of work but less stressful than battling it out in court. Her family is Buddhist, but when she started going with Jimmy, he said he could not date her unless she would become a Christian. Jimmy's family goes to the Lutheran Church. Eventually she became a Christian and was baptized. She asked Pastor Lau Chin Kwee (ERCS) about her baptism since she was baptized by a woman preacher, and she wondered if she should be baptized again. She said Pastor Lau hasn't given her an answer yet.

Ida met Karen through the International Bible Study and introduced her to the Reformed faith. Karen loves it and is growing in her understanding. Our first impression was that Karen is more advanced in her understanding of the Reformed faith than her husband, Jimmy. Jimmy's family is in the Lutheran Church, and that might be difficult for him. I don't know. But wow, did those two ever pay attention and listen during the lectures and sermons. Jimmy also took his father along to all the meetings; his mother passed away some years ago.

The PRF just started renting a room at the YWCA for their church services. It's a small room but just nice for their size group and enough room for visitors as well. The room is air-conditioned and there's a hallway where they can have fellowship and something to drink after the services. The rental cost is 300 RM per month (U.S $90). Their church services are at 10:00 and 5:00. Their order of worship is very similar to FERC. Karen played the keyboard on Sunday. It was really neat; she is just so humble. During the week she is a lawyer, and on Sunday she can get up there and play the melody with one finger and then add some more notes during the singing. We sang some Psalter numbers, completely unfamiliar to them, so we sang slowly, and they all tried their best. In the morning Grandpa preached from Romans 8:35–39 and in the evening "God will provide himself a lamb."

The group had dinner together after the morning service, and then we went with Paul and Ida and the children to visit his parents. The parents attended the lectures on Saturday, and afterward Paul's father came to Grandpa with some questions. Then we had opportunity to go to their home on Sunday and continue the discussion. Paul's parents are Roman Catholic, and on Sunday he wanted Grandpa's viewpoint on a lot of things. He was questioning whether all religions don't ultimately lead to God and it's simply just a different way of worshiping. Another topic was free will and man's

MISSION TRIPS: PENANG, MALAYSIA—OCTOBER 19-25, 2005

responsibility. Grandpa patiently tried to answer his questions and explain to him from the Bible. It was an interesting afternoon and Grandpa ended with prayer. He asked how long we would be staying in Penang, and could he take us out for dinner yet at the Swimming Club along with Paul and Ida? We could still make it on Monday night, so we agreed to that, and the discussion could be continued there as well.

Mr. Tan, Paul's father, was a professor of mathematics in a teacher's college. Judging from the house they live in, the family is quite wealthy. They have four children, a daughter and three sons. When the youngest son was about eight years old, a mother of a poor family approached Mrs. Tan and asked if her thirteen-year-old daughter could live with the Tan family and work for them—in other words, be their maid. The Tans took her in and she has lived with them ever since: "She's like a daughter to us." This person is now forty-eight years old. She takes care of everything; loves to take care of the dog, tend to the flowers, housework, laundry, cooking, etc. Mr. and Mrs. Tan do a good share of traveling and she holds down the fort for them while they are away.

We met up with Joseph Lim after the Sunday evening worship service. He has embraced the Reformed faith and knows of about one hundred people in Penang who are Reformed. He attends the Brethren Church now, and the way he looks at it is, stay in the church where you are and try to influence the people in the Reformed faith and reform the church from within. He says, "Why begin yet another church in Penang without a pastor?" He desires to study for the ministry and has in mind to go to Westminster. He thinks as long as those who are Reformed can meet up with each other, remain committed, and promote Reformed lectures, etc., the cause of the Reformed truth will continue. The PRF is happy to know there are more in Penang who desire to be Reformed, and they can perhaps stay in touch with Joseph Lim too, but their desire is to come out of their former churches and have a full Reformed church life for their souls' sake and spiritual growth.

Before we went to Penang, we really expected that we would have a lot of time to ourselves. How wrong we were! It was literally from one thing to the next. Finally on Monday we thought we might have a quiet day before coming back home on Tuesday. To start off the day, Grandpa and I went for a walk. Not too far from the apartments is a nice park with paths and exercise equipment. On our way there, we met Susan; her family also has a unit in the Lavinia Apartments. She started talking to us, asked where we were from, etc. They saw us Sunday morning waiting at the entrance of the apartments for our ride to church. Another opportunity to explain why we were in Penang, and who knows what may come of it.

We continued with our walk, came home, showered, and during breakfast received a call that two ladies wanted to come and visit at 1:00. Okay, fine. While I was cleaning up after breakfast, someone knocked on the door. Grandpa answered, and there was Susan. It was a nice day, and she wondered if we had any laundry that she could do up for us. Grandpa explained that we were leaving the next day so we really didn't need that. I thought perhaps it would be nice for me to go down later, chat with her a bit, and thank her for her kind offer.

At 1:00 Ruth Law (the tutor) came over with Melissa. Both of them are members of the Methodist Church. Melissa is in her first year of studying at the Baptist Bible Seminary in Penang. She attended the lectures and had questions she wanted to ask. Melissa is married with two teenaged sons; her husband works for a BMW car dealership. Melissa studied in the U.S. for five years in pharmaceutical and had her own pharmacy shop in Penang. She has given that up now and likes to study for some type of church work. One of the things she struggles with is, why does God let certain things happen, for example, the tsunami or Hurricane Katrina.

As you can imagine, there was a lot of talking and explaining and trying to put things in perspective for her. And, of course, the subject of free will and man's responsibility came up again also. They stayed for a couple hours.

After they left, I thought I better go down and see Susan. I was

MISSION TRIPS: PENANG, MALAYSIA—OCTOBER 19-25, 2005

just going to thank her at the door and chat a couple minutes, but she really wanted me to come in and visit. She has three children and takes care of another three. The three she babysits were sleeping. After a bit of family talk, our work in Singapore, etc., I asked what church they go to: Full Gospel Assembly. Then I asked if the church is charismatic with speaking in tongues and faith healing. "Yes, do you have that too?" When I said, "No, we don't," she replied, "When Jesus was about to leave, he said he would send another." "Yes," I said, "that was the Holy Spirit, the Comforter. We certainly believe in the Holy Spirit."

"Then how come you don't speak in tongues?" I explained how in the New Testament, tongues were necessary because the Bible was not yet complete and it proved the authenticity of the apostles, but now God's Word, the Bible, is complete and he speaks to us through his Word and not by extra revelation. I quoted, "Whether there be tongues, they shall cease." I asked if she knew what she was saying when she spoke in tongues. She said, "No, I don't, it's a heavenly language." When someone else speaks in tongues, does it sound the same way yours does? "No, it is different and no one can understand it."

I tried to show her how God comes to us by his Word, through our minds and in our hearts so we can understand the truth of the Bible. I referred her to 1 Corinthians 14, especially verse 19, "Yet in the church I had rather speak five words with my understanding, that by my voice I might teach others also, than ten thousand words in an unknown tongue." It might have been new to her; she shrugged her shoulders. We had a nice little visit, and she asked if we would be coming back to Penang. "If you do come back, be sure to come and visit me again."

And then our last meeting was at the Swimming Club with Paul's parents. It's a beautiful place, right on the sea. Very relaxing. The food was extra good: gourmet. We had more discussion of Roman Catholic and Reformed. Paul's father believes the position that all religions are true. He explained Mariolatry this way: if you are going to speak with a very important person, you may be apprehensive and nervous. It would be much easier to go through someone else and have them represent you. For them to go directly to God in prayer is difficult, but if Mary can help them and go to God on their behalf, why not? One thing we can say for him is that he is willing to listen, and if he is willing to listen, then we don't know if the Lord will use the instruction to speak to his heart.

When you are in situations like this, you just can't help thinking about how greatly blessed we are to be brought up in a Christian home and be taught all the precious truths of God's Word from our very youth. For the PRF people, they are so thankful to God for their deliverance from sin and salvation in Christ, but there are many struggles and questions that they must work through, and especially hard for them are their unbelieving families. Pray for them.

Tuesday morning Ida drove us to the airport, and then we were once again on our own. The whole stay in Penang was very enjoyable with lots of experiences. Ida adds a lot of spark to the group—she is very energetic, vivacious, bubbly, just a real pleasing personality. We're glad we had the opportunity to go. They'd love to have us come back again while we're here, but I don't think that will happen. Pastor Lau and Pastor Goh have their assigned Sundays to go, and it is good for the group to have as much continuity as they can.

We had a good flight back to Singapore, then took a taxi home and settled in once again. We were completely exhausted by evening and went to bed at 8:45 and slept.

The Church's One Foundation

The Church's one foundation
Is Jesus Christ her Lord;
She is His new creation
By water and the word;
From heaven He came,
and sought her
To be His holy bride;
With His own blood
He bought her,
And for her life He died.

Elect from every nation,
Yet one o'er all the earth,
Her charter of salvation
One Lord, one faith, one birth;
One holy name she blesses,
Partakes one holy food,
And to one hope she presses
With every grace endued.

Though with a scornful wonder
Men see her sore oppressed,
By schisms rent asunder,
By heresies distressed,
Yet saints their watch are keeping,
Their cry goes up, "How long?"
And soon the night of weeping
Shall be the morn of song.

Mid toil and tribulation,
And tumult of her war,
She waits the consummation
Of peace for evermore;
Till with the vision glorious
Her longing eyes are blest,
And the great Church victorious
Shall be the Church at rest.

Yet she on earth hath union
With God, the Three in One;
And mystic sweet communion
With those whose rest is won.
Oh, happy saints and holy!
Lord, give us grace that we
Like them, the meek and lowly,
On high may dwell with Thee![*]

---

* Samuel J. Stone (1866).

EPILOGUE

My dear family—children, grandchildren, and great grand-children,

Here we are, July 2022. Many years have gone by since the book *Say Among the Heathen the Lord Reigns* was first published. You grandchildren were quite young when we presented you with your own personal copy of the book. Now most of you are married and some of you have children older than what you were at that time. What comes to my mind is, "O God, our help in ages past, our hope for years to come."

Our living in Singapore and other foreign countries for 10+ years was a great blessing for the whole family. Though children and grandchildren gave up their parents and grandparents for the Lord's work, and we were separated from each other for a while, God remained our constant. He reigns. He reigns over the whole earth and we rejoice. He reigns over the multitude of isles and they are glad (Ps. 97). He rules in America and he rules across the globe. We were separated by many, many miles but we were so close because we worshiped and served the same God. He is supremely sovereign and yet gentle and caring in his love for his people. It was our privilege many years ago to share that truth in a heathen culture.

Dad/Grandpa is no longer with us; the Lord took him to glory on December 20, 2020. How we loved to hear him talk about all the experiences on the mission field and how the Lord gathers his church in other lands. We all personally learned from his experiences, and now the great-grandkids are benefiting too. They listen as their parents retell of the goodness and grace of our heavenly Father in his precious work of calling his own out of darkness into his marvelous light.

Years ago, when we lived overseas, the only way we could be in contact with each other was by a weekly fax or email. Expensive phone calls were out of the question. Now you girls and grandkids can call or text whenever you like. My friends across the world can do the same. (Having the experience of laboring in foreign lands, we rejoice that our family is much larger than you girls, grandchildren, and great-grandchildren. Our family, because we're part of God's family, is large—impossible to number).

I love the video chats on WhatsApp with my "daughters" in Singapore. The quilt some of them made for us kept Dad warm even in his last days on this earth. Just recently I was invited to the home of Marcus and Tze Yan Wee to share a meal with them before they head back to Singapore. It thrills my soul that God has provided local pastors for the Covenant Evangelical Reformed Church there. Pastor Josiah Tan will certainly welcome a colleague in the ministry in that country.

I also am grateful to continue contact via WhatsApp with Rev. Titus in Yangon, Myanmar. Titus is a busy man: translating, teaching, conducting seminars. His heart is faithful and true as he continues to say among the heathen that the Lord reigns. I read the updates from Hope PRC and the work in Myanmar with great enthusiasm.

In October of 2019, our family was blessed with Benji, an adopted son for Rev. Joe Holstege, and his wife Lisa, our granddaughter. Benji's birth family is Burmese. Imagine the joy on Grandpa's face when he held in his own arms a great-grandchild from the country where we spent so much time. I'll never forget his comment. "Who would ever have thought…?" All of us as adopted children of God have learned to recognize that with him as our Father, we have brothers and sisters who, though we may seem very different, are very much the same.

I also get regular reports from Georgetown PRC as they have taken on the care of Paulraj and Kasturi in India. Did you know they have a son named Jason, after Grandpa? That's an honor. Grandpa would be the first to say that a name is only respectable if it brings honor to our God who created us. I pray you kids remember that. When someone hears your name, what do they think? Do you have Christ's name attached to yours? Do people know that? Do people know you're a child of the King first of all? "Not unto us, O Lord…

EPILOGUE

but unto Thy name give glory." Paul and Kas labor diligently for God's church in India. In addition to their work in the Tamil and English-speaking congregations, they also manage Grace Foster Home, an orphanage that is home for approximately forty orphans. Paul and Kas are Dad and Mom to these kids and, in addition to feeding and clothing them, they provide for the kids' spiritual care as well. After all, that's what dads and moms do, right? In America, in India, in Singapore, in Myanmar, and all across the world, may godly parents continue to take their children in their arms, and lead them to their precious Savior.

We are so very thankful for God's provision for these dear people whom we have come to love. What is so very real for all these people, and for us as well, is that true happiness is only in the Lord and it is that which brings joy and peace to his children.

Grandpa's prayer has always been, and mine continues to be, that the Lord may bless and keep each one of you—children, grandchildren, and greatgrandchildren—in the way of truth, walking in his ways, and serving him in whatever he calls you to do.

A song that is very dear to my heart and that has helped me to stay focused on the Lord's leading in my life is "All the Way My Savior Leads Me." May it be true for all of you as well.

> All the way my Savior leads me,
> What have I to ask beside?
> Can I doubt His tender mercy,
> Who through life has been my guide?
> Heav'nly peace, divinest comfort,
> Here by faith in Him to dwell!
> For I know, whate'er befall me,
> Jesus doeth all things well.
>
> All the way my Savior leads me,
> Cheers each winding path I tread,
> Gives me grace for ev'ry trial,
> Feeds me with the living bread.

SAY AMONG THE HEATHEN THE LORD REIGNS

Though my weary steps may falter
And my soul athirst may be,
Gushing from the rock before me,
Lo! A spring of joy I see.

All the way my Savior leads me,
Oh, the fullness of His love!
Perfect rest to me is promised
In my Father's house above.
When my spirit, clothed immortal,
Wings its flight to realms of day,
This my song through endless ages:
Jesus led me all the way.[*]

With love to all,
Mom, Grandma, Great-Grandma
July 2022

---

[*] Fanny J. Cosby (1875).

Less Than the Least:
Memoirs of Cornelius Hanko

The memoirs of Rev. Cornelius Hanko's long, fruitful life of nearly a century (1907-2005). He lived through two world wars, the Great Depression, the Korean and Vietnam Wars, the rise and fall of communism, and the advent of the space age, and spanned the terms of eighteen US presidents, from Theodore Roosevelt to George W. Bush. Son of Dutch immigrants to America, Rev. Hanko served six pastorates in five states. Less Than the Least follows Rev. Hanko from his childhood, school days, and seminary training, all the way to his retirement (1977) and beyond. This delightful book comes complete with photos and appendices.

Available in paperback and ebook format at **rfpa.org**,
or by calling the Reformed Free Publishing Association
at **616-457-5970** or emailing **mail@rfpa.org**.

Just Dad: Stories of Herman Hoeksema
by Lois Kregel

Many people are familiar with the public persona of Herman Hoeksema. As one of the leading theologians of the twentieth century, a seminary professor, the pastor of a large congregation, and a prolific writer, he was well-known in ecclesiastical circles. But to his family he was Just Dad. This anecdotal biography written by his youngest child records many stories about him, some perhaps familiar but others never before told. Included in the book are numerous pictures of Hoeksema and his family, as well as an appendix with several personal letters of Hoeksema written to his children when he took a trip to Europe in 1929. These will show you a side of Hoeksema not found elsewhere.

———

Available in paperback and ebook format at **rfpa.org**,
or by calling the Reformed Free Publishing Association
at **616-457-5970** or emailing **mail@rfpa.org.**

I Remember Herman Hoeksema
by David J. Engelsma

Published originally as a series of articles in *Beacon Lights* magazine, I Remember Herman Hoeksema consists of the recollections of David J. Engelsma, a student of Herman Hoeksema. Written for young people, these articles show something of the man whom many know only as an author and theologian.

Available in paperback and ebook format at **rfpa.org**, or by calling the Reformed Free Publishing Association at **616-457-5970** or emailing **mail@rfpa.org**.

Our Mission

To glorify God by making accessible to the broadest possible audience material that testifies to the truth of Scripture as understood and developed in the Reformed tradition.

Reformed Free Publishing Association
1894 Georgetown Center Drive
Jenison, MI 49428-7137
Website: rfpa.org
E-mail: mail@rfpa.org
Phone: 616-457-5970

www.ingramcontent.com/pod-product-compliance
Lightning Source LLC
Chambersburg PA
CBHW071658170426
43195CB00039B/2223